PRAISE FOR *DO B2B BETTER*

"Does customer experience matter in B2B? Absolutely! Across the hundreds of B2B companies that I've worked with, I've seen it impact renewals and expansions, as well as other areas of loyalty such as providing feedback on new offerings, acting as references with prospective clients, and publishing case studies. B2B firms trail consumer-facing firms in areas like voice of the customer and experience design, so there's plenty of opportunity to improve. With dozens of case studies across different B2B segments, *Do B2B Better* provides guidance on how to close that CX gap."
—Bruce Temkin, Head of Qualtrics XM Institute and cofounder, Customer Experience Professionals Association

"CX professionals must mobilize their entire organizations to deliver high-value customer experiences. *Do B2B Better* draws on Jim's extensive real-world experience and interviews with practicing CX leaders to serve as a guide on how to make the case for CX to your organization, understand customer emotions and desires, and develop a scalable, measurable approach that achieves results."
—Greg Melia, CEO, Customer Experience Professionals Association

"In software and service businesses, we all strive to understand and serve our customers. Unfortunately, over time, the complexity of offerings and scale of business can lead to disconnects. Growing through customer experience requires a solid methodology to understand the specific emotions that matter most and then engaging the entire organization to deliver what will lead to improved loyalty. In *Do B2B Better*, Jim Tincher provides just such a framework, not just to delight customers, but to ensure your solutions are irreplaceable to them and they have the highest level of confidence that the value you provide will continue to increase over time."
—Julie Dodd, board member, Duck Creek Technologies

"CX is difficult and even more challenging to create loyalty when those customers are businesses, requiring you to align all your silos. There aren't many guides available that focus specifically on the B2B or B2B2C experience. This book is packed with real-life examples from CX leaders who bravely lead CX change efforts—driving increased customer loyalty and revenues."
—Lisa Crymes, Chief Revenue Officer, Preventric

"Providing an excellent and differentiated customer experience is as critical to the success of business-to-business (B2B) organizations as it is to business-to-consumer (B2C) organizations. Based on interviews with hundreds of CX leaders and dozens of case studies, *Do B2B Better* provides a compelling framework for how B2B leaders can increase the impact and effectiveness of their customer experience investments."
—Mark Smith, Senior Vice President of Customer Experience, Tangoe

"*Do B2B Better* offers a library of useful case studies and examples showcasing how the best organizations identify, manage, measure, and evaluate customer experiences. The book is filled with practical advice and techniques to accelerate the CX Loyalty Flywheel."
—Tim Gabel, CEO, RTI International

"The B2B customer experience is unique and requires both discipline and the right cross-functional culture to ensure everybody works together to create powerful customer outcomes. In this book, Jim lays out how great companies work together to create loyal customers and measurably healthier businesses."
—Steven Durkee, President, Legrand | AV

"The best way to earn loyal clients is through a compelling customer experience. But doing it in a B2B context is complicated, and there aren't many resources to help. In this book, Jim provides an effective path on how to build a world-class B2B program, using case studies to show the way."
—Frank Berweger, Head of Sales, Lineas

"Truly understanding B2B customers and creating loyalty is a complex, challenging, and ever-changing skill that needs to be learned. Jim takes you on an incredible journey that helps you unlock doors and see around corners, and ultimately provides a deeper understanding of your customers' businesses."
—Mike Marusa, sales executive for Fortune 500 and private equity companies

DO **B2B** BETTER

DO **B2B** BETTER

BETTER

DRIVE GROWTH THROUGH GAME-CHANGING CUSTOMER EXPERIENCE

JIM TINCHER

WONDERWELL

Library of Congress Control Number: 2022902219

ISBN 978-1-63756-018-1 (hardcover)
ISBN 978-1-63756-019-8 (EPUB)

Editor: Don Loney
Cover design: Mimi Bark
Interior design: Morgan Krehbiel
Cover images: flywheel by Graphic Grid / Shutterstock.com;
    wooden blocks by PANsight / Shutterstock.com
CX Loyalty Flywheel graphics and figures 8-1, 8-2, 8-3, 8-4, 11-1, and 11-2:
    Kris LaFavor of Design Ahead
Author photo: Paul Markert

Published by Wonderwell in Los Angeles, CA
www.wonderwell.press

WONDERWELL

Distributed in the US by Publishers Group West and in Canada by
Publishers Group Canada

Printed and bound in Canada

To Sue, my rock.

And to all those CX Change Makers
who inspire me to keep learning.

CONTENTS

FOREWORD

I HAVE SPENT MY ENTIRE PROFESSIONAL CAREER IN CUSTOMER-facing roles, thinking about how to create and translate customer value into brand loyalty. We didn't call it CX back then, and we focused a lot on the transaction. But as those standards became common, I found myself searching for new fields of differentiation and growth.

When I got the opportunity in 2018 to lead the global commercial function at Dow, our leadership recognized a chance to transform the materials industry by aspiring to the types of digital experiences that were emerging in the B2C world, especially around finding and buying products. You can imagine that not too many people were buying chemicals from websites at the time.

One of our first steps was to hire Heart of the Customer to help us map out our current customer experience—both the rational and emotional touchpoints. That's when Jim Tincher and his team came in to facilitate a deep dive into the experiences our customers were having, from discovering solutions to transacting to using our products and getting support through a range of digital and human interactions.

To my knowledge, this was the first systematic approach to customer experience in our industry. We instituted a singular annual customer survey with robust metrics and dashboard capabilities that helped us recognize and prioritize what to change. Now the more data we collect, the better we are at analyzing and decision-making.

We established disciplines for treating our customers according to the value we create for one another, aligned with the experiences that they want from Dow, that strikes a balance between under-delivering or overdelivering. And of course, we instituted a discipline for improving touchpoints systematically across our global and complex enterprise.

In *Do B2B Better*, Jim Tincher, now the leading thought leader in B2B customer experience, shares dozens of stories showing how Dow and other leading companies follow a more systematic approach toward customer experience. With its impactful case studies and proprietary research, Jim's book makes a compelling, evidence-based case for adopting CX in the B2B landscape in a way that drives a competitive difference.

It was an incredible and exciting challenge that Heart of the Customer helped us frame and launch—and we're still using that foundational work and many of those principals in our systems today.

But the credit for what we've accomplished is shared by many people at Dow—from the C-suite to the people who are working with customers every day. It took a vision from the top that started when our executive leadership put customer centricity as one of our four expressed corporate ambitions. Since then, we've added CX scoring as a factor in our annual performance award system. That draws even more people into the effort, which generates new insights and participation over time.

We've had project and change leaders who did amazing work to provide the tools and processes our businesses needed to convert these disciplines into value for Dow. As we gained traction, and the positive impacts of CX revealed itself to people in every role across the company—from manufacturing to customer service—ownership shifted from CX project teams to deeper in our business and functional teams. It helped that the changes we made for our customers clearly improved the employee experience as well.

This all goes to show that even a 125-year-old industrial company (in 2022) can reinvent itself by designing business models around how our customers want to do business. Perhaps the most exciting part is that the never-ending quest for elevating customers' experiences is further enabled by digital transformation and calls for an ever-more sustainable society. For a materials science company like Dow, that opens the door for innovation and new partnerships that will energize our people for the next 125 years.

—DANIEL FUTTER, Chief Commercial Officer, Dow

INTRODUCTION

IF YOU'RE READING THIS BOOK, YOU UNDOUBTEDLY SHARE my passion for customers and the desire to help your entire organization truly understand your customers and their needs, as well as act in the way that best serves them. You want to create an experience that's so good that customers go out of their way to work with you whenever they can!

You have also probably discovered just how difficult this work is. That's one of the reasons why turnover in our field is so high. Most customer experience (CX) teams have only a handful of people who are trying to move thousands of employees to think differently, starting with the client. It's no wonder the role turns over so quickly, as leaders search for greener grass in other pastures.

This difficulty is further compounded if you work at a company that serves other businesses, or a B2B company. In B2B, it's harder to get your employees to see the experience firsthand. You can't send all of your employees out to follow one of your customers' agents as she does her work. While a medical device manufacturer may be able to have its sales representatives visit the operating room with a doctor who purchases its products, it can't send its entire product development, services, and finance teams. So, it's harder to bring the customer experience to life for all of your employees.

If you are frustrated with how hard it is to get the organization to act as a single unit to create a better experience, you're not alone. Whether you read research from CustomerThink, Pointillist, or my own writing at Heart of the Customer, it is the case that about three-quarters of customer experience programs are unable to demonstrably create the kind of customer experience that leads customers to want to stay with companies longer and buy more products and services.

Yet, those few programs that can show impact and be proven successful give us hope! Their organizations are rewarded with higher sales, lower churn, and a reduced cost to serve those customers. In other words, when done right, an improved customer experience program creates a stronger, more profitable company.

This book is the result of my quest to learn the secret sauce of customer experience excellence. You'll read the stories of dozens of Change Makers who can inspire us to do better at sharing the customer experience and igniting change. Ever since I led customer experience at a large health insurance organization (more on this soon), I've been fascinated with trying to understand why some programs seem to effortlessly design great customer experiences while others, such as the programs I led, struggle.

It is this quest that led me and my team at Heart of the Customer to log over two hundred hours of interviews with customer experience leaders in B2B (business-to-business) and B2B2C (business-to-business-to-consumer) companies, plus a few in B2C (business-to-consumer) companies for context. We also talked with CEOs, leaders from finance, marketing, sales, and anybody else who could help us. Then I shadowed great leaders, watching how they talked with employees and where they spent their time. Finally, we surveyed hundreds more. This survey revealed the challenges of building a differentiated customer experience. When we asked participants what gets in their way, there was essentially a three-way tie between organizational complexities, not having enough or the right people, and a lack of leadership buy-in.

All this helped us to identify what separates a Change Maker from a "Hopeful." Change Makers, that one-quarter of great CX programs,[1] are those elite CX leaders who can prove that their efforts produce improved outcomes for their customers and their businesses. This latter outcome is critical; if you can't show that your work is making your company stronger, then you're at risk when the next budget cuts come.

Hopefuls are the vast majority of programs that may be doing adequate-to-good work in customer experience but can't measure and prove the value of their efforts for either the customers or their own company. Thus, they rely on passion-fueled hope that their work is creating a stronger organization.

Hope is not enough. When we do our work right, we create outcomes in which customers *want* to spend more with our companies, stay longer, and interact in ways that are less expensive to serve. But we need to be able to prove this impact to skeptical executives.

We learned that Change Makers have a fundamentally different approach to their efforts, focusing on business outcomes rather than survey scores. From our work with Change Makers, we created the CX Loyalty Flywheel as a visual demonstration of customer experience dynamics that guide their efforts.[2] They then use change management techniques to help the rest of the company align with and advance the flywheel.

When the flywheel is in motion, it shows the business impact of the investments your company makes to improve the customer experience. Rather than *hoping* the investments help create better outcomes, when the company invests in the customer experience, Change Makers:

show how investments in CX
measurably improve the experience that →
creates more emotionally engaged customers, who →
buy more and stay longer, and →
strengthen the company as a result.

Or, they create, as I call it, the CX Loyalty Flywheel.

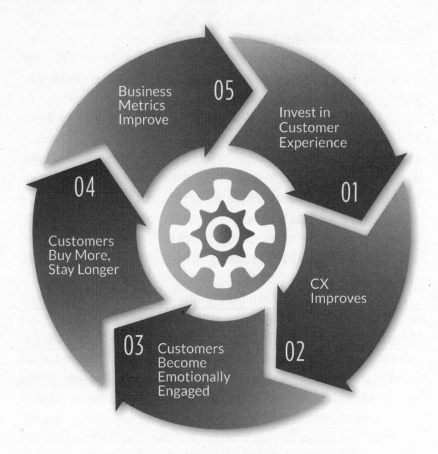

Figure O-1: The five stages of the CX Loyalty Flywheel.

In this book, you'll learn how B2B and B2B2C companies are doing this work every day through four Actions:

1. **Point the Flywheel** in the right direction, creating organizational value.
2. **Accelerate the Flywheel** by measuring and designing for emotions.
3. **Evaluate the Flywheel** using the Customer Ecosystem Data.
4. **Grease the Flywheel** using change management.

B2B Is Different

I am particularly interested in B2B and B2B2C companies like yours. B2B companies, of course, are those that sell to other businesses, such as manufacturers, software companies, service companies, and distributors. B2B2C companies are those that service consumers but sell through separate companies. Insurance companies are a common example of this. Whether they sell life, property and casualty, or health insurance, many insurance companies sell through independent agents and service the consumers brought to them by these agents, meaning these companies have both a B2B and a B2C component. While there's not a lot of business writing focused on B2B, there's even less about B2B2C. I've tried to bring both foci into this book.

According to the International Centre for Trade and Sustainable Development (ICTSD), the B2B marketplace is $7.72 trillion, as compared to $4.01 trillion for B2C.[3] Despite the dominant role of B2B companies in the economy, there are very few resources to help these companies organize their customer-focused efforts. Most articles on the topic cite B2C examples, such as Amazon, Best Buy, Airbnb, and USAA. While these are great companies, it's difficult to apply lessons to the more complex environments of B2B companies.

B2B companies have a host of stakeholders in their client companies, typically including an economic purchaser who is rarely involved with the organization day to day, and dozens—sometimes hundreds—of employees who interact with your company's products regularly.

This isn't to say that B2B is harder or easier than B2C. It's just so different that it's almost impossible to apply lessons from retail or other B2C examples.

Likely as a result of this complexity, B2B organizations as a whole are much less mature in managing their customers' experiences. Qualtrics XM Institute reported that while 59 percent of all companies are in the lowest two stages of customer experience management (out of five), that number rises to nearly 80 percent with B2B companies.[4]

Yet, some companies are able to create great customer experiences that inspire their customers to stay longer, order more, and interact in ways that cost less to serve. In early 2020, we set out to understand what those companies did in order to use the resulting takeaways to create a guidebook for the rest of the industry.

Who Am I?

For whatever reason, I've always had a focus on customers. Out of college, I joined LaserMaster[5] in its technical support organization. I remember that when I went to visit my girlfriend, Sue,[6] I wanted to visit a customer while I was there. I asked a sales manager to arrange a visit with one of our resellers. He was confused, asking, "Why don't you just go on vacation?" But this was important to me.

Years later, I joined Best Buy, where I just loved its customer focus. We would often visit stores just to watch what customers did. At this point of my career, I naively thought that *every* organization was customer obsessed.

Then I joined a large B2B2C health insurance organization, and I learned there were different models, which focused more on operations than customer centricity. I'll share more about this organization in Action 1: Point the Flywheel.

As I look back, this is the book I wish I had available fourteen years ago when I was in that role and I failed to drive customer-focused change. I also wish I had access to *Outside In*, by Harley Manning and Kerry Bodine. It's a great overview of CX, and if you haven't read it, I suggest you start there. *Outside In* is the 101 book—*Do B2B Better* is the 201. You won't find topics like how to do an ecosystem map here. Instead, this book shows how great programs go beyond the basics to become true Change Makers, serving both their companies and their customers well.

Meet Four Great Change Makers

Because being a Change Maker requires different thinking, it's helpful to have guides. I have numerous examples of customer experience programs and tips that I'll share in this book, but I am delighted to have you meet four exemplary Change Makers: Jennifer (Jen) Zamora at Dow, Nancy Flowers at Hagerty, Natasha at an unnamed software as a service (SaaS) company we're referring to as XYZ Software, and Roxana (Roxie) Strohmenger at UKG. These four graciously gave of their time to teach me what they do. In their own words, you will learn comprehensive approaches to CX across a variety of industries that reflect the focus on value needed to differentiate your organization. And, as proof of their impact, during the writing of this book all four were promoted!

DOW

At the time I conducted the interviews, Jen Zamora was the Senior Director of Global CX and Commercial Excellence for Dow, where she's been for over twenty years in marketing, sales, business development, and customer service roles. Jen bleeds Dow red, and her broad background helps her drive change in an organization over 130 years old—not an easy task. Since I initially conducted our interviews, she was promoted to a global change-management role.

She started the CX program in 2018, reporting to Chief Commercial Officer Daniel Futter, a very visible role. It would be easy for her to disperse her efforts across dozens of initiatives, so one of her first tasks was to narrow down her team's approach to focus on three outcomes: (1) deploying a new customer survey process; (2) defining and implementing Dow's Customer Distinction Model; and (3) building customer journey mapping (CJM) practices that deliver improved customer and employee experiences. As a strong sign of her success, Dow's business units also elected to invest in customer experience, creating and funding over twenty roles. They work with Jen's team but report into the business units.

Jen's history also means that she has strong relationships throughout Dow, critical when you consider its global footprint. Based in Michigan, Dow has over thirty-five thousand employees across five businesses, less than half of which are in North America. These relationships are critical as she reorients employees to focus on customers, rather than on operations, where most manufacturing companies focus. She's become a Dow spokesperson, writing a series of articles on LinkedIn and speaking at conferences worldwide about its customer experience transformation.

HAGERTY

Nancy Flowers leads the customer experience for Hagerty. If you're not familiar with the organization, it probably means you're not into cars—especially the classic kind. While the organization began as a niche insurance company for classic and collector vehicles, the company has evolved into an automotive lifestyle brand that happens to offer insurance.

The change of mindset from insurance company to an automotive lifestyle brand helped create the recognition that a game-changing customer experience is central to Hagerty's success, and Nancy has led this charge. She's been with the company for over sixteen years, starting in marketing before creating the customer experience capability in 2011. She has seven employees reporting to her, and her role expanded while I was writing this book. She is now the Vice President of Insights and Loyalty.

As a B2B2C organization,[7] Nancy needs to manage two sets of relationships: agents and members. Both are customers for the organization, as Hagerty sells through independent agents, who can easily take their books of business elsewhere. So, she needs to ensure that agents have a great experience. One way to win an agent's loyalty is to ensure their customers are well cared for and happy, so Hagerty spends even more effort creating great experiences for the policyholder.

Nancy is an active member of the Customer Experience Professionals Association (CXPA),[8] sharing expertise across the organization. She was recognized in 2014 with its CX Impact Award.

XYZ SOFTWARE

Natasha leads customer experience at a global SaaS company that we'll refer to as XYZ Software,[9] reporting to the Chief Design Officer. She was promoted to the Global Vice President for Customer Experience soon after our interviews began. As I wrapped up writing the book, she was again promoted to chief of staff for one of the company's product lines.

Now with XYZ for a dozen years, prior to her customer experience roles, Natasha led operations and finance functions. Her experience in these functions informs her work, as she applies numbers in deliberate ways to measure and implement improvements to the customer experience. Managing a seven-person team, she works across the organization's seventy thousand employees to measure and improve the experience of using XYZ's products.

Natasha shared her thoughts on her approach to CX: "What I love about CX is that it is both an art and a science, a perfect combination for me. And so that's how I landed in this role and have loved it ever since. My goal is this: How do I make XYZ be the best in class with CX from a B2B standpoint, using technology and data to drive better experiences for our customers. And I think there's a lot more that we can do."

UKG

Roxie Strohmenger is the Vice President of Customer Experience Strategy for UKG, a provider of HR, payroll, and workforce management solutions. During the writing of this book, Ultimate Software (Roxie's original company) merged with Kronos to become UKG, with over fourteen thousand employees, and she was shortly afterward promoted to her current VP role.

Unlike our other three Change Makers, who have been with their organizations for at least a decade, Roxie came to UKG from Forrester in 2018, where she led a customer experience practice centered around the CX Index, which she cocreated, that helped organizations diagnose their CX quality and identify how to improve their outcomes. This visibility into what drove other programs' success has helped Roxie bring in new practices that give UKG a more mature program than found in most.

One fun sentiment from Roxie is that she believes that every CX leader should be able to run their own statistical regressions![10] Like Natasha (who can probably do this, too), she's very focused on using the data to diagnose the most efficient and effective way to target resources to improve the customer experience in a way that improves the business results.

Roxie was recognized with the CXPA's CX Impact Award in 2020, and she now sits on its board. She was also a finalist for the CX Leader of the Year in 2020.

Your CX Loyalty Flywheel Journey

As discussed earlier, this book is divided into four parts as you progress through the steps needed to become a Change Maker. That doesn't mean that you'll implement everything from Action 1 first, then move on to Action 2, etc. While a book is an amazing resource, it is limited to a linear format. I hope you'll take a ton of notes, then flip back and forth as you implement the steps and record the results.

What differentiates Jen, Nancy, Natasha, and Roxie from the rest of our Change Makers is that, while most Change Makers effectively implement one or two of these Actions, these four are strong in each. We'll visit them in each of the four sections. Along the way, we'll hear from dozens of others who can illustrate best or unique practices in these four Actions. While most of our case studies are from B2B and B2B2C companies, those of you who happen to work for a B2C business will find that these findings apply to you, too. We'll start by understanding the **CX Loyalty Flywheel**, looking specifically at how B2B and B2B2C programs are able to link their programs to the value that comes out of the flywheel. We'll determine sources of value and give ideas of how you can link to each of them.

Next, we'll look at the idea of creating an **Emotional North Star**, the least common of the four capabilities. This involves measuring and managing against customer emotions, as well as showing how this creates the outcomes identified in Action 1.

Following that, we'll learn how to measure the flywheel in a more comprehensive way through integrating **Customer Ecosystem Data** into your measurement, allowing you to diagnose where the flywheel can get stuck.

Lastly, we'll talk about how to accelerate your impact through **change management**. Change management greases the flywheel, helping everyone in your organization contribute to better outcomes for your customers and therefore your company.

But first, there's someone I'd like you to meet.

Introducing Change Maker Cari

I love stories. They suck me in, and it's not just me, as the research is clear: stories are how we learn best. Humans have told stories for millennia because they stick in the brain and lead to greater understanding than facts and figures. In this book, you'll find a ton of stories of great customer experience leaders, and I hope they inspire you as much as they do me.

To help frame what great programs do, I would like to introduce you to a fictional character we'll call Cari, an energetic, intelligent, and "let's get to it" kind of person who has been plucked out of a perfectly good job and offered an opportunity to explore something new—the world of customer experience. The Chief Revenue Officer of the company, whose name is Dale, is relying on her to solve the company's customer experience woes.

Cari's story, and that of the team she assembles along the way, complements the insightful case studies that populate the book. She is representative of the Change Maker lineup in the book whose voices you will hear: Jen, Nancy, Natasha, and Roxie, but also Darin, Olga, Dave, Marlanges, and all the other Change Makers I've discovered in conducting my research. I hope you enjoy Cari's journey and perhaps you will empathize with the challenges Cari and her team face.

Meet Cari

Dale had a decision to make. Two years into his role as Chief Revenue Officer for Sycamore Software Solutions, he was facing two related problems.

First, it was getting harder to find referenceable clients, which threatened future sales. Dale knew that being a referral was hard work. Prospective clients were known to pepper the referencing client with dozens of questions to learn about Sycamore's products and how the reference company was using them. As Sycamore's main software as a service (SaaS) product was central to running their customers' businesses, prospects typically spoke with three to five references before committing to purchasing Sycamore's product. A lack of referenceable clients could seriously limit growth. And, for him as Chief Revenue Officer, that was critical for his personal success.

At the same time, Sycamore's upselling strategy wasn't as successful as expected. Like most software companies, Sycamore used a Land-and-Expand model, where most profit comes from adding products. But customers weren't adding products to the extent that Sycamore projected.

When Dale spoke with customers, the reason for both of these issues became clear: Sycamore was difficult to work with. Customers consistently complained that implementing the platform was far more challenging than expected. To add insult to injury, issue resolution could be a long drawn-out affair, with issues bouncing around the organization until clients' complaints reached the ear of the CEO. The stress over these issues not only impacted clients but also took a toll on employees, who had to drop what they were doing to fix the issue of the day.

Dale saw the day when Sycamore would lose customers over these issues. They hadn't lost any yet, but that was primarily because the mission-critical nature of Sycamore's software made it difficult for customers to replace them. Doing so would disrupt that customer's business for at least a year and cost tens of millions of dollars. But if Sycamore didn't fix the issues soon, there was no guarantee this wouldn't happen. And word would almost certainly get out into the marketplace, threatening future sales even more.

Dale knew that improving customer experience was no longer a nice-to-have; it was a must-have. And he also knew it wouldn't be easy to achieve. A year earlier, he had tried to build a program by hiring someone from the outside as the Senior Director of Customer Experience. But a year into her role, Dale found she spent most of her time reporting on survey results rather than proactively working across the organization to fix the issues she discovered. Perhaps realizing she was not creating impact, she told Dale it was best to move on, leaving Dale to consider what to do next.

He thought about hiring from the outside again, but his first failure concerned him. He needed someone who had soft skills mixed with some grit—someone who could inspire Sycamore's different departments to step outside their silos and work together to improve customer outcomes. And he didn't have a year for this new hire to learn how to drive change. But nobody in the organization had background in customer experience.

However, there was one person who might work. Cari was the Senior Director of SaaS Operations, and she had led significant improvements in her time in that role. Cari started her career as a software developer, but her natural instincts and customer focus led to her receiving a string of promotions. She had a proven history of working across the company, and Dale was impressed with her tenacity. When he floated the idea of having her lead customer experience, her boss—while surprised at the idea—agreed that she had the skills to drive change that her predecessor lacked.

Finally deciding that they needed a different approach, Dale sent a Teams chat to ask if Cari had a few minutes to talk. Cari responded enthusiastically. She had met with Sycamore's previous CX leader multiple times, trying to learn what she could about the customer experience, and she had specific thoughts about how to use the role to drive action. Dale left the call feeling encouraged he had made the right decision.

ACTION 1

POINT THE FLYWHEEL

MOST COMPANIES BELIEVE IN
CUSTOMER EXPERIENCE. CHANGE
MAKERS PROVE IT WORKS.

"Delivering a great customer experience requires linking your investment to business outcomes. You might
be able to kick off the work without this, but you won't
be able to sustain it for the long term."

—**Beth Hollenback,** Vice President of Customer Experience,
Duck Creek Technologies

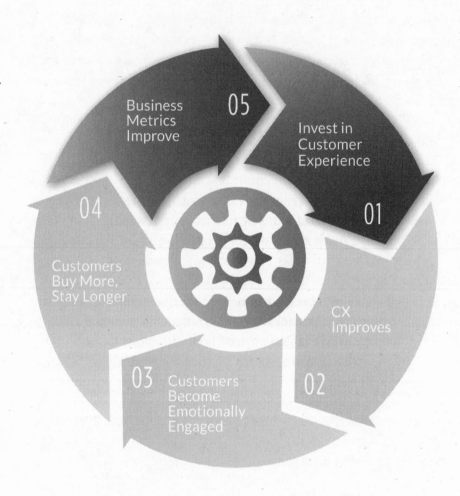

Figure 1-1: The CX Loyalty Flywheel: Prove the value.

THE CX LOYALTY FLYWHEEL IS A VISUAL REPRESENTATION OF the outcomes of investing in the customer experience (CX). As the journey improves, customers are more engaged, and levels of trust and loyalty grow, leading them to buy more of your products and services. This frees up dollars that allow your organization to continue to invest in your customer experience, responding to customer feedback to always make the experience better.

While you and I might see eye to eye on the theory of improving customer experience for the businesses we sell to, we both know that investing in CX requires providing quantifiable proof to the executive team to get their continued buy-in. Relying on faith that investing in customers will help the organization to grow might work in the short term. But sustainable change requires long-term thinking and investment, which is a challenge when executives are confronted with other pressing challenges that can show their impact to the business.

Action 1: Point the Flywheel is all about establishing how the business improves as a result of that investment in customer experience, which in our experience at Heart of the Customer is something few programs design for at the outset. We will show you a great example in chapter 1, in which we present a Change Maker named Olga who explains how she navigates this issue in a global environment. In chapter 2, we'll walk through the various ways to calculate business impact; then in chapter 3, we'll walk through how our four recurring case studies connect their programs to value.

CHAPTER 1

Can I Prove That Customer Experience Matters?

LEADERSHIP CONSISTENTLY HAS TO ENSURE THAT ITS investments are the best use of the company's funds, ensuring that the organization's success continues. Customer experience doesn't get a pass on this. Without showing the value of your work, you'll constantly be at risk of losing budget.

Change Makers deliberately and continually show how their work ties to business success, whether through higher revenue or decreased costs. Let's start by learning how one Change Maker runs her program.

Meet Olga Budieri—Her Challenges May Sound Familiar

Olga Budieri is the Global Customer Experience Lead at Aramex. Aramex provides cross-border shipping services. It partners with other companies to manage shipping requirements across countries and continents, reducing its customers' logistics complexity. Aramex serves customers varying from local mom-and-pop retailers to some of the biggest companies in the world.

Aramex's customer experience incorporates both a B2B and B2C component. Clients outsource their shipping needs to Aramex, so

Aramex's primary commercial relationships are B2B relationships. Yet, Aramex's value proposition is to ensure that a client's customers receive their goods on time. For example, a clothing retailer trusts Aramex to meet its promise to efficiently deliver packages to those who have ordered the retailer's products. The result is that Aramex has both B2B and B2C components to its customer experience, or a B2B2C experience. Aramex needs to track its two experiences separately, yet manage it as a whole.

Olga is an industrial engineer by training. While that may not be the most common background for leading customer experience, it enables her to better understand the complexities of the experience and connect it to Aramex's financial success. As Olga explains, "There is a lot of pressure to connect everything we do with return-on-investment financials, whether it's optimization or what we call an ARC objective, which stands for acquisition, retention, and cultivation, which is a mix between cross-selling and upselling. Success requires finding a true connection to return on investment, as opposed to assumptions based on secondary research."

She nicely summarizes the challenges of showing the impact of customer experience:

> We've all seen those studies where it says a one-point increase of CSAT [customer satisfaction] equals this revenue, but to a commercial officer, a CEO, or a CFO, this doesn't sound real. So, it doesn't put CX in a credible position. We need to prove this based on our own data: "These are the scores for the past year, and this is the revenue or the growth in revenue and the growth and shipments for these exact countries. And this is what it looks like. This is the correlation between the revenue and customer satisfaction and NPS." That's what they care about. An ideal scenario would be when every person in our mix has a customer satisfaction score as part of their key performance indicator scorecard. We are not there yet, but we're making great strides. In the

process, we're introducing different B2B metrics that we had not been looking at before, trying out what resonates the most with our internal organization, and with financials.

Cash always wins. There needs to be a connection. I'm not the only industrial engineer; so is the rest of my team, fortunately or unfortunately.

Olga and her team have invested in statistics and mathematical modeling, used as foundational information for dashboarding. One dashboard Olga's team is developing is a Journey Health Index, which will provide information and insight about which components of the customer experience need to be prioritized—the type of initiative many other Change Makers we interviewed also led. The need for such dashboards doesn't come up in most of the CX literature, so the consistency with which Change Makers focused on them surprised me. It seems many of our Change Makers independently came up with the idea of measuring journey health and using a dashboard to communicate the results. (We'll take a deep dive into dashboards in Action 3: Evaluate the Flywheel with Customer Ecosystem Data.)

Supporting these efforts is segmentation of its B2B customers. Aramex knows that different customers warrant different levels of support and service, and the company created a value-based segmentation to enable that. The four levels of customer segmentation are global key accounts, which Aramex supports with the largest account staff, followed by national key accounts that manage key or strategic customers at a local level. Next is middle markets, and finally SMEs (small and medium enterprises), with accounts serviced with an inside sales model. Each level has specific criteria to qualify, based on ROI, revenue, and size of company.

This segmentation can be anathema to some in customer experience, who want *every* customer to have the best experience possible. But Change Makers recognize that their organizations have limited resources, and the surest way to an undifferentiated outcome is to try to create a perfect experience for all. Additionally, these different types of clients have different needs. Investing in white-glove service to the smallest customers would require increasing prices to an unsustainable level. Segmentation enables the ability to target the right experience to the right client for the right outcome.

Most companies have some sort of customer segmentation, although most only use the segmentation for pricing and allocation of sales resources. Aramex goes further by using segmentation as a guide to create specific customer experiences, based on both needs and the customer's value to Aramex. This ability to target the right level of service to the right customer ensures strong outcomes for both Aramex and its customers.

Like most organizations, Aramex built its model incrementally, as the company hasn't found a ton of good guidance on how to build a world-class B2B customer experience. Olga summarizes what I have heard from many organizations when she shared that "a big piece of our experience is B2B related. And a lot of the CX content out there is B2C. It's relatively easy to find resource to help you map or monitor your journey for consumers, but much less easy to look at a B2B perspective and incorporate segmentation into that."

This lack of a B2B perspective inspires Olga to share her experience with others, and she is a popular speaker at customer experience events, sharing Aramex's CX journey.

Connect CX to the Health of Your Business

Olga is the paragon of a successful B2B CX leader—not despite being an industrial engineer but perhaps because of it. One finding I couldn't ignore as we conducted our analysis is that most (although not all) of the leaders we interviewed who were successful moved into a CX role from other functions or departments. Our research is clear: leaders who differentiate through an improved customer experience start by understanding the business itself—how it makes money and how that connects to the customer experience. Instead of following the conventional wisdom to focus on customer surveys,

Change Makers treat customer experience as a business discipline designed to improve customer and business outcomes. Here we have the start of the construction of the CX Loyalty Flywheel.

This connection to value ensures that customer experience won't become the "flavor of the month" because a successful CX program that clearly contributes to the health of the business will continue to receive organizational support. **It's this missing connection to organizational value that leads to the turnover endemic to most customer experience programs. By showing how you drive value, you can ensure continued impact and continued investment.**

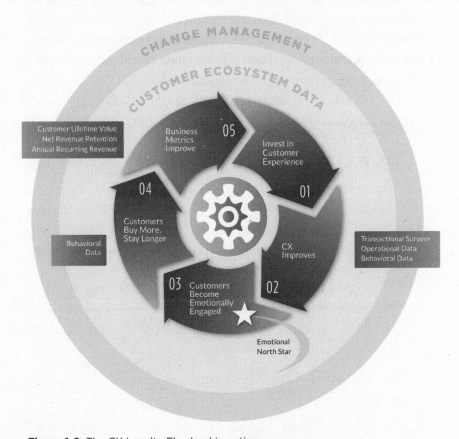

Figure 1-2: The CX Loyalty Flywheel in action.

As an example, journey analytics vendor Pointillist runs annual surveys of customer experience programs, and the top overall challenge for companies for the last three years is not being able to quantify customer experience ROI.[1]

Most guides and articles on how to build a CX program suggest you begin with a survey asking the popular Net Promoter Score (NPS) questions,[2] whereas others argue that NPS is the wrong metric, perhaps arguing for the Customer Effort Score (CES). Other guides and consulting recommend using both. But this debate begins with an assumption that the most important factor in managing your customer experience is the survey. That's a mistake. What matters is not how you measure the customer experience but what you do with the results. Change Makers focus on showing how an improved customer experience results in changes in your clients' behaviors that lead to them buying more, staying longer, and being less costly to serve.

MAKE SURE THE BUTTONS YOU PUSH MATTER

I think back to when I was in college and I was visiting my friend Rick. We headed to his dorm's game room to play some pool. In college I had no money, so pool and video games were rare treats. As we were getting ready to play pool, I noticed a video game playing in the corner and ran over to see if I could get a free game. It was a boxing match, and I mashed the buttons and moved the joystick trying to knock out my opponent. I lasted ten to fifteen seconds before losing the bout, so I headed back to the pool table. But then it started again with new boxers, so I went back to the game. I kept playing, switching with Rick when it was my time to shoot pool. We continued alternating between playing pool and the video game, never lasting more than twenty or thirty seconds before being knocked out but continually trying to do better. Finally, frustrated with repeatedly losing, we quit playing. And that's when I noticed that the game continued to play itself! It was on a recorded loop the entire time, and despite fervently mashing buttons and pulling on the joystick, nothing we did mattered.

Most CX programs are like this. They push buttons *hoping* that what they do matters. But unless they specifically tie their program to business outcomes, there's no guarantee that their efforts are having any impact at all. The CX Loyalty Flywheel may be spinning, and the Hopefuls *hope* their focus on customer experience improvements are leading customers to stay longer, buy more, and be less expensive to serve. But without connecting to the business outcomes, they will have no proof and therefore receive limited investment. They keep mashing buttons, but they don't know if they're knocking out their opponent.

SHOW ME THE MONEY

There's plenty of industry data that show that customer experience pays. The most compelling is Watermark Consulting's tracking of stock prices.[3] Watermark Consulting simulated purchasing the stock of CX Leaders (the ten top-performing companies on annual CX studies), Laggards (the bottom ten), and the S&P 500 (see figure 1-3 on next page). Every year, Watermark "sold" last year's Leaders and Laggards and "bought" the current year's, based on the new index results. Leaders outpaced the market, whereas Laggards returned less than half the value of the S&P 500.

This is a study CX leaders love to quote. Other studies show that improved customer experience leads to increased revenue[4] and a decrease in future cost of sales.[5]

But all of these are general studies across many industries. That doesn't prove that there's any value in *your* customer experience efforts at *your* company. As Olga argued above, "Success requires finding a true connection to ROI, as opposed to assumptions based on secondary research." Establishing that connection is required for CEOs to consistently invest. Even trying to make an argument based solely on secondary data will hurt your cause. Leaders want to know how improving outcomes for *your* customers will help *your* business. By connecting everything you do to value, you earn support for your efforts to improve customer and business outcomes. In this chapter, we'll show you how to make these connections, based on many examples from our Change Makers.

Customer Experience Leaders Outperform the Market
13-Year Stock Performance of Customer Experience (CX) Leaders vs. Laggards (2007–2019)

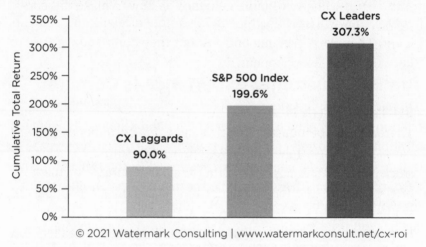

© 2021 Watermark Consulting | www.watermarkconsult.net/cx-roi

Figure 1-3: Watermark Consulting's analysis of CX Leaders and Laggards.[6]

TELL A COMPELLING STORY

Showing progress through improved survey scores isn't compelling for leaders. Disconnects between survey scores and business results are common. I once spoke with a software company that reported extremely high customer satisfaction scores in its quarterly investor calls; at the same time, the CFO wondered why she was seeing reduced retention. She certainly wasn't a believer in the power of customer experience!

This inability to prove the value of CX is common. One report showed that only 14 percent of CX professionals strongly agreed that the return on investing in CX is well established in their firms.[7] In his report, *Customer Experience at a Crossroads,* CustomerThink CEO Bob Thompson shared that most customer experience programs were unable to show value, stating, "Despite much enthusiasm at executive levels and investments in CX teams and initiatives over the past decade, only one in four companies are 'winning'—[that is] able to quantify CX benefits or achieve a competitive edge."[8]

Before we get into more detail on how to show this impact, let's go deeper into the challenges unique to B2B organizations such as yours, as this will give us more guidance on how to make this connection to business impact.

The B2B Customer Experience Is Complex

B2B relationships are more complex than those of B2C. While a B2C relationship may need to consider a buyer and a spouse, B2B organizations have dozens of influencers involved in the customer experience. Consider the client experience for UKG: the Chief Human Resources Officer (CHRO) may be the main decision-maker, but she's influenced by several vice presidents with their own needs; she has multiple locations spread across the globe, involving payroll specialists, benefits experts, and others who all work on UKG's systems. Even the frontline employees can express dissatisfaction with UKG's customer experience and consequently reduce the amount of business the company does with UKG, or possibly even stop doing business with it.

These varied roles also add complexity to measuring the customer experience. For example, whose survey scores matter? The CHRO or other senior decision-maker may make the final decision to purchase UKG, but she doesn't use the software on a day-to-day basis, so she can't always speak to its functionality and ease of use. (Nor is she likely to fill out your survey.)

Connecting surveys with business outcomes is also more complicated in B2B, both because there are fewer survey participants available and multiple roles are involved. While retailers can see thousands of shoppers every day, most B2B organizations have fewer customers. Best Buy sends daily surveys; UKG doesn't. One of our clients is a $250 million B2B organization, but its quarterly survey was only sent to 120 participants. Even if *every* client responded—which won't happen—it's still not a ton of data in which to connect customer experience to outcomes. (Don't worry—I'll walk through alternative ways to show the impact of the flywheel, even in this situation.)

The long-term nature of B2B relationships also confounds an easy connection between survey scores and overall revenue. UKG has relationships that last for years, and losing a customer is rare. If UKG sees ten years of $1 million in revenue from one company, which then becomes $0, how does it correlate survey scores to that?

While it is possible, it requires sophisticated analytic resources that few programs possess. As we'll discuss in chapter 2, there are other ways to show business impact through targeted analysis that are more approachable.

Another complication is that B2B customers vary greatly in size and spend. A retailer's customers might spend anywhere from $100 to $10,000 a year, but a manufacturer's client may order $10,000 or $100,000,000. Purchasing volume can disguise the relationship between CX and business outcomes. Imagine two customers:

- Company A orders $10,000 in widgets a year from you and $5,000 from your competitor and gives you a 9 on your 0 to 10 scale.
- Much larger Company B orders $100,000 from you and $900,000 from competitors and gives you a 6.

Comparing scores and top-line revenue gives you an inverse relationship; the higher score equates to lower revenue. Most programs give up. But Change Makers go deeper. Finding business impact requires you to go beyond top-level revenue to more granular data. And while it's hard, doing so is critical to the long-term health of your customer experience program.

Every year at budget time, leadership is tasked with choosing which initiatives to fund. Imagine that you're a senior executive. Your organization has "customer focus" as one of your pillars, and you truly believe that treating customers right is important. But you have ten budget requests in front of you, and you only have the funds for three. In that case, even though you believe in the power of customer experience, it's tough to pass over one with hard dollar ROI in favor of this "customer" project with its success measured by a survey outcome.

Luckily, there are alternatives that Change Makers use to build the case, and we'll discuss those further in this section.

Why Connecting to Value Matters

A critical component of the CX Loyalty Flywheel is proving that it actually improves business outcomes. If your efforts aren't leading customers to stay with you longer, spend more, or become less costly to serve, you have to ask whether you're truly improving the customer experience in any meaningful way. (Spoiler alert: you aren't.) This value is what your fellow executives care about. They may show some interest in an improved NPS score, but they'll be far more likely to support you if you demonstrate that investments in customer experience result in increased retention or higher cross-sells. Once you establish that link, you know where to invest to improve outcomes.

By linking to business metrics, you also show the impact of your work. I won't spend any time going into what is the right survey metric to link to value, as our research shows that the "right" survey questions vary by industry, and even within players in the same industry. Suffice it to say that if your metric doesn't predict any of the sources of value discussed below, then it's the wrong metric. But even with the right metric, our Change Makers rightly focus emphasis on business outcomes rather than survey results. They don't view the survey results as the score but instead as a diagnostic, helping to explain why the business results are what they are.

Business Growth Can Hide a Multitude of Sins

I would be remiss if I didn't share my own experience in showing the business value of customer experience. Or, more accurately, failing to do so. When I left Best Buy, I joined a health insurance organization as the product owner for health savings accounts (HSAs). Like its name suggests, this is a special bank account for use in healthcare. Our company was growing rapidly, and we led the nation in sales and number of accounts, so everyone was pleased. But I realized that literally nobody in marketing or product development had ever met a client. (Note: A client was the decision-maker in the business we sold the accounts to, while a customer was their employee who opened the account.)

As I talked with clients and customers, I discovered that our products were the most complex on the market because we were creating the products that *we* wanted to buy. When I talked about the need to spend time with customers, the answer was "Jim, we don't need to talk to customers. We *are* customers." Well, yes. The most biased customers on the planet. Whereas we thought about HSAs eight to ten hours a day, our customers didn't spend that much time thinking about them in an entire year!

So, I went on a mission to improve our products, moving from product development to CX. I had the two easiest business problems on earth that I could leverage. First, even though their employers offered them hundreds of dollars to open the accounts, 14 percent of employees didn't open them. That was over fifty thousand potential customers who could receive hundreds of dollars in free money if they just opened the accounts. Since we were a bank, that meant we missed out on over $10 million in deposits! Second, while we led the nation in sales, we also led the nation in the percentage of customers who canceled the accounts.

But I didn't use these business cases. Rather than starting with the business opportunity, I started—and ended—with customers. "Our products are too complex!" I told the team. "No, they aren't" was the reply. I used survey scores to show how customers were frustrated by our product.

But what I didn't do is show the linkage between the survey scores and those business outcomes. Because we were growing so fast, nobody focused on churn. Business growth hides a multitude of sins, and the teams were feeling good about the growth.

Had I worked with finance to show the dollars lost through our poor experience, I'm confident I could have created positive change. But because my only message was that customers were frustrated, executives were frustrated with *me*! Finally, I was called into my boss's boss's office, and he closed the door, telling me, "You create a lot of noise." (This wasn't the first time he had said this to me.) "We're going to have to make a change."

The next thing I knew, I was responsible for writing marketing collateral. Not exactly my strength.

So, I speak from personal experience. If you want to drive customer-focused change, tie it to the strength of the business. Because if your work doesn't lead to customers who *want* to buy more, stay longer, or interact in less expensive ways, then you're doing it wrong.

Showing the Value of Support Interactions

Dave Seaton was the Vice President of Service Level Transformation (Customer Experience) at nThrive, a platform that improves revenue cycle speed, accuracy, and productivity for medical companies.[9] He didn't start in CX; he was previously a programmer with a passion for customers. nThrive won ARCET Global's North American Customer Centricity Award for his efforts to move the organization toward a customer focus. When we asked him how he communicates the value of his efforts, he shared the following:

You can ask what your stakeholders care about, or you can pay attention to what they talk about in business reviews and other reports. So, I know our CFO has his eye on new bookings. And he's got his eye on retention. So, there are two financial metrics that are very, very important to our CFO. If I want to influence him to spend time or money on something I think is important, I've got to tie it back to "this is going to help sell more" or "this is going to help keep customers from churning." That's what he cares about. So, how do you connect those dots?

It's an art and a science. What's effective is aligning to metrics that stakeholders already care about. Rather than trying to get people to care about the customer experience metrics, align those to what they already care about, whether that's financial or operational metrics, depending on where they sit. For example, if you have a stakeholder who cares about revenue, and you can show how improving the customer experience can lead to revenue, retention, and renewals and repurchase, then you've got that stakeholder's attention.

If you've got somebody who cares about operational performance, speed, quality, and cost, and you can show how improving the customer experience is also going to lead to operational efficiencies, you've got that person's attention.

Being aligned with the customer service and support organization, renewals are the biggest indicator of success, where clients are terminating because of dissatisfaction with service and support. Once a client has bought our technology, gone through a lengthy implementation, and gone live on it, their greatest number of interactions is with service and support. One of the things research has found is that each customer service interaction is four times more likely to drive disloyalty than to drive loyalty. So, everything we can do to make those customer service interactions as easy and hassle-free as possible is going to contribute to that customer perception of nThrive and ultimately factor into renewals.

We've had to shift how we think about who our customer is. Is it the CFO of the hospital system? Is it a particular hospital or the user of the software? And it's all of them. And so, in B2B, we found customer experience takes on an almost geometric level of complexity because you're not dealing with a single person and their motivations and expectations and frustrations; [rather], the customer is this entity made up of dozens, or sometimes hundreds, of people who have different motivations, expectations, etc.

But it's all connected. Because that end user who is really frustrated with their customer support experience, they're going to tell their boss, who is going to tell their boss, and if that message is loud enough, the guy who's writing the checks is going to hear about it, and then it's going to become a renewal issue for us. By the time the CFO is saying, "We've got a problem with our vendor," that problem was months in the making over dozens and hundreds of interactions with many different people that's built up this collective opinion within the customer. Shifting those organizational perspectives in your customer is a very long-term endeavor.

Dave shared how he used all of this to make the business case to bring in a customer experience platform:

The idea of regularly surveying customers was new. So, we used our CX results to get funding for a survey platform. We weren't doing any transactional surveys. This came full circle back around to how we convinced the CFO to spend six figures on a world-class survey platform. We said, "These clients are terminating, and here's the price tag on it. They're terminating for dissatisfaction with service. One of the things they most care about is the effort they're spending in working with us. We're not even measuring effort. If we buy this, we can measure effort, and we can improve it.

And we can prevent these terminations and return this money to the bottom line."

Finance said, "Great, I see the ROI. Sweet." So, you start with the financial data. We did the work to figure out what they cared about and why were they leaving, starting with the financial piece and working backward to the root cause.

■ ■ ■

The focus of this chapter is on the importance of establishing how customer experience impacts your organization's success, which is critical to implementing the CX Loyalty Flywheel. Establishing that linkage is critical to gaining the internal support required for sustained investment. How to do it in a systematic way is the topic we tackle next.

Cari's Story

Cari was excited to get started! Throughout her time at Sycamore, she had made it a policy to take every opportunity to meet with customers, learning about them and how they were using Sycamore's software. Her role in SaaS operations had helped her learn where problems occurred and how it impacted them on a day-to-day basis. Over time, she came to realize that many of the problems her colleagues in operations faced were rooted in other parts of the organization. Taking on the role of Vice President of Customer Experience would help her realize her vision of creating better outcomes for her clients—and for Sycamore, as well.

The first thing she needed to do was to make it clear that, unlike her predecessor, she wasn't the "survey person." To learn more about the broader experience, she scheduled a learning tour, meeting with leaders throughout the organization to discover their perceptions of the customer experience and the causes of the negative feedback, and to enlist their help to drive change. When Dale announced her new role, she made sure he sent a separate note to leadership to set up these interviews.

As she met with leaders, she heard a consistent inconsistency. Perspectives were all over the place, with two leaders even claiming that Sycamore offered the best experience in the industry! While that might possibly be true, she had no desire to be the best of the worst. She knew from previous conversations that Sycamore's clients didn't compare Sycamore with their competitors; they compared it to their best SaaS vendors—including those that had nothing to do with Sycamore's product. One customer even compared it to their job posting software!

She considered the feedback; success required getting every leader aligned on the importance of changing the experience. So, she asked Dale to help her create a CX council to guide her work, involving Patricia (the COO and her former boss), representatives from product, as well as marketing and their HR leader. The existing leadership team (LT) meetings had a fixed agenda, and getting on the LT's schedule was difficult. Instead, she met monthly with this subset of the LT to guide her efforts.

There was one more important interview on Cari's horizon—her CFO, Yolanda. Cari began to prepare.

My Thoughts

Dale's decision to hire someone inside the organization was a smart move. While it's possible to drive change through an external hire, our analysis of CX leaders has shown that the programs that had the most challenges were often led by an external hire because they had a difficult time navigating the organization. Where there were exceptions to this rule, those leaders typically had consulting experience, so they already knew how to work across different types of organizations and functions.

A new CX leader needs to be very visible, and these initial meet and greets are crucial to gaining the buy-in needed to improve the customer experience. The CX council is another crucial element of change management: continuing to engage leadership. We'll return to both of these topics in Action 4: Grease the Flywheel with Change Management.

CHAPTER 2

Do I Know How CX Provides Value to My Organization?

HOW CUSTOMER EXPERIENCE PROVIDES ORGANIZATIONAL value is through the CX Loyalty Flywheel. Top-line revenue grows through multiple components, including gaining more customers, improving customer retention rates, and selling more to your customer base. There are also cost savings from an improved experience, such as reducing customer complaints. Start here to understand how your customer experience relates to your company's financials and drives profits.

It's Time to Hug Your CFO

I'm constantly surprised at how few in marketing and customer experience have a relationship with their finance team. I cannot suggest strongly enough the necessity to spend time with finance to become educated on the financial drivers of your business, even if you think you understand them. Asking to improve your understanding will help build the bridge to finance. After all, a supportive finance team offers instant credibility and reassures executives you are focused on business outcomes. Finance also likely has models to give you a head start.

Your ultimate goal is to have finance proactively talking about the relationship between customer experience and financial outcomes. While most of our interviews were with B2B and B2B2C companies, we also interviewed Twin City Federal (TCF) Bank's Director for Line of Business Finance, Noah Jones,[1] who was quite articulate about the relationship between the two. As he explains:

> Where you can really differentiate and make money is if you have a better mousetrap in terms of being where customers want you to be, which is related to CX. So, we thought, "How do we measure this relationship?" And that's all about usage. So, we actually measure direct interaction with TCF. How many times do you swipe your debit card? How many times are you making deposits? How many times are you accessing online banking? What we're finding is that customers, if they're using us more, they tend to be more profitable for us as well. And it's also positively correlated to interaction satisfaction.
>
> And so, we broke measurement into a couple of pieces. We measure NPS on a relational basis, and there are a number of other key performance indicators [KPIs] we measure below that, such as on an interaction. We discovered that customer satisfaction was a lagging indicator of what customers feel, and usage was a leading indicator of what they feel. Understanding that helped us drive what we want to do to engage with customers earlier in the process before any disengagement or unhappiness occurs. It also helped us think of interaction satisfaction, which led to us asking "easy to bank with" questions. These are more of a diagnostic tool because, when we see these types of instances of customers not feeling engaged and they're changing their behavior, we can use the wealth of the data we have on our customers' interactions to help us figure out where we can drive improvements.

We also look at the channels and use types. Are they going through the least friction type channels that we have? Are we seeing a slope in the amount of business that they're doing with us, primarily around the top deposit balances? All of that should then be well correlated with a strong NPS, which is what we see. I think of NPS as being a good diagnostic tool.

When finance has such a deep understanding of the relationship between customer experience and business outcomes, it makes it much easier to get executive buy-in, something we'll discuss more when we delve into change management. In this chapter, we will focus on the metrics that reveal value, and in chapter 3, we will discuss ways of working with finance.

Make Finance Your Ally

It is my experience that building a bridge between customer experience and finance pays solid dividends. When you can create an ally and advocate in finance, it makes your job to prove the value of CX so much easier. While you may believe your CEO cares about high survey scores, they spend far more time talking with your CFO than they do looking at these scores. If your finance teams see the value and benefits to the organization by improving customer experience, they can support CX by advising on the right level of investment. You can't simply ask for finance's support. You need to start by doing the heavy lifting to show that customer experience has a strong impact to your company's financial outcomes, as we discuss here in Action 1.

Valuing Customer Experience

There's no shortage of ways to show value, depending on the nature of your business. However, there are some general categories. I'm going to outline six categories of value, but realize that all these are related. The six categories are client retention, share of wallet, lifetime value, innovation, referrals, and costs to serve.

CLIENT RETENTION

For many, client retention is the first place to turn, and for good reason. Preventing churn is a natural focus for customer experience. If your experience is compelling, why would clients ever look elsewhere? Subscription-based organizations, such as SaaS companies, internet providers, and some service businesses, focus obsessively on improving retention. If you can create great outcomes for your clients, they'll reward you by staying with you to your mutual benefit.

However, retention isn't the right focus for every organization. Many SaaS companies have churn rates below 2 percent. One of our SaaS clients lost only three customers in a year, while onboarding dozens of clients over the same time period. Imagine focusing on churn and reporting that you lowered churn by one-third, and it's just by reducing the number of three lost clients to two. Yes, it matters. But it's hard to prove this didn't just happen by chance.

In other industries, it's almost impossible to know when customers leave you. If a distributor's client doesn't order for three months, does that mean that it's no longer a customer or is it that it just didn't need any of your products in that timeframe?[2] One of our clients assumed that some customers that had gone without submitting an order in the last six months had churned. The client contacted these customers to see why they left. This led to confusing interviews because the customer didn't consider itself as having stopped working with the company. The only way to measure lost customers in organizations whose customers order sporadically is to use assumptions, such as customers who haven't ordered in six months have left you, even though we know assumptions can be wrong. One customer may not have ordered for six months and may still consider itself a customer, while another who hasn't ordered for two months has moved on, but that client's departure hasn't hit your radar yet.

One-and-Done Customers Hurt

A specific type of churn issue is the *one-and-done customer*. B2B and B2B2C programs typically have a higher cost of sales, requiring a long-term relationship to offset those costs. One client requires a customer to stay for three years before it sees *any* profit. By the time you add in the costs to sell and onboard the customer, one-and-done customers may cost you more than those who never buy from you. An insurance client[3] that served multiple channels discovered that, in one channel, its experience was so bad that over half of its agents abandoned the company after working with it only once!

Your first step is to discover your costs of sales and of onboarding a new client. Many organizations document their cost of sales, so this is a good starting point, although tracking onboarding costs is less common. If you can quantify what it costs to land a new customer, and compare that with the profit of the only order, it's a straightforward calculation to show how much each one-and-done customer costs you. Next, identify the causes for this quick attrition and attack that. Improving this will enable you to show the organization strong impact.

SHARE OF WALLET

Share of wallet is the amount of money a customer spends with your company as a percentage of the overall category spending, a common concern for B2B companies. For example, Hagerty and Dow are both keenly interested in winning as much of their agents' or customers' business in their category as possible. They strive to create an experience that is so compelling that customers naturally want to order from them whenever they can.

The share of wallet calculation is simple:

Amount your customer spends with your company

Amount your customer spends in the category

If a customer of Dow's purchases $10 million in chemicals, and $5 million of that is from Dow, Dow's share of wallet with that customer is 50 percent. The math is easy, and the numerator is readily available.[4] But the denominator is harder. Few industries can track the total amount a customer spends in a category. While a Dow account manager may be able to guess at a customer's total spending, Dow has no systematic way to determine how much their thousands of customers spend on relevant products.

However, even when you can't get the actual numbers, there are two ways to create approximate results, including using surveys and analyzing categories.

Ask Customers How Much They Spend

It's less scientific, but to discover your share of wallet, you can simply ask survey recipients how much they spend in your category, including how much of that is with you. When we conducted a survey for one manufacturer, we asked participants their top two vendors in the manufacturer's market and the amount spent with each. We weren't looking for precision but to understand mindshare. This enabled us to show how customer experience reflected the share of wallet, as demonstrated in figure 2-1. This type of reporting works well for most B2B organizations, especially when a more scientific number isn't available.

Impact of "Brand Confidence" on Share of Wallet

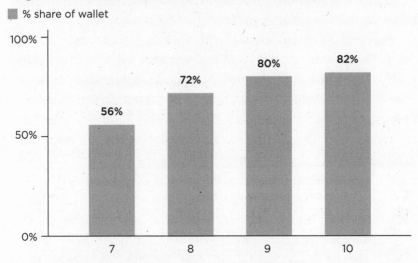

Figure 2-1: Impact of "brand confidence" on share of wallet.[5]

Consider Product Categories Purchased

A common proxy for share of wallet is product categories purchased, particularly for industries where customers order from competitors simultaneously. This is often labeled as "cross-sells." Product suppliers such as manufacturers and distributors offer multiple related products, as do broad-based consultancies or other service providers. Dow's competitors offer unique products that it doesn't, so Dow will never win 100 percent of a customer's chemical business. However, there are categories where Dow competes directly with these competitors. As Dow continues to focus on improving the experience, its customers are more likely to switch purchases they are making with Dow's competitors in discretionary categories to Dow. If a customer formerly purchased products in one category, and then because of your improved customer experience starts purchasing in a second and third category, that's a source of value.

Another client is primarily a distributor that also offers software. This client can prove that customers who rate its distribution experience highly are more likely to purchase its software—a big win, since software margin is much higher. This is the impetus for this organization to focus on customer experience.

Many SaaS companies start with a single product and then sell more, an approach called Land and Expand. These organizations measure the impact of an improved customer experience by showing how it leads customers to purchase more products. The sheer cost of implementing the first solution often makes it difficult to replace the vendor, so long-term retention is virtually guaranteed, even if the experience is brutal. But this negative experience can haunt the company when its clients refuse to purchase additional modules.

I recall a workshop we held with a client, and we showed videos of an interview with its customers to illustrate how much our client's poor customer experience impacted its business. After one interview, the sales rep for this account shared how that client forbade her from bidding on a million-dollar project because of its frustration. That story, combined with the rest of the data, showed the company the costs of its poor customer experience and was a critical reason why it redesigned its experience. We'll talk more about driving change in Action 4: Grease the Flywheel with Change Management.

Order Velocity

While share of wallet is important, it can be difficult to measure. A simpler method is looking at order velocity: Do customers that report a better experience also order more often? If not, then you may not be focusing on improving the right parts of the experience. Improving order velocity typically increases other revenue-related metrics, from categories ordered to overall revenue and margin. But there's something about the specific nature of order velocity that makes it compelling. Here's an example, and while it's B2C, it still illustrates the point: one nonprofit client found that as the customer experience improves, its donors respond by making contributions more often. This organization found that contribution velocity was the best way to show the impact of its experience work.

LIFETIME VALUE

Customer lifetime value (CLV but also called LTV or CLTV) combines retention and revenue into one overall metric. This was the most common metric our Change Makers used to show their impact. One challenge to this metric is the variety of ways in which a "single" metric is calculated so differently. Here's the metric at its core:

Number of years of expected retention ×

Expected annual purchases

For example, if a segment of customers is expected to remain with your company for eight years, spending $12,000 annually, then the CLV is $96,000. The hardest part of CLV is the expected length of retention. It's easy to see how long customers have stayed with you historically; projecting into the future requires assumptions. This calculation can become much more complicated once you consider referrals or when you add costs into the equation, as some do. I spoke at a conference with Lori Laflin, Vice President of Client Experience and Digital Strategy at Compeer Financial. Compeer provides lending to farmers, and Lori explained the complexities in creating a CLV score, asking, "How much credit do you give a farmer for his grandson's loan?"

Change Makers typically report CLV based on categories of survey scores to show the impact of improving the customer experience. The most common way to report it is by NPS levels (Promoters, Passives, Detractors). That makes for a nice slide. But the more powerful calculations often come from other survey questions or from your data, such as satisfaction with issue resolution or confidence in the company. These questions are also closer to the root cause than "likelihood to recommend," suggesting where to target interventions. For example, if you can show the CLV for those who were satisfied with how their issues were handled versus those who weren't, or report on CLV by preferred channel, that becomes very powerful.

While multiplying expected revenue times expected years of retention is the simplest way to calculate CLV, I'm a fan of a more comprehensive approach, factoring in costs to serve. However, this data may be difficult to isolate. For example, can you track customer service or rush-shipping costs back to a specific customer?

One client takes the CLV calculation to an extreme:

$$\text{CLTV} = \sum_{-S} \left[\sum_{p-1}^{N} \left(\sum_{t-0}^{w} \left(\frac{1}{(1+i_t)^{t-1/2}} \right) \left(\left(\prod_{j-1}^{T} R_j \right) \left(\sum_{s-1}^{U} (P'_{p,t,a} - CR_{p,t,a}) + IF_{p,t} - CO_{p,t} - CRe_{p,t} - CocMs_{p,t} \right) \right) \right) \right]_{S}$$

Don't ask me to interpret this for you, because I have *no* idea what they're calculating!

While CLV's expected retention can make this difficult to calculate, there are two related metrics that don't have this issue: net revenue retention and annual recurring revenue.

Net Revenue Retention

Net revenue retention (NRR), also called net dollar retention, combines customer retention with sales volume (but not new customers' sales). The calculation is:

**Number of last year's customers renewing this year ×
Average spent this year**
————————————————————
Number of customers last year × Average spent last year

For example, if last year you had one hundred customers who spent $1,000 and you lost five of them, with revenue staying consistent, your calculation would be:

95 customers (this year) × $1,000 = $95,000
————————————————————
100 customers (last year) × $1,000 = $100,000

Or 95 percent. Note that new customers don't factor into this; this is strictly about retention. To examine a different scenario, let's say that you upsell your remaining 95 customers by $100 on average. In that case, the calculation is:

95 customers (this year) × $1,100 = $104,500

100 customers (last year) × $1,000 = $100,000

Or 104.5 percent.

I like NRR because it directly represents the outcome of your customer experience. While CX can certainly impact new sales, we typically focus more on retention and growth. So, it's appealing to use a metric that highlights those two outcomes. NRR is the metric we often recommend to our clients. It doesn't work for everyone, though. For example, few health insurance companies offer many upsells, so in this segment, it's more effective to focus on retention only. But NRR works well for most industries. Analysis by SaaS Capital shows a direct relationship for SaaS companies between NRR and growth, which makes sense.[6] It's hard to grow if you're constantly needing to replace your existing revenue.

Growth Rate Based on Net Revenue Retention

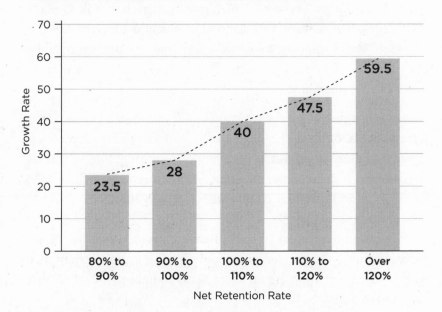

Figure 2-2: Growth rate based on net revenue retention (NRR).[7]

If I were ever to take on a corporate CX role again, my first step would be to own this as a metric and report on it regularly. Everyone in the organization would know our NRR.

Annual Recurring Revenue

Annual recurring revenue (ARR) is the most common metric for SaaS companies. ARR goes beyond NRR to factor in new customers. It is calculated as follows:

$$\frac{\begin{array}{l}\text{Last year's overall subscription revenue} \\ \text{+ New contracted revenue} \\ \text{+ Recurring revenue from add-ons or upgrades} \\ \text{- Revenue lost from cancellations}\end{array}}{\text{Last year's ARR}}$$

Note that unlike net revenue retention, this formula includes new sales. Another key word, which makes this a better fit for SaaS companies, is *recurring*. One-time sales, such as services, are not included. That's important for SaaS companies looking to go public because their valuation is based off licensing sales (revenue from services does not count).

INNOVATION

There's no question about it: innovation is exciting! But what does it have to do with customer experience? Creating a great experience makes it more likely that clients will trust you enough to try your new products and services.

New products typically have higher margin, offset by higher perceived risk. Customers who report having a great experience with your organization are far more likely to have the level of trust required to purchase these new products.

An even better outcome is the willingness of customers to partner with you to create new-to-the-world products. I know of several manufacturers who show how customers who report a better experience are also more willing to conduct joint innovation programs. Those customer experience leaders tell me that this is one of their most compelling forms of impact. When you can generate coinnovation, you typically get a halo effect that creates a more engaged customer, leading to higher order velocity and margin in the rest of your book of business.

Innovation is also a compelling topic for most executives. Any link you can create to innovation will typically find a receptive audience among your peers throughout the business.

REFERRALS

Advocacy is at the core of the popular Net Promoter Score. Despite that, few programs systematically track referrals and connect it to the customer experience. Don't confuse someone who clicks on a high score for "likelihood to recommend" with a customer who will actually refer you, as the two rarely match up. I once met with the leaders of a bank who did this analysis, and they reported that there was very little connection between a customer's "likelihood to recommend" score and actual referrals. Intention does not always carry over to behavior.

A related outcome is a customer's willingness to be a reference. A lack of referenceable customers is a drain on growth. For some industries, such as software, being a reference is a chore, involving multiple calls and potential site visits. Tying the customer experience to referenceable accounts shows the impact of improvements made.

COSTS TO SERVE

Many customer experience efforts are led by marketing, which naturally focuses on revenue. But customer experience can have an immediate impact on cost savings. The most direct route to reducing costs is removing the need for customers to call your contact center by reducing the cause for complaints. As B2B complaints are frequently more complex than B2C, often requiring the use of engineers and developers, they typically have higher costs. Depending on the nature of the complaint, costs can average from $25 to $100 and up per incident, as compared to $3 to $15 per incident in B2C, so reducing volume through an improved experience helps both your customers (who would prefer not to have to call your support team) and your company. An improved customer experience can prevent the need for calls, as well as encourage self-service. Reducing costs is often the fastest way to show impact.

Extended software or hardware implementation is another impact of a poor customer experience. Implementing software can take months, involving teams of individuals and potential time spent on client sites. A poor implementation experience can lead to unnecessarily lengthening this investment; it also delays when customers are able to buy your next product, critical to the Land-and-Expand approach common to most software companies. This measurement is called time to value, and it is an important metric for both you and your clients, neither of whom benefit from a delayed implementation. Implementations are often complex, so tracking and improving time to value is critical to many software- and hardware-based customer experiences.

Few companies track the direct costs of implementation, but it's easy to do a back-of-the-envelope calculation. If the implementation team includes a project manager at $180K (including benefits and related costs), an engineer ($220K), and two implementation specialists ($200K each), then that implementation team costs $800K a year. Shortening an implementation by two weeks will result in saving $31K (800K / 52 weeks × 2 weeks) per implementation. And that doesn't count travel or management time, so $40k isn't out of the question. If your organization does six implementations a year, that's $240K in savings—not too shabby!

Revenue-based outcomes are important and typically enable higher-dollar impact; however, they often take longer to impact (especially when there are long-term contracts). Reducing costs to serve, however, typically requires involving a smaller team and can show quicker impact.

For example, if there are many calls related to understanding invoices, you may be able to address this through a communications program or an invoice redesign. While that's not a quick fix, it involves fewer teams, primarily communications and billing. Involving fewer teams means less coordination and typically less cost.

■ ■ ■

The key plank of this chapter is that, before you can engage finance, it's important to do some of the heavy lifting yourself to identify where you can drive business impact. Once that's done, you can earn the right to get finance to proactively discuss the relationship between customer experience and financial outcomes in the CX Loyalty Flywheel.

Different industries have different business models, so financial drivers vary by industry. Manufacturing involves repeat purchases and regular interactions; software is ordered once and updated frequently; engineering services are somewhere in between. Each industry benefits from customer experience in different ways, requiring you to work with your finance organization to identify the metrics your leadership focuses on.

This may seem obvious. Where else would you discover what drives financial success? But while it's intuitive, it's not common. When we conducted our interviews, three questions we asked participants were:

1. If I were to ask you whether the customer experience is getting better or worse, how would you go about answering that question?
2. How would your CEO go about answering it?
3. How would your favorite finance person go about answering it?

Most were stumped by our third question, but Change Makers had an easy answer because they had already asked the question.[8]

There is an old saying that if you can't measure something, you can't manage it. In the next chapter, we'll talk about how CX can be measured and what measurement tells you about the health of your customer relationships.

Cari's Story

As Cari continued with the interviews, there was one last leader who was difficult to schedule. She wanted to meet with her CFO, Yolanda, to understand her perspective as to how customer experience impacted the organization's financial success. But Yolanda's admin kept canceling the meeting at the last minute. While Yolanda was a popular leader—she'd been with the company since its early days—others shared that she didn't see customer health as part of her role, which is likely why the meeting kept being pushed off. Cari finally asked Dale to intervene, asking for time for the three of them to meet together.

Cari came to the meeting prepared, and Dale was even impressed by her questions. She knew that Yolanda reported on annual recurring revenue, so she began by asking about how the score was calculated and reported and whether the analysis incorporated such factors as their existing Net Promoter Score. Yolanda was aware that Sycamore surveyed customers, but didn't see the relevance to ARR. As she argued, "Our bank doesn't accept NPS points." Cari countered with specific examples of how Sycamore's happiest customers (based on survey results) had higher ARR. Customers with higher survey scores for both decision-makers and influencers averaged 2.5 products, whereas the overall book of business had only 1.6 products and thus, a low ARR. Yolanda conceded that there may be some relevance; when Cari asked for a resource to help with this analysis, Yolanda agreed to assign a team member to help.

Cari also asked about net revenue retention, which she felt better illustrated the impact of customer experience. Yolanda agreed that NRR was important, but countered, "With our current rate of growth, ARR is what our investors are mostly interested in. They want to know that we're growing. So, that's what we report."

This didn't surprise Cari. But she had a ready response: "The data elements are much the same, with the primary difference being that NRR doesn't include new customers. As we look at the analysis, I'd like to include that as a specific measurement, as my role is focused on the loyalty of existing customers."

Yolanda agreed, ending the meeting with "Thank you for setting this up. I don't typically pay attention to soft data like surveys, but maybe there's something here we can learn."

My Thoughts

Cari worked first to establish her credibility and visibility at Sycamore. She has the benefit of a leader who is her advocate and understands the necessity of engaging senior leaders in the company. But most importantly, Cari carefully prepared for her meeting with her CFO.

While the financial numbers express dollars, underneath them is an emotional connection with customers. The flywheel in this book is called the CX Loyalty Flywheel for a very good reason: loyalty is hard to earn and easy to lose.

Once your finance team understands the value of investing in CX, you will have earned their confidence and trust. It will be hard work, so be prepared. Have some client survey results ready that, in their words, speak to the growth in business because of the focus on experience. And once finance is engaged, keep the finance team informed and channels of communication open.

CHAPTER 3

Can I Identify the Best Path to Show Value?

IT IS MY EXPERIENCE THAT CX LEADERS WHO HAVE COME TO that role from elsewhere in the organization intuitively understand how the organization sees customer-related value, so they are able to connect the customer experience to these outcomes. But what is there to be said about the organization's view of value?

If you don't know what metrics have the most priority in terms of how leadership measures business success (or even if you do), it's always a good idea to regularly meet with finance. Your long-term goal should be to create an advocate like Noah Jones from TCF Bank—a finance leader who can speak eloquently about the connections between customer experience and business success. This may be an uphill battle. In our interviews with finance leaders, many were unable to articulate a connection between their work and customer experience. This is a concern: if your finance team doesn't see a linkage between the metrics it tracks and the degree to which the organization is providing a compelling customer experience, finance certainly won't be an advocate for spending resources to improve the experience. When we help organizations build a CX capability, the first thing we do is to have leaders meet with finance to determine how to connect the dots.

Having finance validate your work—or, even better, *present* it—will go a long way to building credibility.

To do this, as Noah outlined (see page 24), you must understand the connections between customer experience and business success. Let's begin to explore the process by understanding your customers, measuring customer value, and using your best thinking to implement value.

Getting Clear on Customer Value

You can't build a great customer experience if you don't know who those customers are or how they recognize value—and provide value back to your organization. Once you understand that, the next step is to segment customers based on the value they give. Let's be clear: Your best customers *should* both receive and give more benefits from their relationships with you. That's the best way to ensure that value is sustainable.

Sales and marketing likely have a segmentation system already. In fact, both may have their own and even contradictory segmentations. Sales typically segments based on customer size because it wants to target the right sales approach to the complexity of the organization. That makes this a good place to begin, as your organization likely grasps the relationship between customer size and potential value. Marketing may segment based on industry, size, or a host of other factors. Your goal isn't to tell marketing to stop using its own segmentation for communication but rather, to create one for service design.

We heard in chapter 1 how Aramex used customer segmentation to develop specific service levels for its customers. Similarly, Dow created three levels of segmentation: key customers, who represent its most strategic accounts; priority; and foundational, with the foundational customers representing over 90 percent of its customers. Although the company originally targeted fifty customers for its key segment, through a multiyear process of negotiating with sales and leadership on the criteria for the three levels, it settled on seventy-eight. While that's quite a bit bigger than fifty, it's still just a fraction of its more than fifteen thousand customers. Doing this foundational work of segmenting customers based on value opened the door for Dow to a host of service design opportunities and helped align the organization on the importance of customer experience through a deliberate process of distinction or designing specific levels of customer experience for each.

Trying to improve the experience for everyone dilutes your efforts. One key phrase Change Makers often use is "I don't want to boil the ocean." Often the fastest way to show impact is to isolate a set of high-value customers and deliberately design improved experiences for this group. That first design is often resource intensive but pays for itself by increasing engagement for these high-margin customers. You'll likely learn from this activity and often will be able to design a more scalable version for the rest of the customer base once this is complete.

MEASURING CUSTOMER VALUE

Customers experience you through journeys. Once you understand how the organization gains value from customer experience, the next step is to understand which journeys are most critical to establishing that value. Research from both CustomerThink and from my firm, Heart of the Customer, shows that effective organizations first map the end-to-end experience to understand the entire customer landscape. This then shows which individual subjourneys are more likely to create—or detract from—that value.

The onboarding journey is a Moment of Truth for many B2B firms. *Onboarding* is the general term that describes the time immediately after the sale, where customers learn to work with you and discover your value. In software companies, it's often referred to as installation or implementation. When onboarding goes well, customers learn to trust you and discover how your products make them more successful. It is tremendously difficult to recover from a failed onboarding experience. One large reason for this is the cognitive bias called excessive coherence, where the emotions that were initially formed remain consistent even when disconfirming evidence is found. It is very hard to turn around a failed onboarding experience.

In one particular instance, we mapped the onboarding experience for a distributor and discovered that two weeks was the magic number. If onboarding was not successful within two weeks, customers had a lower order velocity throughout their tenure; the impacts of a poor onboarding lasted for years. Showing this connection between an effective onboarding process and business outcomes presents a compelling reason to invest in improving the experience. In another case, a company that installs diagnostic systems for hospitals discovered that the success of the installation journey (equivalent to implementation) predicted whether that customer would renew at the end of the five-year contract. Much as with the distributor, showing this clear linkage between customer experience and business outcomes accelerates the business case to invest in this experience.

You may not be able to measure the impact of journeys immediately; many organizations find that they need to map the end-to-end experience to better understand how each journey impacts the financial outcomes of customer experience, then come back and work on specific journeys.

IMPLEMENTING VALUE

Once you understand the big picture, your next step is to isolate the best opportunities to connect an improved customer experience to business value. I am regularly asked how to utilize all the different ways that CX can help a business prosper. My advice is to analyze all the financial impacts in chapter 2, then focus reporting on the three or four with the greatest impact and appeal.

This is done in two ways. The first is to connect customer experience as a whole with financial outcomes, typically through connecting surveys to business value. Show the connection between your relationship survey and the business outcomes listed in chapter 2. While getting access to the financial data can be tough, once you have it, this analysis is straightforward. This step is necessary but not sufficient to become a true Change Maker because it often leads executives to say, "So what? I get it—happier customers spend more money with us. But that doesn't give me any direction on what to do next."

Change Makers do deeper analysis to give clearer direction, the second method of connecting to value. They go beyond the top-level survey metric to see where connections to value are even deeper, typically in individual journeys. Perhaps it's satisfaction with a claims experience or dissatisfaction with issue resolution that leads to lower scores, and then decreased spending. Finding where poor experiences destroy value helps isolate where further investment is needed.

Also, by showing specific connections, such as the link between customer satisfaction and order velocity, the value of customer experience to business outcomes becomes more believable and actionable. Increasing the number of specific connections to your organization's outcomes increases your credibility. For example, it's compelling when you can show how an ongoing issue continuing past a certain number of days leads to reduced order velocity. Alternately, if you can connect how customers with six or more claims have a higher or lower renewal rate, this makes a compelling claim for executives. These efforts also help focus where to invest your time and the company's resources.

For most organizations, the quickest path to show business impact is cost savings, often through preventing the need for clients to require customer support. Start here to show quick impact, but the best path to strategic change often lies in increasing revenue, even though it takes longer to see that result. Using the example of the organization that installs diagnostic systems into hospitals, improving the installation journey created higher retention, meaning millions of dollars in new revenue. But since contracts were five years long, the payback for an improved installation journey by definition took five years to see the impact. Reducing costs to serve earns you the permission to create that five-year plan.

This entire approach requires a partner who can analyze the data and find these connections. While Roxie Strohmenger argues that everybody leading the customer experience program should be able to do this work, I find that few people have both the skills needed to transform the organization around the customer *and* the ability to do in-depth numeric analysis. While all of our Change Makers have departments of at least five people, they didn't start that way.[1] Nancy Flowers and Jen Zamora both have team members whose specific role is to do this analysis; doing it right is how they grew their departments.

Once you have access to the data, go deeper to see where that value grows and diminishes. Which customers are giving you greater share of wallet? Which journeys link to higher or lower costs to serve? Look to past surveys—is there a link between specific survey questions and churn? Answering this will help you determine where to focus.

Dow, Hagerty, XYZ, and UKG Show Value

All four of our ongoing case studies clearly illustrate how CX connects to business value and across these different industries.

DOW: FAITH ALONE WILL NOT CONVINCE SENIOR LEADERS

While Jen Zamora, Senior Director of Global CX and Commercial Excellence, knew that an improved customer experience links to business impact, she also knew that faith alone wouldn't convince leaders at her company; she needed proof. To create this proof, she worked with her data science team to establish the connections between Dow's customer experience and organizational value. The team captured the customer experience both through behavioral data (which we'll discuss later in this book) and survey responses. It took her about a year of surveying customers to have sufficient data to show the connection.

Product ordering and delivery is the most common interaction between a manufacturer and its customers. Given the global nature of Dow's program, it's also complex. Now Jen can demonstrate the linkage between on-time delivery and financial results. She uses survey results to diagnose issues in the process, demonstrating how failure to meet on-time delivery schedules causes client frustration, which is documented in lower survey scores and in client comments. These lower survey scores are predictive of fewer future orders. Jen establishes cause and effect: a failure to meet on-time delivery is the cause, and the effect is fewer orders. The survey creates the connection.

Most programs point to survey scores, and a few may connect NPS with high-level results such as churn. But that doesn't provide any direction on how to improve the results. Change Makers view surveys as just another piece of the data and focus on the granular connections to the CX Loyalty Flywheel. I interviewed Jen for a Reuters conference, and she provided more of her thoughts on loyalty:

What does loyalty mean? For Dow, loyalty is beyond just the day-to-day customer relationship that we have. Loyalty opens the doors for innovation, for really changing the game with the regard to the extent of value we can bring our customers. You open that door to have conversations about next-generation products. And that ultimately is where we grow. That's where we innovate with customers on advancing their capabilities in the market, but we also work together to solve for world problems. And that's what really gets us excited. It's great to transact business on a daily basis, and we absolutely need that. But when you start having conversations about sustainability, and things that are really going to change the future, that's when you and your customers can get excited together.

Contrast this with a customer experience leader I interviewed in preparation for the same conference. I asked her what metrics her performance was based on, and she responded with "loyalty." So, I followed up, "Oh, so decreased attrition and increased ordering?" And she responded, "No. Loyalty for us means our Net Promoter Score." For many organizations, a customer's survey score indicates success, but for Change Makers, it's about the ongoing relationship with customers and their behaviors.

For an advanced manufacturer such as Dow, innovation is clearly an outcome of interest. But joint innovation is relatively rare, and even when it happens, it takes years. So, while this is a big deal, it's only one outcome that Jen tracks. She also considers in her work more routine metrics, such as order velocity and margin—the same metrics her internal customers obsess over. She continues, "We've been able to prove that improving on-time delivery, as well as its related customer complaint experience, adds financial value through improving revenue, margins, and price in future orders." Few companies take the time to prove this linkage. But it's no coincidence that the companies that can do this—such as Dow, Hagerty, and UKG—also have thriving customer experience practices. The proof enables the investment needed to sustain such positive outcomes.

One area that Jen has a keen focus on is per-unit margin. It may seem odd that customer experience can lead to customers paying more on a unit level, but a deeper analysis shows why. When the experience improves, customers' increased trust leads them to buying newer (and higher margin) products, which increases the average margin overall.

HAGERTY: TALK ABOUT NPS AND NOBODY LISTENS; TALK ABOUT RETENTION AND LEADERS CARE

Nancy Flowers, Vice President of Insights and Loyalty, launched her program as many do by measuring and focusing on the Net Promoter Score and using these survey results to identify where her company should target improvements. But after a few years, she could see that NPS wasn't the whole story. More importantly, NPS wasn't a business outcome that showed the ultimate financial value to the company, which is what her fellow executives care about.

As she explains, "Linking our customer experience metrics to business results—retention and growth—were critical. That put us on the map in terms of creating an enterprise KPI. When an executive asks, 'Why do we care about this?,' it's an easy answer. We know that if we see NPS points drop, we're going to see retention drop, and that's money, right?"

It's not that NPS isn't related to value. It's that leaders care more about the outcomes—happy customers who stay with Hagerty and choose to purchase more—than a survey score. Before you can even start discussing survey results, you must prove a direct connection between them and a healthy business, which is how executives judge success.

Nancy has learned that engaging executives requires her to speak more in terms of revenue and costs than survey scores. She analyzes NPS and uses it when appropriate, but she bases her work on impacts to customer lifetime value. Nancy can prove that customers who rate Hagerty higher in NPS stay with the company longer. Her survey is a diagnostic instead of the outcome. Customer lifetime value is the score—NPS is a metric that predicts it. This enables her to create a compelling business case to improve survey scores, as she can show the linkage to the business outcomes that in turn frees up more dollars to further invest in customers—the CX Loyalty Flywheel.

She can also link improvements in NPS to customers purchasing additional products, CLV's second component. By linking her team's efforts to improved customer engagement, reflected in survey scores, then showing how those scores impact retention and purchasing additional products, captured in her CLV, she proves value.

Over time, Nancy has had a surprising change in her role. For the first few years, she was in a central role, working with a small team to build and advocate for a formalized approach to customer experience. Now, by linking to business success, *everybody* at Hagerty is an advocate for creating an industry-leading customer experience. Instead of Nancy focusing on find-and-fix initiatives, everyone in the organization does this daily. This enables her to focus on more strategic issues, such as building membership products that go beyond Hagerty's traditional insurance offering.

This widespread acceptance enables her to create a more strategic relationship with her fellow executives. **By representing the voice of the customer and showing how it relates to the voice of the business, she's driving a customer-focused strategy.** As she explains, "Now, I've become the business sponsor for initiatives, something that's not common for a CX role. Not just for our loyalty program, which was a big change to the experience, but also when we launched the next stage of our membership products. If I had just kept talking about the survey scores and launching 'find-and-fix' efforts, I'd have been moved to the side. But sharing the health of our customers and how that reflects our business outcomes greatly increases the impact we're able to have."

XYZ CREATES CLV

While B2B companies typically have fewer customers than B2C, XYZ is one of the world's largest SaaS companies. The size of its customer base makes it almost like a B2C company in terms of modeling journeys and financial outcomes. For example, it creates a CLV calculation at the customer company level, which is how its CX program shows value.

Natasha, Global Vice President for Customer Experience at XYZ Software, came from a finance and operations background, so the linkage of customer experience to business success comes naturally to her. In an early stage of her life, she worked as a financial analyst for a joint venture between Toyota and General Motors. She recalls:

> I spent close to nine years there. And that's where I ended up implementing their cost accounting system, and that was where I fell in love with data and systems and technology. Then I went into consulting with KPMG, where I helped CFOs transform their finance organization, and I loved it because it was such a great way to learn how companies solve problems. And then I joined XYZ because I was helping the CFO, and XYZ invited me to join them. So, I joined as a finance business partner. And in that role, leaders kept saying, "You're really good with data." And you know, just that strategic vision of what you do with information, I ended up implementing our analytics tool.
>
> From there, I went to work for the office of the CEO. I didn't know I was doing customer experience until one day, when I was doing a journey map, someone said to me, "There's something called customer experience." I had never heard of it! And I just fell into this role, and I felt like everything that I was doing led me to this point.

XYZ is all about customer success. Its Customer Success Managers are CX's cousin. They focus on individual accounts instead of customer segments, with a similar goal of creating outcomes in which customers decide that it makes the most sense to their business to work more with the company. As such, the natural way to measure this is customer lifetime value. As Natasha explains:

We've developed models tying NPS scores to customer lifetime value, so we can connect the dots internally. This allows us to also understand key drivers of customer loyalty and their impact on our financials. With models like this, we can make investment decisions on where to improve.

While CLV is the end goal, we break it down. For example, we analyze ACV, which is annual contract value, as well as annual order value, but we also look at renewal rate, as well as retention rate. Those are ultimately what we will work toward, knowing that if we do well there, CLV will take care of itself.

One metric we've seen that strongly predicts these is time to value for new accounts, especially for our smaller clients. We use our Journey Builder product to deliberately create a strong beginning because we know that when customers start on the right foot, they're much more likely to stay with us longer and add on more products, the key components of CLV.

By identifying the sources of value from customer experience, reporting on these, and working with teams to improve these drivers, Natasha and her team show the impact of an improved customer experience, receiving approval for continuing investment.

UKG: UNDERSTAND THE INITIATIVE AND THE IMPACT
Soon after joining the company, Roxie Strohmenger, Vice President of Customer Experience Strategy, analyzed the descriptive, behavioral, operational, and financial data[2] to understand what was truly happening in the customer experience and how it affected customers and the health of UKG's business. Let's look at three business outcomes she targeted.

The first was **protecting revenue**. Replacing a core HR systems provider isn't an easy decision and is very disruptive to an organization. UKG's first customer experience outcome is to ensure this

doesn't happen. Next was **expansion**. Most clients begin by purchasing UKG Pro, the organization's HR and payroll offering, which
serves the core HR function. UKG offers multiple upgrade possi-
bilities, and Roxie can show the relationship: when the customer
experience improves, clients are far more likely to purchase more
products or services. Roxie shows the math. She starts with survey
results, but rather than tying a high-level metric like overall satisfaction to high-level revenue, she can show executives exactly how
an improved CX creates confidence in their customers, for example,
which influences their willingness to purchase additional products
and other positive outcomes. Said differently, she documents the
specific inputs and outputs from the CX Loyalty Flywheel.

While protecting revenue and expansion are more long-term
focused, her third outcome is more immediate: the **cost to serve
customers**. Reducing cost to serve isn't a reactive "we have to cut
costs to make budget" move. When technology providers spend
more time on-site to finalize a software implementation, or have
ongoing support issues, it's a negative outcome for both customers and the vendor. In the case of UKG, Roxie dives into extended
services to see what causes it and works with her fellow executives
to mitigate those causes, whether that's through product or service
improvements. The organization measures recurring revenue as
one of her critical outcomes. But, as Roxie states:

> I've been saying, "Recurring revenue is king, but let's break
> this apart because there are factors we contribute to directly
> on the services side that are about the protection of the rev-
> enue." So, we break that apart and say, take into account
> cost to serve and all of those elements, which is what we
> need to be able to measure that piece. And then, what's that
> formula? What if we move away from just OSAT [overall sat-
> isfaction, a relationship survey score] and instead, get down
> to things that really matter within the experience? This is
> how customers perceive the interactions or the quality

dimensions—those drivers that surfaced either in the journey mapping that we did with Heart of the Customer, the competitive benchmarking study that we did last year, that we know can move the needle the most, and let's quantify that and then build the model so that, when we track them, we can say, "If we want to do this initiative, we know it impacts A, B, and C pieces. We can calculate quite easily the potential revenue uptake and control for cost."

To summarize, rather than using a high-level outcome metric, such as satisfaction, Roxie uses her more detailed questions in her relationship and transactional surveys to diagnose what's happening in the customer experience and link it to business outcomes. In a theme that we'll revisit throughout the book, **the survey isn't the ultimate score**. The true score is your organization's growth through customers extending their relationships with your company. The survey is a diagnostic, showing why some customers have more service issues, how that impacts how customers feel about UKG, and the business outcomes for both customers and UKG.

■ ■ ■

Connecting customer experience to value is critical to influencing how your company thinks about and delivers its products or services to clients, and for innovating those practices. By discovering issues that impact customer satisfaction, customers are happier and more loyal. As Nancy says, "Sharing the health of our customers and how that reflects our business outcomes greatly increases the impact we're able to have."

In Action 2: Accelerate the Flywheel by Measuring and Designing for Emotion, we will discuss how technology and data tell a story and how you can use that information to map your customers' journeys and where you can improve their experiences.

Cari's Story

In Cari's next one-on-one with Dale, he began by saying, "Great job in the Yolanda meeting! She's a tough nut, but you were obviously prepared. It's great that she agreed to have a team member help you with the analysis. But you're not really a numbers person. How are you going to do that?"

"That's something I was hoping to discuss," Cari responded. "While I'm fine with the occasional Excel analysis, you don't want me spending my days sending surveys and reading the results. That's why I targeted my first hire as an analyst for just this type of work. They'll certainly run the surveys and analyze the results. But the real impact will come when we can tie in to the financials.

"We also need a more comprehensive customer feedback platform. That free software we've used works okay for one-off surveys, but it doesn't enable the type of analysis we'll need to truly understand the role of CX in driving business results. For example, I have no doubt there's a link between engaged customers and NRR, but we don't have the data, or the right survey questions, to discover this. This new hire will help me put together a more comprehensive approach than we've used historically. I want to make sure that we embed all the data that we need to truly understand our customers. Not just their sales but also whether they've had complaints, how long they've been a customer, which products they've purchased—we're going to need all of that to successfully understand our customer experience and how we can improve both their outcomes and ours."

"Ah," Dale responded, "that explains why this analyst requisition is at a higher rate than I initially expected. But I agree. Yolanda is one of the most influential people in the company. If we can gain her as an advocate, that will help all of us be more successful."

Cari continued, "I'm also going to need access to data from our operations, CRM, and issue-resolution platforms so we can analyze the impacts on our customers, and vice versa. One example of these siloed systems is that individual departments have been sending one-off surveys through the CRM, and operations also sends one when we close a ticket. As a result, a customer can get three surveys—our relationship survey, the ad hoc CRM surveys, and issue-resolution surveys—all in the same month! Plus, there's no process to consolidate and compare results to learn the full story of their experience. If we can combine all surveys into one platform and integrate the surveys with the associated data, we can learn much more about customers and their experiences."

"Sounds like a plan," Dale responded. "I've already approved the hiring requisition. Let me know the costs and the business case for the new platform. Yolanda may be interested, but she won't let us buy a platform with six-digit costs if we can't show how it will impact either revenue or cost savings."

My Thoughts

One early effort should be to build agreement to centralize surveys and data into a single platform. This isn't sexy, exciting work! The effort to do so will take time, and doesn't directly show impact. However, once you have the results, it will enable you to create visible dashboard reporting, as well as help you dive into specific issues without having to constantly ask for updated data. (More on dashboard design and reporting in Action 3.)

It's also critical to have an analyst on your team. As a leader, it's nearly impossible to drive organizational change if you're spending your days reviewing survey results. This takes valuable time away from higher priorities, and you will be tagged as an analyst instead of an executive. You can bet that Yolanda isn't spending her time calculating days sales outstanding! She has a team to do that. While some of our Change Makers are comfortable digging into the data, this is rarely the highest and best use of their time.

Lastly, let's talk about survey platforms. While it's tempting to use free survey software, it doesn't allow the comprehensive analysis needed to understand your best opportunities to improve the experience, something we'll come back to in Action 3: Evaluate the Flywheel with Customer Ecosystem Data.

Takeaways

Identifying Sources of Value in the CX Loyalty Flywheel

Please use the workbook that you can download from DoB2BBetter .com/workbook to complete the exercises and activities. Completing this work will result in a playbook that will help you accelerate your CX program and provide insight into questions and challenges that your fellow CX colleagues everywhere are facing. We will continue to use the story of Cari, and we will see how she responds to questions from her colleagues. If I were to help Cari think through her customer experience strategy, these are the questions I'd ask her.

What are two or three sources of revenue-based outcomes of the CX Loyalty Flywheel and how will you calculate them?

CARI: First is annual recurring revenue: this is a key metric that is reported internally and to stock analysts. ARR is tracked by finance, and we need to establish the link between customer survey data and ARR. This analysis will need to go beyond our Net Promoter Score, as I don't have confidence this is the right measurement. We need to see which of our existing questions most predicts ARR. Further, we need to isolate the factors making up ARR, such as an increase or decline in revenue for existing customers and adding customers, and tie our data in to these individual outcomes. This will help us get smarter.

Also, net revenue retention: this metric isolates the impact of customer experience because it zeroes in on retention and growth. The analysis is similar; it just lets us more specifically target the outcome of our experience work, since it isolates existing customers' outcomes from sales activities.

What are two or three sources of cost-based outcomes that you can connect your customer experience efforts to, and how are they calculated?

CARI: First, the length of implementations, which are painful. Sometimes implementation takes months beyond the plan, much to the understandable annoyance of our customers and to Sycamore because of the extra costs involved. These costs need to be projected and tracked, and to do that, we estimate the cost through salaries plus benefits of the implementation team and multiply this figure by the length of the implementation. We can get estimates from HR and the implementation team.

The second is issue resolution: at Sycamore, our severity 1 complaints take an average of ten days to resolve and can involve multiple teams. We need to set up a tracking mechanism to calculate these costs as these issues work their way through the organization. Finding ways to reduce issue-resolution time will increase customer satisfaction and presumably our costs.

Cari, you have a firm grasp on the metrics to use. What are the implications for your plans as you get more data when you measure the outcomes? How do you plan to persuade other departments to use your measurements?

CARI: Leadership and finance both report on ARR. And, as a public company, this is something that stock analysts expect of SaaS firms, including ours. I need to make sure we can measure ARR. But since this involves sales of new customers, I plan to use NRR for our team's reporting. We'll need to educate audiences on how these metrics relate and the distinctions between the two. We'll also need to show how integrating our CX data into their analysis will help the organization make better, more-informed business decisions.

Are there internal reports that finance has agreed to provide into which you can incorporate customer data?

CARI: For internal reporting (and perhaps external), I think we can get Yolanda and her team to report on customer impact if we can prove a strong relationship. We need to create consistent surveys and give her enough data to earn her confidence. Luckily, we have two years of historical survey data. Even though we're going to need to redesign our surveys, we plan to keep the questions that have a strong relationship with our financial outcomes. Once we do the analysis, I'll know what data impacts ARR and NRR, and as a bonus, I'll know what questions I need to keep in our current surveys. But until we can prove the linkage, it is unlikely that Yolanda will include customer data.

Will access to a finance analyst help you integrate financial metrics into your analysis?

CARI: Yolanda agreed to connect me with a member of her team who can help us integrate their data into our reports. Once I've hired my analyst, the two working together should be able to prove the linkage between our CX data and the business results. That is, assuming there is a linkage. If not, we'll need to redo our survey to find out what *does* link to value.

How can you integrate financial data into your reporting?

CARI: Once we show the link, we'll need to update our reporting to incorporate it. I plan on changing our reporting, since my predecessor simply presented a PowerPoint with a *bunch* of graphs with no context. I'm moving to a more story-based presentation, anyway; this will just be another element of that story.

Are you going to set up regular meetings with finance?

CARI: Once I get an analyst on board, I'll have that person meet regularly with the finance analyst to ensure we get their support. I'll also meet with the Vice President of Finance quarterly and try to include him in my CX council once that is established.

Let's talk about the financial analysis for a moment. How can we create a feed of the top revenue and cost information into our survey platform to assist with the analysis? For example, number of calls to support, average costs of those calls, and annual purchases.

CARI: We have account-level software and service revenue from our enterprise resource planning (ERP) system incorporated into our customer relationship management (CRM) system. By connecting our survey platform to the CRM, we will have what we need to calculate both ARR and NRR. Cost data will be trickier, since there's no central data repository where we track the length of implementations and staff involved.

Can you create a feed to supply your survey data to the finance team for use in their reporting?

CARI: We can technically do that through a built-in integration to their system from our survey platform. But until we can get them interested, it's not yet a good use of our time.

ACTION 2

ACCELERATE THE FLYWHEEL BY MEASURING AND DESIGNING FOR EMOTION

IMPROVING EMOTIONAL OUTCOMES IS
THE FASTEST PATH TO LOYALTY.

"Something we introduced at my former employer [a life insurance organization that provided products through companies to their employees] was the concept of designing for emotions, especially when helping employees at client firms who were getting laid off. I wanted our marketing and legal teams, everybody really, to understand the emotions that people go through, like the stages of grief, when they find out they're getting laid off. Some people are ecstatic, some are angry. There's stress, and they go through all these emotions even before they even call and talk to us, and so I wanted to make sure that the call centers knew this. We don't want to sound tone deaf. Emotion is huge, so you need to stop and assess and make sure that everything you're doing is aligning to the emotions. The last thing you want to do is come off like you're tone deaf."

—**Margaret-Anne Heyland,** Customer Journey and
Strategy Analytics Manager, Ally

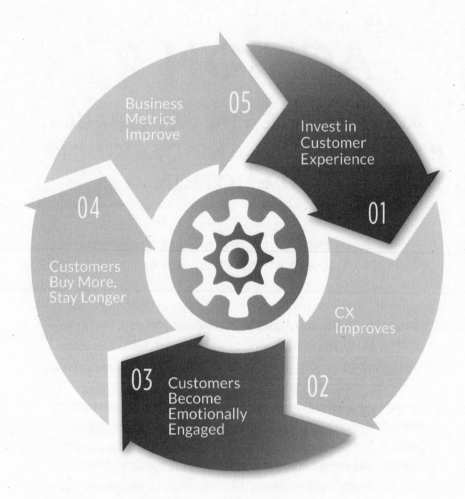

Figure 4-1: The CX Loyalty Flywheel: Engage through emotion.

LINKING YOUR WORK TO VALUE SHOWS HOW THE CX LOYALTY Flywheel works, identifying specifically how investments in customer experience lead to a healthier business. Once you make that connection, the next question is: What accelerates the flywheel? Is there a way to move customers through it more effectively to lead to more business value?

The answer is yes. By identifying the top emotions created in your experience, and redesigning it to create stronger emotional outcomes, you can capture more of your customers' business—because they will *want* to work with you more. Emotions are the most powerful influence on the decisions people make, including decisions your clients make about continuing to do business with you. When I talk with CX leaders, they see this as obvious. They tell me, "Of course emotions matter in the experience!" Then I ask them how they measure those emotions, and I get a blank look. Most leaders acknowledge the importance of emotions. So, why do so few programs deliberately measure and manage the emotions in their customer experience?

Like most, I've always known that emotions matter. But it never occurred to me that you could measure and manage them, let alone connect emotion to business value. But many of our Change Makers do just that. Learning how they connect customer emotion to value enabled me to go deeper into our Change Makers' mindsets.

One outcome was the concept of an Emotional North Star—the use of one emotion to measure CX and focus on as a design target. It shouldn't have surprised me, since at Heart of the Customer, we regularly report on the emotions customers feel in our journey mapping. But the notion of selecting one key emotion and measuring it was something I hadn't run across.

In this section, chapter 4 will go into the impact that emotions have in the customer experience. Chapter 5 will go through how to identify the emotions specific to your business's experiences, and chapter 6 will go deep into UKG's approach and connecting emotions to the sources of CX value identified in Action 1.

CHAPTER 4

Do I Know Which Emotions Are Created through Our Customer Experience?

WHEN I SPEAK WITH B2B LEADERS, THINKING ABOUT EMOTIONS seems like a foreign concept. But emotions are critical to a successful experience. In fact, they're often even more important in B2B than in B2C. There have been voices calling us to measure and manage emotions for years, but few have taken up the challenge. According to the 2015 *Harvard Business Review* article "The New Science of Customer Emotions":

> Given the enormous opportunity to create new value, companies should pursue emotional connections as a science—and a strategy. But for most, building these connections is more guesswork than science. At the end of the day they have little idea what really works and whether their efforts have produced the desired results. . . .
>
> Although brands may be liked or trusted, most fail to align themselves with the emotions that drive their customers' most profitable behaviors. Some brands by nature have an easier time making such connections, but a company doesn't have to be born with the emotional DNA of Disney

or Apple to succeed. Even a cleaning product or a canned food [or, I would add, a B2B company] can forge powerful connections.[1]

To be fair, most programs and even most Change Makers *don't* do this. But as the case studies we highlight in the book—Dow, Hagerty, XYZ, and UKG—show us, some organizations do this very well and provide a pathway for the rest of us. You may be more familiar with this concept in the B2C world, so I will draw on some B2C examples to illustrate how this works.

■ ■ ■

Creating Trust at the Veterans Administration

Barbara C. Morton is Deputy Chief Experience Officer for the US Department of Veterans Affairs (VA), where she oversees its focus on improving veteran outcomes. Barbara's background is a bit different. She's the only customer experience leader I've met who is also a practicing attorney.

Customer experience is a growing concern for government agencies. In fact, during the writing of this book, President Biden signed an executive order designed to strengthen the government's "customer" experience.[2] This order went into place about a year after I interviewed Barbara.

The concern about the VA's experience went public over a wait-time scandal in 2014, in which a significant number of veterans had to wait for more than one hundred days to receive care, particularly in Phoenix. The then secretary of the VA was fired and replaced by Bob McDonald. Secretary McDonald identified one highly concerning factor of the problem. As Barbara explains, "We did not have a mechanism to hear what veterans were telling us about their experiences. So, for example, in Phoenix, the operational metrics looked fine, everything looked fine. We didn't have a way to read the signals outside of operational metrics at an enterprise level. At the same time, we had veterans saying, 'Something is not quite working smoothly from an experience perspective.' So, he established this office in January 2015. And in 2016, I was asked to come over and help hardwire customer experience across the department."

Nurturing Veterans' Trust

Barbara's team began to examine veterans' healthcare journeys from the veterans' perspective, utilizing human-centered design methodology to build journey maps as both a diagnostic and communications tool. The VA supplemented their journey mapping by creating design capabilities to ensure that the organization was able to construct the current journey and build new journeys based on the feedback, which required interviewing hundreds of veterans.

The team discovered one central idea that became the cornerstone of its continuing work: The core of the VA's work is all about emotion, particularly trust. The VA offers one of the most dramatic examples of designing for emotions and incorporating technology, data, tangible tools, and change management to transform the organization. For example, the VA created "Own the Moment," customer experience training that was deployed to over three hundred thousand VA employees using a train-the-trainer model to scale, emphasizing the importance of emotional resonance and empathy.

The VA started its CX work on behalf of veterans by measuring ease, effectiveness, and emotion, akin to what Dow and UKG practice.[3] But as the VA worked with more and more veterans, one emotion was referenced more than any other: trust. As Barbara explains:

It's interesting in government, but probably in other industries as well. Trust is really your currency. It's ultimately your North Star.[4] If somebody doesn't trust you, they probably are not going to want to engage with you. Phoenix was our wake-up call. Trust was what we focused on when rebuilding after Phoenix. So, ease, effectiveness, and emotion. That's how we explain the drivers of trust. And that's a simple way for us to communicate so people really understand it. It's that North Star, chosen because of Phoenix, but also because we're public servants. We're here to serve the people, and especially veterans. That's why trust has become our North Star because of the mission and, frankly, our role as stewards of public trust as members of the federal government.

The VA surveys millions of veterans each year, asking participants to rate the following items:

- Ease: "It was easy to get the care or service I needed."
- Effectiveness: "I got the care or service I needed."
- Emotion: "I felt like a valued customer."
- Trust: "I trust VA to fulfill our country's commitment to veterans."

The organization goes deeper on its website:

Customer experience is the product of interactions between an organization and a customer over the duration of their relationship. VA measures these interactions through Ease, Effectiveness, and Emotion, all of which impact the overall trust the customer has in the organization.

- **Ease:** VA will make access to VA care, benefits, and memorial services smooth and easy.
- **Effectiveness:** VA will deliver care, benefits, and memorial services to the customer's satisfaction.
- **Emotion:** VA will deliver care, benefits, and memorial services in a manner that makes customers feel honored and valued in their interactions with VA.

VA will use customer experience data and insights in strategy development and decision-making to ensure that the voice of veterans, service members, their families, care-givers, and survivors inform how VA delivers care, benefits, and memorial services.[5]

Trust is the VA's Emotional North Star, a concept we're going to explore deeply in this and the next two chapters. Once the VA discovered how critical trust was to veterans' outcomes, it added a question on trust to its CX measurement. It also trained its teams on ways to build trust, confident this would improve veterans' outcomes. It did, as we will see.

The VA discovered that trust is not only important but also a leading metric, one the organization could use to guide all its experiences. The VA transparently reports the level of trust to the public quarterly; as you can see on the report below, trust has increased over the years. When the VA began measuring it, 55 percent of veterans agreed that they trusted the VA.[6] That figure grew to 80 percent during the pandemic and is just below that at 79 percent as of this writing.

VA-Wide Trust over Time

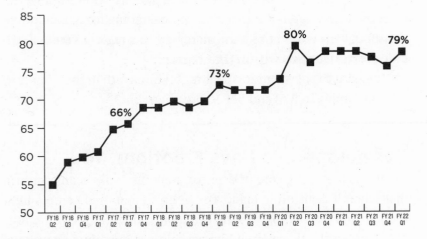

Figure 4-2: VA trust report.[7]

An example of how the VA designed its experience to create trust is the VA Welcome Kit,[8] which showcases for veterans where the VA fits into their lives based on the veteran's life journey, rather than showing them the VA org chart and having the veteran figure out where to apply to get benefits. As Barbara explains, "It's a great example of tangible tools that show how we're bridging that connection between data and insights and creating tangible outcomes—which is the most critical piece of any experience program." The VA also created the *CX Cookbook* for other agencies, helping share their best practices.

This effort has also improved employee morale and engagement, and the VA has scored sixth among all large government agencies in the annual "Best Places to Work" survey, climbing eleven places.

So, the VA measures trust, educates employees around the drivers of trust, designs for trust, and has seen survey scores improve. All well and good, but let's return to the evidence of outcomes as part of the CX Loyalty Flywheel. The VA is a government agency, so it is not looking to increase share of wallet. How does this help it accomplish its goals?

One notable outcome of the VA is that veterans who use the agency are much less likely to die by suicide. In the most powerful example I have seen of measuring and designing for one emotion, the VA discovered that as trust increased in a region, **veteran suicide alerts dropped within that region**.[9]

It's hard to show a more meaningful impact than that. But how does this apply to B2B and B2B2C organizations?

Businesspeople Have Emotions, Too

Emotions are at the core of decision-making. Brain scans confirm that when a decision is made, the brain's emotional centers light up first; the rational part of the brain only kicks in once emotions have guided the decision. While we think of ourselves as rational beings first and emotional beings second, behavioral economics tells us otherwise. We are first and foremost emotional beings. This cognitive bias is called the affect heuristic. This is where you determine what you think through consulting your emotions.[10] All this means that, even in B2B, we make our decisions through the lens of emotions.

In his book *Thinking, Fast and Slow*, Daniel Kahneman identified two methods of thinking: System 1 and System 2. System 1 is the quick-thinking process people use for the majority of decisions they make, and this system relies on emotions. System 2 allows for more rational consideration, but most decisions bypass this more deliberate approach. Our early ancestors who deliberated whether a sound in the forest was that of a saber-toothed tiger or just the wind were eaten—those who reacted quickly survived. As a result, most of our decisions are System 1 processes.

While I've always known that emotions matter in the customer experience, it turns out that they have impact far broader than one might expect. Would you believe a link has been established between emotions and stock market performance? It's true! In a study that compared the positivity and negativity of songs played on Spotify in a particular country, the researchers found that the stock market rose in lockstep with positive songs.[11] If emotions can impact investments in the stock market, surely emotions can affect your customers' loyalty, too.

Earning loyalty requires you to create an emotional experience that leads customers to *want* to spend more with you, stay with you longer, and try out your new products. Creating an effortless experience—the goal of many customer experience programs—will reduce *dis*loyalty. But customers' emotions in the experience have far more impact on future behaviors.

Understanding whether your customers feel positively or negatively toward your brand and their experience with you is just the start. Success requires getting more specific, understanding exactly which emotions lead to those organizational outcomes. Your operations impact the emotions that customers feel, which then impact their behaviors, including those that impact the sources of value. Emotions are the most underutilized measurement for understanding your customers and their behaviors.

Emotions are central to every experience, but the specific emotions that drive behaviors vary. While some Harley-Davidson customers sport tattoos of the company's logo, B2B customers don't. But that doesn't mean emotions aren't critical. There's a common misperception that B2B decisions are more rational and price-focused than those in B2C. Nothing could be further from the truth. B2B decisions have at least as much emotional impact as those in B2C relationships. The emotions are just different.

Consider two scenarios. If a consumer chooses a cell phone that she finds difficult to use or causes her problems, she'll be annoyed with the product and will likely leave that brand the next time she selects a cell phone. While it's frustrating for her, dissatisfaction with a phone isn't a major factor in her life. But what if, at her workplace, she chooses the wrong software partner on behalf of her company? The installation drags on longer than expected, it costs more than budgeted, and users don't adopt it. In that scenario, she'll have to live with that decision for years, assuming she isn't fired over that mistake. Which experience is more emotional?

Compliance and Trust: Wolters Kluwer Compliance Solutions

Let's look at a real-world example of the role of emotions in the B2B decision-making process. Early in his CX career, Darin Byrne,[12] Vice President of Client Experience and Delivery at Wolters Kluwer Compliance Solutions,[13] collaborated with the company's marketing department to understand how bankers decide on a compliance solutions partner. This work was inspired by a study carried out by CEB,[14] which reported that 57 percent of the B2B purchase process happened before a sales representative was involved, primarily involving digital channels. The report showed that potential B2B customers review websites and self-educate before engaging with a vendor's sales team.[15]

So, Wolters Kluwer began its study of customer-buying behavior by documenting its hypothesis of the customer-buying journey. The teams assigned to the project first identified steps potential customers might take, like reading case studies, reviewing capabilities on websites, and watching videos of the products, all digital activities used to decide which products to consider.

After this, dozens of leaders at banks were interviewed to uncover the real story. The result? Bankers did all the things the Wolters Kluwer teams hypothesized. And these activities mattered. *But something else happened first.* Something far more important than these digital activities. As bankers considered selecting a new partner, the first thing they did was *contact another banker*—someone they had met at a conference, for example—and ask that individual about compliance providers that had won their trust. This referral was critical.

Bankers cannot afford to make mistakes. Compliance is critical to lending, and the right system makes compliance almost invisible, fitting into the workflow and helping a bank comply with state and federal regulations without effort. Implementing a system that frustrates users and even lengthens the loan-origination process is the worst possible outcome for banks and their customers.

When someone searches online for software providers, the digital tools look essentially the same between providers. *Every* company's website says that its systems enable easy compliance. So, how does a banker determine the right partner?

The big finding from this research may sound basic, but it's profound: banks don't purchase compliance solutions— bankers do. It's critical to separate the question of *how a bank selects a partner* from *how a banker selects a partner*. Banks conduct requests for proposals (RFPs) and credit checks. Bankers use social proof,[16] outsourcing the selection to trusted peers. If another banker doesn't recommend Wolters Kluwer,

the company has almost no chance to win. This recommendation was a critical Moment of Truth in the purchase journey,
assigning some vendors as potential winners and the rest as
losers. Only when this was settled and the list was narrowed
down to a few providers did the digital tools come into play.

In order to continue its strong growth trajectory, Wolters
Kluwer needed to continue to raise the *trust* level among its
current customers, which would result in more and even more
robust referrals to capture new customers.

A B2C Example: Compassion International

The high-stakes nature of many B2B relationships necessitates
measuring and managing emotions. Yet, it's amazing to us that so
few programs do this, even in B2C. Nearly every program discusses
the importance of emotions, but very few actively measure it. In
fact, it was difficult to find organizations that specifically measure
and manage emotions in *any* industry. One organization that does
an exceptional job is the nonprofit Compassion International, one
of the largest charities in the United States. Compassion's mission
is "releasing children from poverty in Jesus' name," and it recruits
sponsors to support individual children suffering from poverty.

The organization's research into the supporter experience indi-
cated that two emotions were critical for sponsors to feel: happiness
and delight. Compassion integrates questions that focus on these
emotions with likelihood to recommend and other measurements
into what it calls Heartshare, which is one of Compassion's best predictors of retention.

Ben Webb, Senior Director of Global Experience, says, "When
you look at the nature of an experience, emotions are the catalyst
for giving. It's absolutely critical for Compassion to create an experience where our supporters, which are crucial to our mission, feel
happy and delighted with their outcomes. So, we started to measure
this, and we found it absolutely matters."

Compassion knows the importance of connecting emotions to an improved experience, then tying that to organizational outcomes. Not only does the company measure the Heartshare and publish it continually, it invested in a sixty-person organization to design stronger connections with its sponsors and donors, knowing that this investment will pay for itself by creating stronger connections, leading to more funds coming into the organization and resulting in more children released from poverty. It isn't B2B, but it's definitely the CX Loyalty Flywheel in action.

Emotions Are the Strongest Predictor of Loyalty—So Start Measuring Them

By now, you may have noticed that several Change Makers measure customer experience through variations of effectiveness, ease, and emotion, a common framework—originally developed by Forrester—that isolates distinct components of the customer experience. Each is important but in different ways.

Effectiveness speaks to a customer's expectations that the product or service will perform as advertised. It won't win you customers, but it helps keep the ones you have. If expectations are not met—for example, if your software's interface is difficult to navigate, you frequently miss your shipping dates, or veterans do not get access to the care they need—this diminishes effectiveness, which can lead to churn, stopping the flywheel in its tracks.

Ease speaks to the effort it takes for someone to accomplish a goal. Being easier to deal with than your competitors will prevent customers from leaving you and may even win you new customers, but primarily in situations where customers order from multiple competitors simultaneously. For example, if a customer orders from multiple distributors with similar products, it'll likely centralize much of its purchasing with the one that is easiest to order from. But winning just through an easier interface isn't sticky. A company may win business today, but tomorrow someone will develop an even easier interface.

Emotions are where you win longtime loyalty. Effectiveness and ease are table stakes. Emotions are the heart of loyalty, as it speaks to how customers feel about themselves and your company as a result of their engagement with you (the affect heuristic). When customers feel that a company has their backs, they're more likely to stay with the company when there are problems or when someone else offers a cheaper price (the excessive coherence cognitive bias). Customers will spend more money and put in more effort to work with a company they feel a connection with. In their studies of national brands' customer experience quality, Forrester and Qualtrics XM Institute independently report that **emotions are the strongest predictors of loyalty**, which makes it surprising that so few organizations measure their emotional experience.

EASY COME, EASY GO

While emotions are proven to be the strongest predictor of customer loyalty, most B2B businesses focus on ease—likely because it is a metric easier to measure and manage (rim shot!). If customers complain that a form is too difficult to fill out, that can be easily fixed. Emotions are perceived as intangible and difficult to measure, so measuring for emotions is dispensed with. Effortless experiences capture the imagination of the CX crowd, despite the overwhelming evidence that ease has less impact on loyalty than a positive emotional experience.

This focus on ease was inspired by *The Effortless Experience*, a book by Matthew Dixon, Nick Toman, and Rick DeLisi that analyzed customer service calls from multiple companies to discover the best approach to create loyalty. The writers explored creating a "wow" experience versus quickly and effectively resolving the problem, and they reported that enabling a customer to solve a problem easily was the best predictor of self-reported loyalty.

But what most people missed in this book is that the authors only studied customers *calling in to the contact center with a problem.*

Let's stop for a minute and analyze this. Calling in to a contact center is a big deal—I don't want to minimize this. It can be a make-or-break moment in the customer experience. But it's a very different experience from the rest of the customer life cycle.

If you're the manager on duty at a store and your point-of-sale system isn't functioning, you can't help your customers. They're probably waiting in line, trying to give you money, and you can't take it. You're frantic about resolving the issue immediately. You call the help center. If the customer service agent asks how your kids are doing, you're going to give him an earful (and likely in language you wouldn't want your kids to hear!). But that type of polite inquiry is perfectly acceptable and demonstrates empathy, which is a good thing in almost any other situation.

A customer's needs when their software isn't functioning are very different from that same customer's needs when interacting with a sales rep to buy a product, implement software, or select a new solution provider. So, while accessing customer support needs to be effortless, focusing exclusively on reducing effort during the rest of the experience will not earn long-term loyalty. As with effort, reducing friction will prevent *dis*loyalty. But it doesn't inoculate customers for when eventual problems occur. Doing that requires a positive emotional experience.

MAKE GOOD EXPERIENCES GREAT

There's another reason to focus on emotions instead of reducing friction: removing negative emotions created by the friction does nothing to build positive ones. As Matthieu Ricard reports in his book *Happiness*, "In 1969 the psychologist Norman Bradburn showed that pleasant and unpleasant effects derive from different mechanisms and therefore must be studied separately. . . . The suppression of pain doesn't necessarily lead to pleasure. It is therefore necessary not only to rid oneself of negative emotions, but also to develop positive ones." While Bradburn and Ricard were speaking of personal happiness, the same applies to creating emotions in your customers. **Eliminating friction doesn't drive the powerful feelings that create loyalty—that requires a different approach.**

We can learn more by identifying the sections of the brain involved with different emotions. While the science isn't completely settled, it's generally considered that anger, fear, frustration, and similar emotions are generated when the amygdala stimulates the hypothalamus. Positive emotions, such as happiness, occur in completely different parts of the brain, in the limbic cortex and precuneus, the latter of which is home to many complex activities.[17]

The net result is that reducing the activation of the amygdala (that is, reducing frustration) doesn't create happiness; rather, it just prevents the negative emotions from charging. You aren't activating positive emotions—and the loyalty that results—by reducing friction. This requires a different approach.

When companies create a strong emotional connection, something powerful happens. This connection inoculates your company against problems that crop up in any experience. By showing that your organization is more focused on solving customers' problems instead of your own, you build a bank of goodwill that will protect you. Qualtrics XM Institute found that when customers rate the emotional experience highly, 74 percent are willing to forgive a brand when problems occur; when customers give a low rating to the emotional experience, only 19 percent are.[18]

In their book *The Power of Moments*, Chip and Dan Heath further illustrate why it's more important to create a strong emotional connection than to improve effectiveness and ease. They used data from Forrester to look at the impact of moving a customer's survey score from negative (1, 2, or 3 on a 7-point scale) to neutral (4) versus moving a rating from 4, 5, or 6 to a 7 (suggesting a strong emotional connection).

The authors report that 80 percent of organizational efforts focus on improving results for those on the lower end of the spectrum; in other words, moving customers from negative to neutral.[19]

That makes sense. But fixing problems isn't your best place to focus. When companies move customers who give a 4, 5, or 6 on the survey to a top score of 7, it returns *nine times the organizational value* compared to moving low scores to neutral. Qualtrics XM Institute documented how this works, showing that improved emotional relationships lead to increased future orders, reduced churn, and an increased willingness to try new products. Yes, you got it—the CX Loyalty Flywheel.

Emotions can drive a beneficial form of irrationality, in which customers choose to continue working with you even when it seems they shouldn't, utilizing the excessive coherence heuristic we discussed earlier. The strongest example I've seen of the power of an emotional connection occurred when we studied CT scans at a health system. I interviewed a longtime patient who came in for a scan every year for his cancer. I asked him to rate his experience on a scale of 1 to 5, and he gave it a 4. So, I asked why he gave that score, and he shared, "Well, the radiologist reported I was cancer-free, but when I went to the doctor, he told me, 'Here's the tumor. I'm not sure why the radiologist said you were negative because we can see the tumor in the scan plain as day.'"

Baffled, I asked, "Let me see if I have this right. You had a screening for cancer?"

"Yes. The radiologist missed it."

"And you're giving them a 4 out of 5?"

"Yeah," the patient replied. "It's no big deal. They'll find it next year."

Not many patients would give the health system a 4 out of 5 when they missed their cancer! But this patient had earlier shared his positive experiences with this health system, which had been with him throughout his early stages of cancer. They earned his trust, and in return, he forgave them for their mistakes. While few patients are *this* willing to forgive, it does speak to the power of an emotional connection to sustain relationships when problems occur.[20]

A Note on the Net Promoter Score

While many of our Change Makers use a variation of effectiveness, ease, and emotion, this is not to say that Change Makers don't use NPS. You may remember that Nancy Flowers at Hagerty and Natasha at XYZ Software have found NPS to predict retention, whereas Roxie Strohmenger at UKG found no relationship between NPS and business outcomes. No one metric is the right answer for every organization. The right metric is the one that shows how *your* company's CX Loyalty Flywheel works. If a particular survey metric doesn't show that outcome, then it's the wrong one. No matter what article your CEO has read.

That said, the interviews we did for this book demonstrated a negative connection between organizational success and the use of NPS. While both successful and unsuccessful organizations used NPS, when we saw a program that was not having impact, it *almost always used NPS*. The poor results occurred because of an overall lack of a strategic approach to the customer experience. Hopeful organizations never stopped to consider whether NPS was the right metric to measure that company's unique customer experience. This lack of a disciplined approach toward customer experience was the cause to both the usage of NPS and the lack of impact.

Conversely, those organizations that were committed to win by customer experience took the time to assess what specific combination of metrics best measured their individual customer experience. As a result of this discipline, they measured more effectively, they rallied teams more effectively, and they designed better experiences that created more loyalty that accelerated the flywheel.

Digital Experiences Can Also Be Emotional Experiences

It's easy to assume that you can only create these positive emotions through in-person impact and that digital experiences should work to improve effectiveness and ease without damaging emotions. It's certainly true that most digital experiences are designed this way and that can work. But leading digital experiences also differentiate through an improved emotional experience. Intuit is a great example. Whereas most organizations streamline digital experiences to reduce every unnecessary click, Intuit's TurboTax deliberately adds "unnecessary" steps to create an emotional connection, as you can see in the screenshot below.[21]

Figure 4-3: TurboTax adds emotions.

Few experience designers would consider adding this screen, since it slows down the customer's outcomes. But Intuit understands that doing taxes is as much emotional as rational, so it adds this step to build its customers' confidence that TurboTax is helping them complete their tax returns—it's on the customer's side.

Similarly, on a call with Audible, our CTO, Shawn Phillips, reported that one of its three questions was "Did the representative make you smile?" A great example of understanding the role of emotions in the customer experience.

■ ■ ■

Now that we have explored the role of emotions in customer experience, chapter 5 will talk about how to discover your customers' highest value emotions, and chapter 6 will explore how to design for emotions in your experience. And you will be surprised at some of the findings from our research and case studies.

Cari's Story

Cari was excited to find Stephen, an analyst who combined the ability to pore through numbers with the understanding of customer experience necessary to apply the results. Once Stephen was on board, he identified implementation as one of Sycamore's biggest opportunities to improve the customer experience, based on customer feedback. Both surveys and the customer advisory board identified implementation as one of the biggest pain points in working with Sycamore.

Customers who had reported a negative implementation experience continued to have issues well past that implementation. In fact, some of the customer advisory board participants had been implemented three years earlier, and they *still* complained about it. Since Sycamore hadn't materially changed its implementation process in years, and it was still getting negative feedback, it seemed like this issue would continue unless Sycamore focused on it now.

Cari's history in SaaS operations told her one thing very clearly: different customers have different journeys. While Sycamore had hundreds of customers, it seemed like she spent most of her time in operations talking with the same twenty. But she didn't know why these customers had more challenges than the rest, although it seemed that focusing on implementation would help get to the bottom of this.

To understand what was driving these differences, she commissioned a journey mapping initiative to meet with customers and learn more about their experiences. She engaged team members from across the company in the initiative (although Yolanda resisted offering a finance member until Dale asked). They met in a hypothesis mapping session to share what team members thought the outcome would be. Most attendees felt the most common reason for a negative experience was if the system integrator (or the SI, the company the customer hired to lead the implementation of Sycamore's platform) wasn't very good.

Cari asked the members of her CX council to participate in the project, assigning individual leaders to different customer interviews. She knew that most of Sycamore's employees had never personally spent time with customers. Even the leadership could learn. While leaders frequently talked with customers, it was usually in either a sales or an issue-resolution context. Taking a step back to learn about customers' overall needs, and how Sycamore's implementation impacted its success, could only help to build customer empathy.

She looked forward to getting the teams out to hear from customers, and learning how they could best improve their current implementation processes.

My Thoughts

Journey mapping is an effective way to learn about how your customers feel about your experience and what is causing those emotions. And recorded videos are highly effective at communicating both the emotions and their causes.

Journey mapping identifies candidate emotions, both positive and negative. But that's not sufficient to start measuring, as qualitative data doesn't link the emotions to organizational impact. You need to pair those emotions with your operational, behavioral, and financial data to understand their impact and what may be causing those emotions. The operational data often show what causes the emotions, and behavioral and financial data show the outcomes. (We'll introduce this in Action 3 as Customer Ecosystem Data.)

Do annoyed customers open more tickets, whereas confident customers use more self-service? Or do annoyed customers give up on your service processes, escalating to sales immediately? Do customers who see you as a trusted advisor order more products? All this helps you to build the change management processes we discuss in Action 4 of the CX Loyalty Flywheel: Grease the Flywheel with Change Management.

CHAPTER 5

What Are My Customers' Highest Value Emotions?

WHEN THINKING ABOUT THE DESIGN OF CUSTOMER EXPERI-ence, it is dangerous to assume that all emotions are equal and that you just need to add some good emotions to your survey. Identifying the emotion that creates the most value for your customers enables an Emotional North Star—one emotion that your organization can rally around in designing game-changing customer experience. This accelerates the CX Loyalty Flywheel, as you create even more value for your customers, who return the favor by ordering more from you and staying longer.

Determining the Emotions of Interest

Determining the right emotions to measure and manage depends on the company and type of experience. If UnitedHealthcare elected to create enthusiastic consumers, that would be confusing, and likely frustrating, for both the company and its customers. Similarly, if Disney elected to use customer confidence as its Emotional North Star, that wouldn't accelerate the CX Loyalty Flywheel to the extent that joy does.

The right emotions also vary by brands within a market. Compare Publix with Aldi. While both are excellent grocery stores, they deliberately create very different emotional outcomes for shoppers. Publix works to create an inspiring experience, offering amazing sub sandwiches[1] and cooking demonstrations that Aldi would never consider. For its part, Aldi focuses on enabling shoppers with low prices and high quality, likely driving for an outcome of confidence that Aldi has what they need. Both are maximizing emotional outcomes but focusing on different ones.

The same can be said about Walmart and Target, IKEA and Ashley furniture, and Ruth's Chris Steak House compared to Buffalo Wild Wings. Even Amazon and Zappos, while under the same corporate umbrella, design for different Emotional North Stars. Zappos is famous for focusing on happiness. It's even the title of former Zappos CEO Tony Hsieh's book, *Delivering Happiness*.

It's tempting to think that Amazon focuses exclusively on creating an effortless experience. The company does work very hard to streamline interactions. But Amazon's Emotional North Star is trust. In his comments to Congress, Jeff Bezos reported that Amazon is the second-most-trusted company after Apple.[2] Bezos consistently talks about developing customers' trust; in a letter to shareholders, he shared, "Our pricing objective is to earn customer trust, not to optimize short-term profit dollars. We take it as an article of faith that pricing is the best way to grow our aggregate profit dollars over the long term. We may make less per item, but by consistently earning trust we will sell many more items."[3]

Amazon has learned that to build loyal customers, it must go beyond creating easy experiences. Earning trust requires consistency in every element of its experience. Amazon not only makes ordering easy but also provides updates on progress and includes third-party references on the quality of books and other products. There are two types of trust—functional and emotional—and Amazon works to improve each of these.

Another example is Amazon's efforts to ensure customer data security, which doesn't typically factor into a focus on easy experiences. As Bezos explains when talking about customer data, "[Trust is] very valuable, and so you would never do anything to jeopardize it. . . . It's what allows you to expand the business."[4] While you can argue whether trust can truly be classified as an emotion, it is certainly an emotional *outcome*, as Amazon makes plain.

Design for *One* Emotional Outcome

Even when organizations do focus on emotions, they rarely identify one in which to focus on a clear direction and use it to guide their experience design. This can lead to conflicting outcomes. Imagine what would happen if you asked each executive in your organization to design for customer emotions and build a customer experience plan that incorporates that emotion and then set them loose. Marketing might create a plan to build trust. Product might design for desire by adding features to differentiate your offering. Finance might opt for simplicity because fewer options probably mean lower costs, while IT focuses on creating an easy experience. None of these is an incorrect approach in and of itself, but the combination leads to a Frankenstein experience—which happens at most companies today—and will handicap your efforts to earn loyalty.

From my personal experience, when I was at the health insurance company, we didn't consider emotion at all, innovating instead on features. Marketing focused on creating informed customers through detailed communications on tax savings that were rarely read. Product felt that options were critical, providing multiple pricing tiers. While product was adding pricing options, sales focused on ease based on feedback that the pricing options were confusing. Sales removed product's pricing options. Predictably, these uncoordinated approaches created unsatisfactory results, increasing costs without delivering an improved outcome.

Instead of designing for emotions in general, focus on *one* emotion, such as confidence. While teams will still come up with distinct ideas, they will be more congruent.

Or, instead of confidence, imagine that you asked teams to design for enjoyability, as Dow does. (Yes, you read that right. When you think of enjoyable experiences, you probably think of Disney instead of Dow. Stay tuned to learn how it's the right emotion for Dow!) Creating enjoyability requires a different experience than one that builds confidence. Confidence requires consistent outcomes, so customers know that, when they use your products, they will be consistently successful. Enjoyability speaks more to the power of the relationship and that your staff is thinking about the customers' needs and going above and beyond for them. Both confidence and enjoyability have the *potential* to drive better customer and company outcomes. But you need to understand which is right for you and *your* customers. UKG provides software that the customer uses, whereas Dow works more directly with customers to find products for their specific needs. These different types of customer experiences lend themselves to different Emotional North Stars.

As we'll see later, Hagerty has its own Emotional North Star of happiness. This would be a nonsensical goal for most companies that sell insurance, which was Hagerty's original product. But remember that Hagerty isn't an insurance company; rather, it is an automotive lifestyle brand that sells multiple products, with insurance being just one. Its focus on happiness led the company to create programs that were alien to competing insurance companies, such as the ability for members to rent each other's cars. Hagerty's mission is to help its members get the most out of the hobby as possible, so happiness is congruent with this mission.

Hagerty has used NPS for years. Happiness predicts NPS; the happier the company makes its customers, the higher the NPS and (more importantly) the more likely members are to stay and purchase additional products. Happiness is a leading indicator of both NPS and financial outcomes (as the CX Loyalty Flywheel predicts). More importantly, happiness is the company's design target. Rather than asking teams to design toward a higher NPS score, which is hard to conceptualize, Hagerty is more successful when it asks teams to target happiness.

My point here is not just that you need to design for emotions. That is obvious. There is no shortage of writing that talks about the importance of designing for emotion. But most of that same writing misses something compelling: to build loyal customers, you need to align on *one* Emotional North Star and then measure it. Doing this enables you to align your organization toward that emotion, marshalling all your energy toward a shared outcome. Measuring and managing the emotional experience requires four steps:

1. Identify which emotions your customers frequently experience when working with your company today.

2. Use those emotions in quantitative research to show which emotions most impact customer outcomes, positively and negatively. This will give you insight into both where your customer experience is at its best and where your customer experience is letting customers down.

3. Measure the ongoing emotional experience. This enables you to track how your customer experience design is impacting customer emotions and how that is growing business and revenue, or not. This shows the impact of the CX Loyalty Flywheel.

4. Create initiatives to increase positive emotional outcomes and mitigate the negative ones.

Let's go into more detail on how to accomplish this.

DISCOVER THE EXISTING EMOTIONS YOU CREATE AND THEIR IMPACT

Begin the process by carrying out qualitative research to discover how customers feel about the customer experience your company currently provides and, within that experience, which emotions matter most. Do not simply outsource this important step. Engage in it and be a part of it. To capture those emotions, listen to how customers talk about their experiences. You can use open-ended survey feedback, but one-on-one interviews are more effective at uncovering those emotions and their impact. Even better, share those recorded interviews with employees, which helps bring these emotions to life for them. And yes, you can get your business customers to participate. We've done it at every level of leadership, up to (and including) the CEO of global companies.

The next step is to categorize emotions into what we call Emotional Gainers and Emotional Drainers. Emotional Gainers are those that build positive outcomes, such as repurchase, retention, cross-buying, or reduced costs to serve, and Emotional Drainers lead to customer churn and high costs to serve.

Next, separate customers into loyal and less loyal categories. *Don't use survey scores* to segment between successful and unsuccessful customer relationships. Instead, look at the sources of value. The criteria should be familiar by now: customers who give you a higher share of wallet, stay longer, and cost less to serve receive higher scores. The simplest way is to put customers into two to four categories, then see which emotions are prevalent for each. But my preference is to assign each customer a score based on a combination of outcomes (repurchase, share of wallet) and behaviors (number of support calls, escalations).

Once that's done, identify which emotion(s) creates these outcomes. Of course, isolating that emotion isn't so easy. That's where quantitative research comes in. After you have identified loyal and less loyal customers, distribute a survey that asks about the emotions they feel in engaging and working with your company. Offer twenty or thirty different options, including both extreme and milder forms, such as Compassion International's "delight" and "happiness." I often find that more extreme emotions, such as delight, create greater separation than more moderate emotions, but that varies by experience. Send the survey to your entire customer list, including users and decision-makers.

Once the survey is complete, analyze those emotions to see which are most predictive of loyalty. What you are looking for are those emotions that separate your loyal customers—where you have a higher share of wallet, longer retention, and lower cost to serve—from the rest. This shows not only what emotions you create today but also their impact in a way that your CFO can appreciate. The core of this initiative is that emotions impact behaviors, which impact customers' likeliness to stay with your company, order more, and participate in less costly engagements, such as using self-service tools and avoiding service escalations. In other words, this shows how emotions accelerate and slow the CX Loyalty Flywheel.

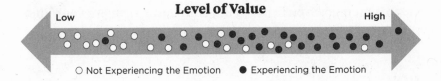

Figure 5-1: The level of value spectrum.

What you are looking for is a pattern, such as in figure 5-1, where loyal customers feel the emotional impact of your experience and less loyal customers don't. While the right emotion will vary by industry and company, good candidates for Emotional North Stars that will be predictive of loyalty include confidence, enjoyability, happiness, and trust. It's also worthwhile to test for negative emotions that you can measure for and design against.

MEASURE THE ONGOING EMOTIONAL EXPERIENCE

Once you identify your Emotional North Star, the next step is to update your relationship and transactional surveys to measure how well you create that emotional outcome today. Many organizations ask about the Emotional North Star with a standard 5-point scale.

Another approach, which I recommend, is to ask about the presence of multiple emotions through a "select all" type of survey question, showing the full set of six or eight emotions and allowing customers to select all that apply to them.

Be deliberate about where you ask these emotional questions. Relationship surveys—which are surveys offered on a periodic basis, typically once or twice a year—are a great way to do this because they allow you to track results regularly. Be thoughtful about asking emotional questions in transactional surveys, as we'll discuss when we share Hagerty's experience (see page 94).

Update your reports and customer health dashboards (we'll talk more about customer health dashboards in Action 3: Evaluate the Flywheel with Customer Ecosystem Data) to communicate to the organization how you're doing in your quest to achieve your Emotional North Star.

NOW, CHANGE THINGS

The whole reason we identify an Emotional North Star is to identify where in your experience you need to drive change. Use your Emotional North Star as a design target as you improve the experience, deliberately creating interventions to emphasize this positive emotion. But understand that you can't create these strong emotional outcomes through one-off or occasional work. Improving the emotional outcome can only happen by rallying the entire organization toward the emotional outcome. Doing so requires change management, which is the topic of Action 4: Grease the Flywheel with Change Management.

Dow = Enjoyable

You might think that the chemical-ordering process is the last place to focus on emotions, but you'd be wrong. I first met Jen Zamora, Senior Director of Global CX and Commercial Excellence at Dow at the time, when we were mapping Dow's complaints experience. Customers told the company that the way they managed complaints was cumbersome, with no clear ownership of issues and limited transparency on progress. Jen told us her goal was to create a complaints process that was *enjoyable*.

I was pretty sure I heard her wrong. Not effective or easy, but an enjoyable complaints experience? She confirmed that was exactly her goal.

Dow considers an effective and easy experience to be table stakes. So, Dow designs for enjoyable experiences. When I interviewed Jen at a conference, she shared the philosophy behind this approach:

> Everybody who transacts business wants an easy and effective transaction, and we strive to deliver against that. But when you take it to the next level and understand what makes the experience enjoyable, you start to tap into a different aspect of the customer's psyche. You tap into the emotional connection. And that's what we've been able to prove out over the last couple of years. Easy and effective are table stakes. But the enjoyable aspect is when a customer has to choose a supplier. If your experience is enjoyable, nine times out of ten, you're going to go back for the enjoyable experience.

Jen doesn't just claim this; she has the data to prove it. Effectiveness and ease matter, but they don't lead to those loyalty outcomes that Dow is looking to drive. When Dow creates an emotional connection, customers order more often and at higher volume, the true definition of loyalty. Dow also measures trust, to provide more context as to how it is doing in creating this emotional connection. The customer experience team worked closely with the analytics group to understand what customer experience efforts led to these outcomes. We'll explore Dow's analysis of customers' behavioral data in Action 3.

Dow's survey work provided valuable insight into improving customer outcomes, its top opportunity being to better manage complaints. This focus on creating an enjoyable experience led Dow to completely revise its complaints process, establishing a dedicated team charged with resolving complaints in a timely manner and keeping customers informed about progress. This focus increased customers' trust, leading to a more enjoyable experience.

Hagerty = Happiness

A key moment in Hagerty's history was the epiphany that the company wasn't really an insurance company but rather, an automotive lifestyle brand featuring many products to support clients through their automotive journeys, one of which happened to be insurance. This opened the door to thinking differently about the company's customer experience, including how emotions matter. As Nancy Flowers, Vice President of Insights and Loyalty at Hagerty, explains:

> We're an automotive lifestyle brand. Our roots were in insurance, but we offer much more than that. We offer valuation services, we have a peer-to-peer renting platform, a marketplace where clients can buy and sell cars, and much more.[5] We don't position ourselves as just insurance. We're a lifestyle brand. And we do a ton to build community and camaraderie. Our mission is to save driving and car culture for future generations, and to do this, we help our members get the most out of the hobby as possible. So, when we looked at these emotions, it was really funny, because let me tell you, car guys aren't so good with saying what their emotions are. But we finally got to it. And the emotion we landed on was this: we want to leave our clients feeling happy. So, we measure how strongly they agree that they left the experience feeling happy.

She went into more detail on how she made the connection between emotion, customer success, and financial outcomes. It started when Hagerty brought on a new roadside assistance vendor. When collectible cars break down, it's a much bigger deal for the owner than when your 2018 sedan fails on your daily commute. This car is their baby, and they're typically taking it out to enjoy the day in their vehicle. And when an enthusiast's car breaks down, it affects not only the driver but also others who are on the trip—and it could be part of a planned vacation or multiday event, even taking place many miles from home. This calls for a special—and special-ized—customer assistance process.

So, Hagerty designed its roadside assistance program to support these classic-car drivers with a high-level, almost white-glove, experience, knowing how disappointing a breakdown can be. It took time for Hagerty to come to understand this emotional connection because Hagerty had been soliciting feedback from drivers on its quality of service and had received positive feedback. However, when the company changed its roadside assistance partner, the NPS took a dive. At first, Hagerty could not figure out why. All the operational data looked fine. The calls were being answered in the same amount of time and the roadside assistance vehicles were showing up as promised, so nothing seemed to be any different.

To discover what was happening, Nancy and her team monitored phone calls between the drivers and the roadside assistance provider. And the light bulb went on when Nancy's team understood that the car owners felt an absence of empathy when they called for help with this new provider. Of course, we all should feel empathy from our service providers when we need help, but for classic-car drivers who are disappointed and frustrated that their trips were interrupted, lack of empathy at the other end of their calls was a big deal. While the functional service level—responding to a call and towing the vehicle—had not changed, the emotional experience was far worse. Hagerty learned that providing an empathetic emotional experience to drivers would restore previous customer satisfaction levels. More importantly, it made the Hagerty team curious about what other emotions could be behind customer satisfaction and NPS scores. Nancy walks through how the company aligned on happiness as its Emotional North Star, which wasn't easy:

> We started out with some focus groups, where we did almost like a card-sorting exercise, showing our customers a feeling and asking them, What feeling does that relate to? But on the first day, I don't think we got anything, and we had to regroup. Remember, we're working with a bunch of car guys—and they are mostly guys—and they're not really used to talking about their emotions. So, we tried to focus on passion because we think there's a lot of passion around that automotive lifestyle. But when we kept trying to key in on passion, they could only relate it to intimacy! It took hard work to get people to express what emotions in an automotive lifestyle matter, but eventually, we were able to land on happiness.
>
> We were surprised about happiness, honestly. But even in some of the transactions, it's happiness. This is a hobby. Even when they call Hagerty for a new policy, happiness popped. We tried to understand: "Why would that be?" One of the things is, they drive these cars for enjoyment. And we understand that, and we get that passion. So, when they call, we can say, "What a beautiful car," "Oh my gosh, I've always wanted a '67 Chevy," or "My dad had a '66 Mustang," which validates what they're doing. That's what we call the virtual thumbs-up. When you see a cool car on the road, you give them a thumbs-up, right? And so, they feel good [about their experience with us]: "I'm happy now that I've got my policy. I can go and drive my car."
>
> We measure happiness at the relationship level and some transactions. At the relationship level, we ask [members to rate], "My experience with Hagerty leaves me feeling

happy" and use a 5-point scale from strongly disagree to strongly agree. It is definitely our Emotional North Star and is highly correlated with loyalty. We also find that feeling supported and valued are important and measure those at the relationship level.

The big difference emotionally comes in with transactions. For example, after a claims or roadside incident, we do not measure happiness. We are currently exploring what emotion correlates with satisfaction/loyalty in those "negative" service incidents. We hear a lot of verbatims in claims surveys regarding feeling cared for, or whether the adjuster shows empathy, and yet roadside seems to be a little different.

Notice how Nancy thinks about when and how to ask about emotions. She understands that, while happiness is Hagerty's overall Emotional North Star, different target emotions fit different journeys in the overall experience. This distinction is critical. Asking a customer whose car was totaled if their experience with Hagerty leaves them feeling happy is just asking for trouble!

Hagerty continues to use NPS as its relationship metric, as it's been proven to predict both retention and purchases of additional products, but the company also asks about happiness, which helps it to see how its design is working. In addition to asking about specific emotions, Hagerty also measures effectiveness, ease, and emotion, and it has discovered that the transactional emotion scores also predict NPS, which in turn predicts retention and cross-sell, completing the CX Loyalty Flywheel.

Moving on as to how Hagerty creates a happy experience, Nancy shares:

If you don't have great service, you cannot make an emotional connection. So, we say, "Hagerty starts with our phenomenal people taking care of what clients need, creating those flawless interactions and engagement." And then we really shift to that sort of more lifestyle focus. It really is just about building emotional connections around those moments that matter in the life of your customer. When we're designing experiences, the question is, How do we elevate? How do we celebrate that moment?

One of the more recent examples is, when people get in a total-loss claim on their collector vehicles, it's really emotional. It's even worse in a vehicle that might have been in your family for fifteen years. So, we designed Total Loss Care Kits. It's all about getting the car back on the road because often, these collectors keep the car whether it's totaled or not, and rebuild it because it's their baby. This total-loss care package is to help them rebuild the car. It's a headlamp, there's magnetic poles for bolts and all your metal stuff. The response has been overwhelming.

Nancy goes on to talk about building emotional connections at events:

A great example is Pebble Beach, the flagship of the automotive world. Pebble Beach overlooks the Pacific Ocean, with the absolute best cars in the world, and they're competing. And many years ago, Hagerty started to go out on the lawn because it's on the Pebble Beach golf course. At, like, 4:00 a.m., we would watch these cars pull onto the field. And I get chills talking about it. It's incredible to see this. The ocean's in the background, it's steamy, it's kind of dark, the sun's coming up. And customers started joining us, just organically, and it became known as Dawn Patrol.

We decided if you were committed enough to get up at 4:00 a.m. and get out there, Hagerty would give you doughnuts and coffee and a really cool hat. So, last year, because of the pandemic, we knew our clients were mourning the loss of that experience. So, we did it virtually, we challenged our clients to do a drive at dawn on the day that [the Pebble Beach event] would have been and send us photos. It was such a success and such a great way to build that emotional connection.

Measuring happiness is the first step. Creating happiness—and the customer and business outcomes that come from this—that's the potential of an Emotional North Star.

XYZ Software = Trust

XYZ has focused on trust, its number one value, from the very beginning. The company has developed different ways to measure it. Unlike our other three case studies, XYZ doesn't ask specific survey questions about trust, but it does measure it indirectly. As Natasha explains:

There are two components to trust. First, there's trust from a technology standpoint, which we break down into site reliability and availability. We have a few technical metrics that our engineering team owns. The head of our engineering group owns system uptime of 99.99 percent, for example. So, those are the technical trust metrics that we look at. Because we're a cloud company, we want to make sure that customers do not experience any downtime. And so that's one part of trust that we do.

The other part of trust can be fuzzy because it's based on emotions. For example, "Do I trust that you have my best interest in mind when you're working with me?," and that is something that's not often tracked in B2B. We look at trust based on sentiment and what customers are saying through surveys at different points in their journeys. We analyze sentiment when they buy, where they provide feedback on our sales behavior. We look at it again when they renew, how they're feeling with our renewal team or sales team, as well as the value they're getting, whether it's one, two, or three years out from the original contract. But we also look at it in intervals of every three months, every six months, every year, in their feedback from our annual survey. So, rather than using a survey, we analyze trust from our relationship, and that emotional perspective through our sentiment analysis of the surveys that we've deployed.

We keep our surveys short and sweet. And we always have an open-ended question, which allows them to write in the comment, elaborate on why they support us the way they do, whether it's satisfaction or advocacy.

We look at it through two things. One is manually combing the sentiment, but we also automate the sentiment analysis, using our AI tools to determine how our customers are feeling. What are emotional words that we can pull from their comments to gauge if they are happy? Is there a high level of frustration? We use an emotional wheel, and we categorize sentiment based on that emotional wheel. It's not perfect—it's a little manual. We're moving toward automation, but it gives us a sense of what our customers are feeling in terms of their relationship. That's a gauge for us in terms of, Do they trust us? Do they trust our sales team? Do they trust our renewals team? How about our success team, when it's engaging with them through services or through accelerators, or even through helping them through tickets with our support team? So, that's how we create a measure of trust.

Once we measure trust, the next step is working to expand it. For example, for the sales organization, when we onboard a new hire, we always talk about the customer experience, and how you behave matters to a customer. This comes through in terms of enablement and driving the right behaviors with our sales team. We create and design those types of enablement and coaching programs for our customer-facing team, whether they are an account executive or a customer success manager.

When our teams design the customer success program, they look at the customer journey and design the desired emotion. We want customers to feel that we have their best interest in mind. But we also want to make sure that they're getting value from their investment, which varies depending on whether they're a small or large customer. The teams are really cognizant in terms of how we create plays, that we show the customer feels that we have their best interests in mind. That means, Do we have the right programs, assets, and tools to help them deploy, to help them get easy support, to get them articles that are easy to find? We want to help them when they need it wherever they need it, and however they need it. So, those are the things that our teams think about when they're designing journeys [for] post-sales engagement. That's how we think about building trust into the design of the product itself, as well as the experience, end to end.

The company deliberately thinks through both types of trust—functional and emotional—and designs experiences to ensure these positive outcomes for customers.

■ ■ ■

Aligning on the one emotion that delivers the most value to your customers has proven to have enormous impact on how companies relate to their customers. Dow, Hagerty, and XYZ aligned on their distinct Emotional North Stars, which resulted in huge benefits to customer loyalty and internally, to company culture. However, there is the final challenge to do with emotions, and that is quantifying the impact.

To be more specific, I mean that B2B programs often have a difficult time acknowledging the importance of emotions, so reporting on them in isolation is a nonstarter. Yes, some customers feel trust and others feel frustration, but so what? Isn't that common? But when you start with the important outcomes—upsells and service issues—and then use the emotions to explain why they happen, that opens eyes across the organization, and lends itself to action. In the next chapter, we'll spend some time with Roxie at UKG and learn how she uses the results to drive change.

Cari's Story

Stephen's musings that the information provided by the journey mapping could lead to unpleasant surprises came to pass. The journey mapping results actually hit the organization pretty hard because they showed significant client frustration with Sycamore on many levels. While many in the organization knew customers were frustrated, seeing their frustrations laid out so clearly forced the organization to look at its challenges head-on.

The candor recorded in the customer interview videos caught Cari off guard. After all, she'd been with the organization for years, and hated to see the clients' frustration. But she also knew this opened an opportunity for everyone to come together to improve the process. As she explained to Stephen, "It was tough to hear customers talking about how frustrated they were with our service and support. It was even harder once all the feedback was consolidated into one report and to sit through ninety minutes of brutal feedback. But this opens up some opportunities.

"What really hit me was when one customer told us how she doesn't feel like we know her, and that, if she left, she wouldn't be letting anybody down. That's tough. That's where we need to start—by building relationships with our customers.

"Let's not waste a good crisis. Even Yolanda recognized that the current experience is untenable, and we need to figure out how to improve it."

"Definitely," Stephen responded. "The journey map showed us pretty clearly our customers' emotions. Let me go through the comments in our surveys to see if we can't go deeper and identify which customers are experiencing which emotions. In the journey mapping, we identified that our goal is to reduce the annoyance and frustration and create an experience where we're their trusted advisor. Let me see if I can quantify how often we're hitting those marks today.

"It will be more efficient if we actually ask about emotions right in the survey. It may seem a bit odd asking a CIO about emotions, but they certainly didn't hold back from identifying them in our interviews!"

Cari agreed. "Well, why can't we? Let's include emotions in the survey," she said. "But first, let's make sure we have the right emotions. So, let's start with the journey map and the surveys to identify fifteen or twenty emotions that customers share. Then, let's put out a separate survey and tie it to our data, to see which emotions are creating higher NRR and which cause it to drop. We may even be able to see how longer implementations or ineffective customizations create distinct emotions from others, showing why those longer times and customizations lead to fewer upsells. Then we can monitor those emotions and intervene when needed."

Stephen concurred. "Sounds like a plan! We can send it to our customers who didn't get the last relationship survey, so we get a good sample size without overwhelming customers, and it should give us enough responses to understand what's happening."

My Thoughts

Emotions are the core of decision-making; that's fairly well accepted. But what Cari and Stephen did—asking about specific emotions in relationship and transactional surveys—isn't common practice. But it should be.

However, simply asking about emotions isn't enough because how do we know which emotions matter? While qualitative research helps identify candidate emotions, it's quantitative research—combined with data—that helps determine which emotions are the right ones. That also makes it easier to get other executives—even the CFO!—on board, since you're showing outcomes that matter to the organization.

CHAPTER 6

How Can I Measure and Manage Emotions to Create Value?

THE EFFORT REQUIRED TO FIND AND MEASURE YOUR EMOTIONAL North Star, as we have seen, is layered. It takes hard work and team effort. But you may be asking, and rightly so, How do we use the information we have discovered to innovate and create better results? In other words, Once we have the results, how does this help us accelerate the CX Loyalty Flywheel? Or, closer to home, How do I communicate its importance in a way that my skeptical executives will listen?

Using Your Customers' Emotions to Drive Action

Emotions show up in every touchpoint of the customer experience journey. Our Change Makers learned how to create experiences to minimize the negative outcomes and maximize the positive ones, then use them to create more value for both customers and the company.

APPLYING EMOTIONS TO SEGMENTATION

Customer values, needs, and emotions all apply to segmentation. The lens of emotions is particularly useful when you focus on designing new experiences. It's worth considering that your most valuable customers are often looking for a different experience than customers who interact less often and therefore drive less revenue. While Dow's best customers want an enjoyable experience (even if they probably wouldn't articulate it in this way), it's likely that some of their lower-volume customers value efficiency and speed over experiencing an emotion such as "enjoyable." They may not be looking for a partnership, preferring instead easy access to Dow's products. And, of course, it takes investment to create a stronger emotional outcome. Where should the company invest in order to create the right emotions for the right customers for the right outcomes?

Of course, this opens up an intriguing possibility. While lower-tier customers may not wish for an emotional experience today, could Dow create—and receive—more value if the company did create a stronger emotional outcome? The first step in this conversation is to see how emotions, particularly your Emotional North Star, vary by your segments.

MAPPING END-TO-END AND CRITICAL CUSTOMER JOURNEYS

This isn't my journey mapping book. But I do have to share this: if you aren't including emotions in your journey mapping, you aren't doing it right. Roxie used journey mapping to help bring the emotions to life for her leaders—by listening firsthand to customers as they discussed what made them confident versus what frustrated them.

In its research report *Customer Experience at a Crossroads*, CustomerThink found that "Winning" programs—defined as those programs that can prove they have business impact—were more likely to have mapped the end-to-end experience first and then continued on to map individual journeys after that. As CEO Bob Thompson wrote, "What's notable is that Winning CX initiatives have a more consistent focus across the journey." I found the same outcome in our surveys, with over half (55 percent) of Change Makers having mapped the end-to-end experience, versus just 36 percent of other organizations.

Mapping the end-to-end experience shows you the emotions your customers feel across their life cycle; this in turn helps you to understand where you need to rethink your experience to create better outcomes for both customers and your company. Without doing this, it's possible to get caught up in focusing on a part of the experience where there's plenty of noise but no real customer impact. For many organizations, invoicing is an example of this. Heart of the Customer's B2B Practice Leader Nicole Newton states, "At a previous company, we mapped the end-to-end journey and discovered that, while our confusing invoices annoyed customers, it wasn't a driver of retention or churn. So, we focused elsewhere where there was more impact, until eventually we were just too embarrassed and went and fixed our invoices."

We often find this. For whatever reason, many B2B companies have frustrating invoices.[1] For example, it can be difficult to match up the invoices with what customers purchased. But it's rare that this becomes one of the most critical areas to design experiences.

I'm often contacted by companies looking to journey mapping, and many ask me where to focus first. My answer is this: decide on what you're trying to optimize. If you're trying to create long-term impact over the next three to five years, then map the end-to-end experience first. This may not be as immediately actionable as focusing on a subjourney, but it will make sure you focus your efforts in the right area to improve long-term results. Alternatively, if you need to show immediate impact, start with a specific subjourney, such as onboarding or issue resolution. This narrow focus can enable you to fix specific problems and show a quick win. However, it might not lead to as much long-term impact because you may not focus on the most important issues if you do not look at the overall journey first.

Don't quit after mapping your end-to-end experience, though. Our survey revealed that Change Makers mapped almost twice as many journeys as average companies. Mapping your subjourneys helps you find new ways to improve the customer experience and keep up the momentum.

THE LINK BETWEEN ONBOARDING AND LOYALTY

For many organizations, the onboarding journey is the most predictive of ongoing loyalty. For example, in our last book, *How Hard Is It to Be Your Customer?*, we wrote about how the YMCA focused on onboarding to improve retention. Onboarding is even more important in the long-term relationships inherent to B2B. B2B companies typically have fewer clients than B2C, so you can't afford a misstep. The onboarding journey is where you set expectations for the rest of the experience. If it doesn't go well, it will be like rolling a rock uphill to build trust and confidence with that unhappy customer. The pattern of behavior that leads to loyalty will not develop.

Onboarding (or implementation) is especially critical for software companies; if onboarding doesn't go well, a customer will have little faith in your platform and be disinclined to learn how to use it. As a result, it doesn't impact the success of the business, and it becomes an easy target to cut at budget time. As Karin Moffett, former Chief Customer Officer at software company Brainshark shares, "If we don't make [customers] successful in their first year, then we have failed. But if they're seeing value and ROI from the solution during that first year, it significantly increases their likelihood to renew."[2]

LinkedIn found the same thing. As reported in the book *Upstream* by Dan Heath, LinkedIn focused on recreating its customer-onboarding process. The resulting change so improved engagement that the company increased revenue by tens of millions of dollars through improved retention of customers who went through the new onboarding journey.

UKG Creates Confidence

While all our case studies can talk at length about the power of measuring and managing emotions, Roxie Strohmenger takes it to a different level at UKG. She studied emotions in graduate school. Probably my favorite comment from her is this:

> My neuroscience professors in grad school, they would be upset that I'm using survey questions to get to emotions, but this is the only way I can do it. I can't hook up my customers to a galvanic skin response system, although it would be awesome.
>
> From my perspective, measuring emotions isn't rocket science. It's just not been done in a systematized, consistent way. So, by developing this system, UKG is bought into it, and it's helping UKG to be smarter in the decisions that it makes.

Roxie started with emotions at the very beginning once she saw that the organization's pre-existing measurement didn't capture and connect to value. She began by using her financial and behavioral data to distinguish success, breaking customers into successful and unsuccessful buckets:

> NPS isn't the most ideal metric to leverage. It isn't a direct measure of experience. And it's critical to understand the experience from the customer's perspective, the quality dimensions like effort, or how we make our customers feel, or specific elements of the experience: Did we clearly communicate with them? Do we keep them informed of status updates? Those are better measures that are easier to tie to either descriptive metrics or even outcome metrics, like revenue or recurring revenue.

To understand which emotions were most critical, Roxie began with a blind competitive benchmarking survey[3] sent to HR decision-makers across both customers and noncustomers. She asked respondents about their relationship with their HR process or software provider, including a battery of thirty emotions to identify which emotions loyal and disloyal customers reported.[4]

Identifying the emotions was only the start. The next step was to isolate which emotions matter most. If most of your customers report being "happy" through their experience with you but their behavior (repurchase, retention, etc.) isn't any different from those who aren't, then managing happiness won't matter. So, Roxie went deeper.

For noncustomers, she asked for self-reported loyalty. But "likelihood to repurchase" only measures *intention*, which is inherently unreliable. To get around this, for clients, Roxie compared their reported emotions with behavioral and financial data to see which translated into action. For example, when clients frequently escalated service issues, what emotions were linked with this behavior? When clients purchased additional products, was this associated with client overall satisfaction, happiness, confidence, or ease of working with UKG? She narrowed the list to four loyalty-building emotions, such as confidence, and four loyalty-weakening emotions, such as frustration. Roxie then identified "confidence" as most critical to success—their Emotional North Star. She went further into confidence and its critical role for a SaaS software company:

My favorite emotion for our sector is confidence. If clients don't feel confident that they can use the solution in the manner they need to, to execute to be successful in their job, or if they don't feel confident in how we engage with them in terms of the services, things break apart, and it becomes this ripple effect. So yes, in B2B, emotions matter. Now, is it confidence in every B2B sector? No. And that's a piece that you have to investigate.

After identifying the top emotions, we worked with Roxie to kick off a journey mapping program to learn what it was like for existing customers to work with UKG and how the experience created or degraded confidence. She invited UKG's leaders to visit customers to learn about their goals and ambitions, how UKG helped achieve these goals (or didn't), and how customers felt about their relationships with UKG.

When leaders talked directly to customers, it brought those customers' emotions to life. The interviews were video recorded for the benefit of those who did not go on the trips, increasing accessibility to the results. Roxie used these recordings to communicate what led to confidence, and contrasted this with what led to frustration or annoyance. From there, she had her teams create experiences amplifying loyalty-building emotions and mitigating loyalty-weakening emotions, and then measured the changes in outcomes. Once she identified the most critical emotions and how they impact UKG's business outcomes, Roxie's next step was to evolve her customer experience measurement. Overall satisfaction worked well to measure the experience, but the complementary metrics were less effective. She replaced NPS and developed more granular measurements of CX quality, including expectations, ease, and emotion in the experience, and then targeted specific drivers of the experience.

This enabled Roxie to produce far more powerful reporting to help the organization better manage and improve customers' emotions and thus, outcomes. Imagine two scenarios. Most organizations have reports that say, "The Net Promoter Score for your product is 20, compared to our overall NPS of 35." While that's data, it's not actionable information. This reporting raises the follow-up questions "Why?" and "What should I do about that?"

Compare this to a report that Roxie might deliver (numbers used here are hypothetical): "Overall, 46 percent of our customers are confident, but that's true for only 25 percent of customers using your product. Worse, while only 15 percent of our overall customer base is frustrated, for your product line, it's 40 percent." While you'll still want to dig in to find out what's driving confidence and frustration, this type of reporting more directly leads to customer-focused change.

This reporting also enables Roxie to track progress on the initiatives that came from journey mapping. Did the ideas create the confidence expected? If not, this reporting enables her team to iterate on the results more quickly. When it comes to driving customer-focused change, Roxie's detailed emotions-based reporting gives clear guidance on how to build out change. As she explained in a webinar with me:

> It's not like we sit around and ask, "Okay, how do we activate confidence?" It's "What are the behaviors and the actions we can do that would help a customer feel more confident?" So, for example, with confidence, we create confidence when we communicate clearly. Why did an issue happen? If there's a break-fix issue[5] that manifested, what are our next steps?
>
> Demonstrating that we're knowledgeable engenders more confidence in the customer, that they are connected with somebody who knows how to help them, and that we've got their back. When you talk about it, from that standpoint, it becomes easier to digest.
>
> Instead, you train on "these are the behaviors." If you follow these behaviors, we will then see these upticks in activation and profit and downticks in frustration. We found that when we communicate clearly with our customers, we see a fifteen times improvement in confidence and a twelve times decrease in frustration. And that reporting helps everyone to lean in and go, "Okay, now I get it." Emotion is the byproduct of these behaviors.

Roxie's approach differs from most in that she didn't start with a common score, such as customer satisfaction or NPS, and simply *hoped* it would work for UKG. Instead, she began with what was most important for UKG to understand: Will they stay a customer of UKG, will they decide to purchase additional products and services, or have a high cost to serve? She then worked backward to determine which emotions most influenced these outcomes.

Confidence is now UKG's target emotion for experience design— its Emotional North Star. UKG prioritizes efforts that will increase confidence while reducing loyalty-weakening emotions such as frustration. It's rare to find an organization as aligned against specific emotional outcomes as UKG.

Change Makers embed emotions into their measurement systems and look for evidence as to where an emotion most impacts the journey. Sharing your Emotional North Star regularly helps create awareness around its importance, aligning teams against this critical outcome.

Another reason to incorporate emotions into your measurement is its predictive power. Hagerty found that happiness predicted NPS, which predicted retention and new product purchases—again, the CX Loyalty Flywheel at work. Dow and UKG found that enjoyability and confidence, respectively, predicted customer-loyalty behaviors. If those disparate organizations found this predictive power, odds are that you can also discover predictive emotions in your customers' experiences.

Innovation

Once you have identified your Emotional North Star and built it into measurement, it's time to innovate toward it. The first place to begin is in establishing an overall framework to create that emotion, as the VA does with trust. The VA can measure the effects of its flywheel; when it improves trust, more veterans come to the VA, meaning its mission is more fully utilized.

Next, focus on individual journeys, using communications and other interventions to further reinforce the desired emotional outcome.

FUTURE-STATE JOURNEYS SHOULD FOCUS ON EMOTIONS

Your Emotional North Star needs to be the centerpiece of your design. CustomerThink also found that the most effective organizations—which it labeled "Winners"—created a future-state vision of their journeys to guide their innovation efforts. Ensure that the touchpoints in your future-state journey align with your Emotional North Star, which will lead to loyalty. Every interaction you have with a customer either builds or degrades loyalty. By targeting every step to create that emotion, you can accelerate your CX Loyalty Flywheel.

CREATE INNOVATIONS THAT BUILD ON POSITIVE EMOTIONS AND REDUCE NEGATIVE ONES

As mentioned in Action 1, the most common place for customer experience programs to begin to show value is in reducing the cost to serve. Emotions give us another lens to approach the same issue. Often, the quickest way to show impact is to identify the places in the journey where customers are feeling those Emotional Drainers. Of course, start with those most tied to loyalty degradation from your survey work.

One common source for frustration is a lack of communication. As we'll discuss in the technology section, B2B customers are regular consumers of goods and services in their personal lives, and so will expect you to communicate with them as effectively as Amazon does. Often, providing an Amazon level of transparency helps to mitigate frustration. As I have emphasized, going the extra mile to be transparent is rarely enough to win customers, but it can help stem churn and reduced share of wallet.

For long-term impact, spend time with your customers and get to understand how they experience your Emotional North Star. Where or how are confidence and trust generated? Can you isolate what is unique about customers who experience high levels of confidence and trust versus those who do not? Common reasons can be grounded in the specific teams managing their account (as we heard from Change Maker Cari) or in specific products. If one product has a majority of clients showing confidence, but another shows very little, then here's a good clue for where to focus innovation. Learn why the difference exists, and target interventions in the weaker product to close the gap.

Measuring emotions can also help with coaching. Once you collect enough data, look for trends in emotions by a sales team, account manager, or customer success manager. It's possible that the sales team is setting higher expectations and achieving them for some accounts and not so much for other accounts, leading to this discrepancy. Or one account or success manager may be more effective at helping build confidence than others. What can be learned from this individual to drive overall success?

While the specific initiatives will vary by company and experience, using emotions as a diagnostic can help you isolate where you need to focus, and its ongoing measurement can ensure that the interventions are accomplishing their goals before having to wait for the client to churn or reorder.

■ ■ ■

Action 2 has covered a lot of ground, from asking if your company is linking emotions to value to discovering your customers' highest value emotion to measuring that emotion to apply to innovation strategies. The key takeaway is that your company's future state depends on knowing your customers' emotions and keeping your finger on the pulse.

Cari's Story

At their one-on-one a few weeks later, Stephen shared the results of their relationship survey. "Just as we discussed, I added a pick list of emotions to help us understand what emotions our clients are experiencing, and it was close to what we hypothesized," he said. "For example, when I looked at customers who selected annoyance and frustration, they required far more support calls to resolve problems—and longer-lasting calls—than our customers who reported experiencing positive emotions. The frustrated clients were also far less likely to purchase additional modules from us. And, like the journey map predicted, they had longer implementations and more customizations than happier customers.

"But then I found something surprising. We did have some complex customers with harder implementations, but they said they felt trust with us. And they purchased more products from us, too."

"Really?" Cari responded. "Normally, complex customers don't have as good of a relationship with us because of those difficulties. How do you explain the trust?"

"Well, that was a surprise. But when I looked at how they were implemented, they all had the same systems integrator, Creative Consulting. We have a great relationship with Creative, and it seems it's figured out the secret sauce to complex implementations and how to create a sense of confidence in our customers."

"Excellent!" said Cari. "Let's get together with the SI team to see if we can identify what Creative does to create such trust, and let's see if we can learn something to help all of our SIs. In the meantime, I want to communicate the role of emotions to everybody. Let's build a road show across the organization to share the most critical emotions, and add them to our dashboard, too. We'll start with the CX council, and then work with each department to communicate the results from the journey map and the emotional research."

My Thoughts

Like many companies that have discovered the power of designing for specific emotions, Sycamore started with journey mapping. Done right, journey mapping identifies the specific emotions customers feel as they go through the journey of interest.

Once that's complete, the best practice to identify the emotions that matter is to use a survey asking about the emotions, and to tie the resulting emotions to your financial and behavioral data, a topic we'll go into more deeply in our next section.

Takeaways

Identifying Sources of Value in the CX Loyalty Flywheel

Please use the workbook that you can download from DoB2BBetter .com/workbook to complete the exercises and activities. Completing this work will result in a playbook that will help you plan your CX program and provide insight into questions and challenges that your fellow CX colleagues everywhere are facing. We will continue on from Action 1 and use the story of Cari as an example of how she would respond to questions from her colleagues. Here's how I would help Cari think through her next steps.

What qualitative research do you have that can help you understand more about your customers' experience working with you?

CARI: We have qualitative interviews from our journey mapping. In addition to the emotions highlighted in the map, we can review the original transcripts to mine the interviews to find which are most common. I don't manage our win/loss interviews, but I can see whether they keep transcripts. If nothing else, maybe the reports will give us some clues.

I know our CABs [customer advisory boards] aren't recorded, but I'll have Stephen interview the organizers to get their perceptions of those emotions. Maybe I can join the next CAB, and we can do an exercise to surface some of them.

How can you separate your customers into higher- and lower-loyalty tiers for comparing the emotions?

CARI: I used two pieces of data: sales of add-on products (who has purchased additional products after their initial implementation) and those with ongoing support issues. Specifically, those who have had more than two severity 1 issues in the last year. I created four tiers of customers:

1. Purchased additional products, fewer than three severity 1 issues in the last year.
2. Purchased additional products, more than three severity 1 issues in the last year.
3. Have not purchased additional products, fewer than three severity 1 issues in the last year.
4. Have not purchased additional products, more than three severity 1 issues in the last year.

Group 1 is clearly positive, and group 4 is negative, so I'll group categories 2 and 3 into a "neutral" bucket and see what emotions separate among the three levels. I can bounce these ideas up against the Customer Success Managers to make sure they agree with the categories and that the ones on top are more positive than the rest.

Now that you've conducted your survey, let's take some time to examine the results. Which positive and negative emotions rose to the top? In taking the next step of the analysis, are you able to isolate the positive or negative results to specific journeys or products?

CARI: Our top positive emotions were confident, excited, proud, and encouraged, while our top-impact negative emotions were frustrated, tired, annoyed, and angry. We found that those who had added additional products were more likely to be excited, while confident and proud drove customers to be a reference. This was most common for customers who had been with us for two years. It seems that it takes a while for the experience to stabilize before they get excited or confident.

Those negative emotions were more common early in the experience, especially while they were implementing our products. Tired, for example, was almost exclusively felt by those who were actively implementing a product.

Those who were frustrated or annoyed were more correlated with clients who escalated issues quickly.

Of course, we can only correlate the current state right now. I plan to have Stephen look at this again in a year and see whether these emotions led to change in any of our crucial outcomes. It's possible (and I hope it's true) that those who are confident in the implementation become excited after it's done and become references for us.

How would you assess our leaders' state of readiness to talk about emotions?

CARI: I can't say that they're ready to talk about hopefulness. But I think they will understand that the more frustrated our customers are, the less likely they are to purchase additional modules. We can have a good conversation on causation. Does having multiple severity 1 issues cause frustration (likely) or does being frustrated cause you to escalate issues to severity 1 quickly (also likely)? As we track results over time, we'll want to see how the emotions change as we resolve issues, and new ones pop up.

Have you thought about how you can build these emotions into your communications?

CARI: I'm going to hold quarterly town halls on customer experience and emotions, and share recordings of customers sharing those emotions. This can be a powerful way to get this message across.

Can you tie the emotions to any financial outcomes yet?

CARI: As expected, those with positive emotions on average buy more products than those with negative emotions. Again, I'm not certain about the causation arrow, but it's important to recognize that. And yes, those who show frustration take that out on our support teams, opening more tickets and escalating to leadership more frequently. We don't have costs for escalations, but everyone knows they're expensive.

What about integrating the emotions data into your analysis and reporting?

CARI: We don't want to put this into the CRM! That's a little too much exposure. We've agreed not to report individual customers' emotions, but instead look at the macro level. But we can report on the overall level of positive and negative emotions in our journey and show the average number of products associated with each emotion, as well as the average number of severity 1 tickets. That should get attention!

ACTION 3

EVALUATE THE FLYWHEEL WITH CUSTOMER ECOSYSTEM DATA

CHANGE MAKERS DON'T RELY ON CHANCE.
THEY UNDERSTAND THE CUSTOMER
ECOSYSTEM DATA AND USE TECHNOLOGY
TO ENSURE CUSTOMERS RECEIVE A
CONSISTENTLY GREAT EXPERIENCE.

"If you want to effectively measure the experience, you look
at some of the operational data to find out what's happening.
Like, for example, how many people read the emails. You look
at sentiment. And then you look at the outcome or financial
data, which are the outcome of the work. And perception
as well. You have CX typically looking at the sentiment and
you have analytics or operations looking at the behavior and
operational data."

—**Emerson Tan,** Director, Financial Planning and Analysis,
Lone Wolf Technologies

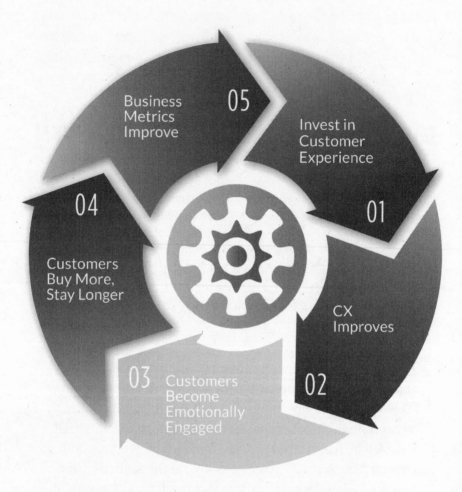

Figure 7-1: The CX Loyalty Flywheel: Engage through data.

DATA IS A MISSING ELEMENT IN MANY CX PROGRAMS. JUST like emotions, customer experience leaders acknowledge the importance of connecting data to their work but rarely do a thorough job.

Data gives you a more solid understanding of the true customer experience. Asking customers about their paths is an unreliable way to understand the truth, as customers frequently misremember their previous activities.

Using your organization's Customer Ecosystem Data—the descriptive, sentiment, behavioral, operational, and financial data—provides a scalable way to understand what truly occurs in your customer experience. Rather than asking customers in a survey whether they logged into the portal before calling customer service with an issue, Change Makers embed that behavioral data into the survey, so they can compare the sentiment of those who tried the portal first, as compared to those whose first step was to call, providing more actionable data to understand the true journey.

In this section, we'll start in chapter 7 by identifying the various types of Customer Ecosystem Data to consider. In chapter 8, we'll look at how technology uses this data to help better understand and improve the customer experience. Finally, in chapter 9, we'll apply this learning to discover how to create a great dashboard to show the right data to the right audiences.

CHAPTER 7

Do I Understand the Role of Data in Designing a Great Customer Experience?

DATA ARE EVERYWHERE IN AN ORGANIZATION! STOCK PRICES often show on the intranet and office entries. Sales data are published regularly. Profitability is known by all. Every part of the organization uses operational, behavioral, and financial data to drive their decisions.

Except, sometimes, for customer experience, which often has its own set of data—survey scores—that is isolated from the rest of the organization's data. But not with Change Makers. Great programs know that data is the secret to both better understanding the customer experience and communicating it in a way that executives want to hear it.

Using Data to Drive Experience

Minnesota's Metropolitan Airports Commission (MAC) owns and operates Minneapolis–St. Paul International (MSP), one of the top-ranked airports in the country and five-time winner of the Airports Council International (ACI) Best Airport in North America in the twenty-five- to forty-million-passenger category between 2016 and 2022.

Being a B2B2C organization is challenging for a commercial airport because many different businesses—and travelers—make up its ecosystem. Travelers can avail themselves of services provided by a variety of MSP tenants, such as restaurants and local specialty and national chain stores, and travelers also receive service from another MSP tenant—the airline on which they're flying.

The MAC has a strong operations culture and knew it could utilize data to better understand the current traveler journey and discover opportunities to improve outcomes for MSP's various customers: travelers, tenants, and airlines. Spearheading efforts to do just that are Phil Burke, who leads the MAC's customer experience program; Steve Gentry, in charge of analytics; and Cassie Schmid, who directs strategic marketing. Working together, they combine journey mapping, persona development, data, and technology and consult with tenants to provide a comprehensive view of the MSP traveler experience.

The MAC has robust dashboards, and analysis starts with the end consumer and flows to the MAC's direct customers—the airport tenants. As with many other B2B2C companies, the MAC requires a more complex analysis of the customer experience than B2C companies. B2B2C companies have multiple types of clients with distinct needs, often leading to fragmented and limited information. In this case, the MAC wants to improve outcomes for travelers but has imperfect data about the interactions between MSP tenants and customers.

It's a familiar challenge for other B2B2C companies, such as insurance. While insurance companies "sell" directly to agents, those agents bring consumers to the company, which then services their needs. As such, the insurance company needs to track how the end consumers fare in their journeys and provide visibility on their successes back to the agents who brought them.[1]

Many B2B2C companies struggle to determine who their "real" customer is. Some insurance companies consider the agent as their primary customer, as that's who is responsible for their revenue. For others, the consumer is the primary customer because they pay the rates that generate the revenue. The reality is that it's both the agents and the consumers, and their different journeys need to be coordinated. Few B2B2C companies can be successful without a comprehensive—and distinct—approach to different types of customers.

It's similar for the MAC. The airlines and other tenants operating at MSP are siloed, and they focus on just the part of the traveler experience that involves them. In order to improve outcomes for its direct customers, the MAC has to measure and manage the traveler experience. To better understand and communicate the traveler experience, the team worked together to create dashboards that show how travelers experience MSP, including their interactions with tenants and experiential factors like wayfinding, restrooms, and parking, as well as how they feel throughout their journeys in the airport. Steve explains more about how the dashboards came to be:

I've been with the MAC for nine years, and there was no dashboarding when I got here. And I was in no rush to dashboard anything because the first thing we needed was getting reliable, actionable data sources. So, the majority of my early work was finding the data sources and being able to utilize them efficiently. My pushback to my management team was "I'd rather we don't do dashboards right now because I think we would do it poorly." And the worst thing in the world is having a dashboard that is not representative of what you're trying to share.

We are now getting pretty far along in a customer experience dashboard, having created one where if somebody wants to know what a customer is feeling about their experience, they could go to this one dashboard and look at this score. And then if they wanted to drill down, they could do that without having to play Where's Waldo? to figure out where everything is on this dashboard.

A critical step in the dashboard is to select the right data, and I sometimes struggle with that because it doesn't really matter what I think, but what my customers [MAC management] want to know. My first job is to figure out what my internal customers need to do their job. Once I understand that, I can go out and see if I can marry their needs with what data are actually out there. The bigger question of how we are successful in getting to where we are now is through champions. There are a few champions within very senior management at the airport who realize that this is what we're going to have to do to be successful. And they are the ones who have made us successful because they've taken the data and integrated into their decision-making process.

Cassie notes the MAC's CEO, Brian Ryks, wants to implement strategies and initiatives that are rooted in data:

That was one of the big pushes with me coming on board: How do we get to that point where we start to really use the data that's available to make key decisions and drive our goals forward? We're utilizing dashboards to manage a variety of marketing initiatives. To Steve's point, we have a lot of data, but we need to refine it a little bit better before we can get to that full funnel view. We have a very robust Travel Confidently program within the MSP community that was launched in response to the pandemic that we do have a dashboard for, and we're looking at several different KPIs, whether it's our web, digital channels, or in-terminal tactics.

Steve points out how using data can benefit decision-making:

Our traveler persona has so dramatically changed over the last few years. I gave a presentation a few years ago about who our travelers were. . . . All our customers were building their models around the thirty- to fifty-year-old man who travels for business, and all he wants is to painlessly get from point A to point B. And, in recent years, the persona is shifting toward women who are traveling for both business and leisure, but leaning more toward leisure. . . . They are in their fifties and older, have disposable income, and want to enjoy what they're doing. There were people in that audience who just swore I was making all this up, but the population changes, and getting our heads around the persona is very, very important.

Sharing information about that change in the traveler persona improved outcomes for both the MAC and one of its airport tenants. Cassie explains:

We had a store dedicated to upscale men's clothing. And there's a lot of money being spent developing this space, and staffing and operating it. Upon learning more about the changing of the customer, we talked with one of the owners of that store and said they should dedicate a section of the store to women's clothing. They swore that it was just not going to happen. "We can't afford it; we will lose revenue." But we convinced them to try maybe a fourth of the store, and suddenly that fourth of the store was generating more money than they had ever thought. Understanding the persona changed how one of our tenants operated and added to the financial success of both the MAC and our tenant.

The MAC is an excellent example of using Customer Ecosystem Data to make more informed decisions. It uses surveys combined with behavioral data—such as how long customers spend at the airport—and other research to get a comprehensive view of how travelers experience MSP. This was one of the big surprises in my interviews—how Change Makers refuse to limit their analysis to surveys, taking the time to bring in data to provide a nuanced understanding of the customer journey.

Imagine the MAC team shares this hypothetical statement with its senior leaders: "Our overall NPS increased by five points over the last quarter." That's interesting, and hopefully, it has some verbatims to help shed light on what caused the improvement. But by combining survey analysis and behavioral data, the team could say, "Our overall NPS increased by five points over the last quarter. That was accompanied by an increase in restaurant revenue in this same time period. It seems to be that the addition of three new higher-end restaurants is creating a better traveler experience. We also see that the average time spent at the airport has increased by twelve minutes, likely because of more visits to these restaurants." The addition of restaurant revenue and time spent at the airport—which comes from operational and behavioral data—provides insight for strategies to improve outcomes for MAC customers, both tenants (the restaurants) and travelers.

Through the deliberate combination of data, research, and surveys, the MAC is able to help its tenants make far better decisions, creating improved outcomes for tenants, travelers, and the MAC itself—an ideal outcome for any customer experience capability.

I Didn't Sign Up for an Analytics Job. Why Should I Care about Data?

Data enable an enormous step forward in understanding your customer experience by showing you a clear picture of the customer's actual experience. Change Makers have varied backgrounds, but a common denominator is that they have a clearer understanding of their customers, driven by the use of Customer Ecosystem Data.

Applying this to the CX Loyalty Flywheel, data help you identify how the flywheel moves. Once you invest in customer experience, it helps you identify how (and whether) the customer experience actually gets better; it also allows you to determine whether customers truly buy more and stay longer and whether the business actually becomes stronger as a result.

It reminds me of the book and movie *Moneyball*, in which the Oakland A's abandoned the intuitive approach of selecting players used throughout baseball's history. Traditionally, baseball teams evaluated new players by observing their looks, stances, and performances in a few games, which meant they suboptimized their outcomes because sometimes the best players didn't match the image scouts expected to see. The protagonist, Billy Beane, was actually the opposite; he looked the part but was unable to build a successful career. This caused him to realize there was far more to the science of finding baseball players than had been realized.

It's similar in your customer experience. Customers with high survey scores look like healthy relationships. But quite often, those good survey scores don't relate to happy, loyal customers. For example, I once worked with a bank, and we tested eight different measures of customer experience, such as NPS, customer satisfaction, Kordupleski's value framework, ease of doing business, and others. We then compared those results to revenue and profitability, and *every metric* had no relationship to, or was inversely correlated with, financial outcomes.

By restricting yourself to survey scores to evaluate the customer experience, you're the functional equivalent of a scout who watches a player in a few games and uses that limited data to judge the player's likelihood to become a major league player. The A's taught the rest of the league that uncovering the true story requires looking at data. It's the same with customer loyalty.

Few CX leaders have an analytics background, so it may sound counterintuitive to ask a CX leader and their team to focus on data. This tendency to shy away from data is exactly why, when I want to evaluate whether a marketing, operations, or customer experience leader is a Change Maker, I first ask them how they assess and use their data. Looking at data isn't the only thing that makes one a Change Maker. But taking the effort to link the Customer Ecosystem Data with survey results is a common step for Change Makers that is not utilized by Hopefuls. You'll recall that I define a Hopeful as a company that may be doing adequate to good work to drive the customer experience but can't measure and prove the value of its efforts for either the customers or the company itself. Hopefuls believe in the power of customer experience, but by not being able to quantify it, they put their capabilities—and their jobs—at risk.

Data isn't a sexy concept, but without data, you will be limited in your understanding of your customer experience. Mining the right data will tell you when customers are having problems and, when combined with technology, can enable both automated and in-person interventions to resolve the issue. When the customer does call with a problem, data allow you to see how the issue has been addressed to date, not only through customer service but also through any interaction with your website and across your operational platforms. Data also allow you to connect your customer experience efforts and outcomes with finance, as we discussed in Action 1.

I separated the discussion about data into different parts of this book because their use cases are different. Action 1 focuses on how to use the link to financial results to show value. Action 2 discusses sentiment data, particularly emotions. Here in Action 3, we turn to how to add the Customer Ecosystem Data—descriptive, operational, and behavioral—to create a more comprehensive analysis of the overall customer experience.

Most Organizations Use a Limited Approach to Understanding the Customer Experience

Beyond Net Promoter Score: Customer Experience Measurement Reimagined, a global survey, conducted by Harvard Business Review Analytic Services in collaboration with Genesys, interviewed 437 global executives. The report showed that only 38 percent of respondents say they are "very proficient" at measuring the customer experience, although 81 percent agree that being able to measure CX along key points of the customer journey is important to their organization's business strategy. Yes, most companies say it's critical, but most also say they're not very good at it. One of the most critical outcomes of the report showed that Leaders[2] used a whopping 61 percent more data to measure their customer experience than Laggards. Leaders are more likely to use such data as retention, average time to resolution, customer lifetime value, and first contact resolution in measuring their customer experience.

Data give you a more comprehensive view of your customers than relying only on survey scores, which capture only a small percentage of customers. A typical B2B survey is lucky to get 30 percent of customers to respond, which means you're missing feedback from 70 percent of your customers. But *every* customer is a source of data. Use the survey as a diagnostic to understand why issues exist, but use data to show what is truly happening.

Data are also the language of your business. Finance talks about revenue and costs. Operations talks about the cost of claims, percentage of on-time delivery, or defects per one thousand orders. Sales talks about, well, sales. All speak in data. No other department uses survey outcomes as a primary KPI. In many organizations, CX has become its own silo, using its own measurements (survey data) and its own definition of success (those scores improving).

Let me give an example from a conversation I recently had. A company that processes healthcare claims contacted us to request a journey map of its customers. Its business problem was that physicians' offices were calling the company for information on their claims. It required five minutes just to authenticate the caller, let alone answer the question, whereas the problem could be answered in less than a minute using the company's portal. Our prospective client wanted us to interview the physicians' offices to understand why they were calling. While I love a good journey map, it seemed that there were some very basic data to assess first. I asked what percentage of the callers had gone to the company's portal first, and I had three possible scenarios in mind:

1. **Very few callers went to the portal first.** If this were the case, we'd want to find out why people calling for information about claims were not using the portal. Were they not aware of it? Did they try it in the past and find it wasn't useful?

2. **Most tried the portal first.** If this were the case, then it's not an awareness issue and likely related to the quality of information or ease of navigating the site. In this case, we would ask different questions, regarding how they maneuvered through the site and why they were unable to find what they wanted.

3. **Most tried the portal but had login issues.** Healthcare websites have high security protocols. This wouldn't be the first time I ran across a company where security protocols prevented customers from being able to use its site.

My prospective client couldn't answer whether its customers tried to use the portal first. The information it had was provided only through surveys, which didn't give the client enough context to know where the problem originated. This is a common problem. Reviewing the data first would enable us to target the journey mapping more effectively.

We'll talk more about change management in Action 4, but one requirement to inspiring employees to improve the customer experience is to show how these improvements will impact their metrics. Your motivation may be to improve the customer experience by ensuring clients receive the right products at the right time, but you will be more persuasive with your internal partners if you can show how doing this will remove significant rework for operations, for example. Change Makers naturally think through the implications of an improved customer experience in a way that shows impact to the business. Then they use technology to show that linkage, as well as a way to change that experience.

Let's first discuss what constitutes the Customer Ecosystem Data, and then we'll look at key technologies enabling change.

A Customer Ecosystem Data Primer

When I talk about the Customer Ecosystem Data, I'm referring to the internal data that are distributed throughout your organization but rarely incorporated into an analysis of the customer experience. Some critical data include how long a client company has been your customer and what products and services it has purchased, or how many times representatives from the company have called you and whether they were bounced from department to department three, five, or six times. Data can tell you how well you have performed at delivering a customer's products on time and the frequency of product defects. Incorporating this information into your survey analysis helps to create much richer reporting that shows that customer experience isn't simply a feel-good program to make customers happy but creates better outcomes for them *and* for your company.

Change Makers use data to discover each story of their customers and their companies, a story with a past and hopefully a future, and this data-focused story leads to a deeper understanding of the customer experience and its implications. Relevant data will vary by industry; manufacturing relies on different metrics than does SaaS companies. But data are always helpful.

The complexity of the B2B experience flows down to the data. Most B2C companies focus on the individual consumer, but this doesn't work in B2B. Seeing an average of two calls on an issue from a client sounds acceptable, until you discover that multiple people at the client company called twice, meaning the clients' employees average six calls altogether. B2B organizations need to report on the individual contact, the contact's location and region, and the overall company. When the team at Dow analyzes the results from its customer L'Oréal, it needs to look at the company's interactions across Dow's different business units, as well as across L'Oréal's global footprint.

There are five categories of Customer Ecosystem Data to consider: descriptive, sentiment, behavioral, operational, and financial. Many customer experience programs separate these into two categories: experiential (X) data, which equate to sentiment, and operational (O) data, which describe the rest. However, I find it more instructive to combine sentiment and behavioral data into the voice of the customer, then financial and operational data into the voice of the business. Descriptive data sit outside of these two categories.

Descriptive data describe who the customer is and often sit in your customer relationship management (CRM) database. Examples include the length of time the client has been with your organization, the products it owns, revenue, geographic region, and placement in your customer segmentation. These data sets enable you to segment your reporting; for example, if the data show that customers with a national footprint have fewer issues than global customers, this would be informative. Or showing how customers in the eastern region have higher product returns and lower trust will help guide your actions to solve the problem.

Sentiment data show how your customers feel about the current experience. Nearly every program has survey results; mature programs include text and speech analytics, which supplement the surveys and provides a more robust assessment of how customers feel across contact center calls or other unstructured sources of data. For example, when Jiffy Lube analyzed what differentiated its most and least successful locations, the company found that survey results didn't show any differences—stores with high NPS didn't perform any better financially than those with lower scores. Taking a deeper dive, Jiffy Lube applied text analytics to survey verbatims and found something that did matter. When customers in a location's survey used a variant of the word *easy* 1 percent more often, that store earned $14,000 more in annual revenue. Similarly, when customers used words like *boss* or *manager*, revenue declined.[3] Sentiment data can help diagnose why an experience is going well or badly, as well as show its impact.

Behavioral data show what a customer does, so I include it as a version of voice of the customer, as clients give you feedback based on their behavior.

For an ordering journey, common types of behavioral data include categories of products ordered (more categories typically suggest a higher share of customers' wallet), order velocity, orders within lead-time windows,[4] rush orders, canceled orders, and channels used (in person, phone, or online, for example).

Software companies can track usage of self-service channels or logins and software usage. Organizations undergoing digital transformation (and who isn't) track individual customers' adoption of digital and analog channels.

Customer service behavioral data can include open tickets, number of complaints from one individual on a specific topic, channel(s) used, number of severity 1 complaints, and how many times a client has contacted you about the same issue.

Customers leave signals in the data showing when they are having problems, and these signals can help you to resolve these problems before it's too late. Behavioral data show the direct impact of your experience change efforts. As you make changes to the journey, does your customers' behaviors change? Do more customers use self-serve options, for example? Do complaints per thousand customers decrease? These behavioral data tie directly to cost outcomes, as self-service orders are less expensive to serve, and reduced complaints also decrease costs. These outcomes have direct cost-based impacts and often lead to revenue improvements, although this may take some time to appear.

Operational data show what happens inside your walls, often as a reaction to the behavioral data. For example, while behavioral data show the number of complaints, the operational data might show the average duration of an unresolved complaint, how many transfers of ownership were required to resolve the issue, and how many total resources were involved.

Operational data vary across the customer journey, scattered throughout disparate sources. The data are often siloed, sequestered to the department directly responsible for that operation. For example, we worked with a B2B2C life insurance organization, and as part of our journey mapping effort, we created an operations scorecard to communicate the health of the journey. As we presented the scorecard, the Vice President of Operations told us that she already had a dashboard with nearly identical data to what we recommended. Yet, none of the other departments present had access to this critical information.

Change Makers use operational data to show what the organization does that causes the customer impact. For example, customers discovering bugs in their software may not renew their contracts. Or a decreasing percentage of on-time deliveries can explain customer dissatisfaction and decreasing orders. Other examples of operational data include the length of time to resolve complaints, time waiting to offload products at a customer site, length of implementation, product defects, and unplanned outages.

Financial data are the outcomes of your customer experience, as we discussed in Action 1. Revenue is the most obvious, but it is often easier to tie your work to more granular financial outcomes, such as product or order margin, customer churn, product categories ordered, innovation (new, higher-margin) products, unit margin, and costs to serve, such as through customer service.

Applying this use of data to the CX Loyalty Flywheel, you can see the areas where each comes into play.

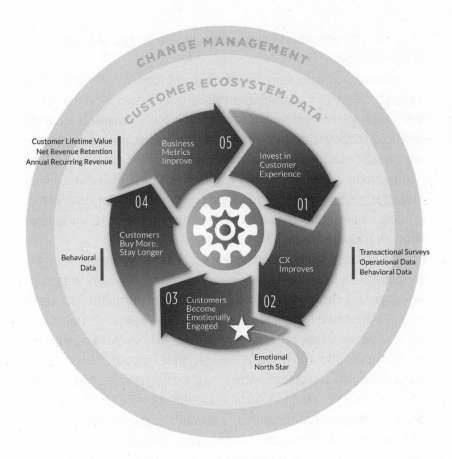

Figure 7-2: Sources of data in the CX Loyalty Flywheel.

GETTING ACCESS TO THE DATA

Discovering the right data and setting up access takes time and support from both leadership and IT, which is why many customer experience capabilities limit their analysis to the survey data they own. However, one key reason most programs have limited impact is this tendency to ignore the Customer Ecosystem Data. Unless you can show the relationship between customer and business health, you're limited to telling stories about customers to motivate others to change. But when you connect your work with improved business outcomes, it becomes much easier to convince internal teams of the need to change.

Identifying the linkages between these types of data often goes beyond the skill set of customer experience executives. This is why building partnerships is so critical. While some programs have the required analytic skills embedded in their teams, most rely on their data analytics or business information teams to lead these efforts. These teams already have access to this data and build models. However, they may not be accustomed to using survey data as part of their models. Survey data provide additional context, sometimes providing early warnings to the financial outcomes.

As an example, we worked with a B2B2C insurance company to map its claims journey. As we talked with customers who were undergoing a claim, we heard a repeated theme of calling the agent and the insurance company to discover the status of the claim, which was one of the biggest friction points. As we worked with the company to build a dashboard, we identified "touches" as being the most important data to measure, and the company set a stretch goal of 1.5 touches per claim. It turned out that the touches were spread across multiple silos, so nobody had visibility to the total number of times policyholders and their agents called. Once the company put the data together, they discovered that the average claim had 4.7 touches—far more than anybody expected. Surfacing this data helped create the sense of urgency to create a more streamlined claims experience.

USE DATA TO CREATE OPERATIONAL TRANSPARENCY

Even when we work with the most hard-nosed B2B journey, one of two analogies continually comes up: the Domino's Pizza tracker and/or Amazon's communication of a package delivery. As we shared with one manufacturer, "Customers have an easier time tracking a pizza than a $100,000 order of your products." The concept is called operational transparency, and it matters to your customers. As discussed in a *Harvard Business Review* article with the same name, "When customers are cordoned off from a company's operation, they are less likely to fully understand and appreciate the value being created. As a result, they are less satisfied, less willing to pay, less trusting, and less loyal to the company over time."[5]

While the technology used to create this operational transparency varies, it relies on the operational data around an order and its fulfillment, which has two implications for you. First, in building a "pizza tracker," somebody may have already pulled together the critical data on an ordering and fulfillment journey that you can leverage for your analysis. And second, if they haven't, then your efforts to identify this data for your dashboard can help your organization create such an offering.

■ ■ ■

Remember what Cassie said about data and the Metropolitan Airports Commission: "How do we get to that point where we start to really use the data that's available to make key decisions and drive our goals forward? We're utilizing dashboards to manage a variety of marketing initiatives. . . . we have a lot of data, but we need to refine it a little bit better before we can get to that full funnel view."

The MAC story is a perfect example of leveraging data that existed, taking the steps to build a robust dashboard that provides this information, and getting results that surprise people but that make clear the new directions required to provide an excellent customer experience.

In the next chapter, we will dive deeper into types of data and how they connect to customer experience.

Cari's Story

All told, during its journey mapping, the Sycamore team met with fifty individuals who represented thirty of Sycamore's clients to understand (a) why some customers were very happy with Sycamore; (b) why some customers were indifferent; and (c) why some customers were downright frustrated. The team's analysis showed that the system integrator (SI) mattered, but the SI wasn't the most important factor in terms of customer experience.

Cari learned there were three common issues that could delight a customer and inspire them to become an advocate or conversely, set them on a path to continuing issues.

The first issue, which seemed to be the biggest, was customizations. The more a product was customized, the more likely that client had issues. There was also some cross-correlation with timing, in that customizations extended implementation timelines. Worse, this time crunch encouraged teams to rush implementation, which led to even poorer outcomes, since testing was less rigorous than it needed to be.

The second issue was time based. Implementation was a Moment of Truth in the overall experience. Even customers who had been with Sycamore for years seemed to have lingering issues carrying over from the implementation of Sycamore's products. Clients that implemented in fewer than six months were far happier than clients with extended timelines. Whether the lengthy implementation was the cause of the problem or a symptom of another issue was unclear, but timely implementation correlated with ongoing success, as measured by ARR. Clients with an extended implementation took out their frustration by refusing to add new software.

The third was the SI team that led the implementation, which employees believed was the most important issue. Certain SIs surpassed others in creating better outcomes. The same names kept popping up in conversations with happy customers. Cari made sure those partners received the recognition they deserved!

Cari and Stephen met to discuss the findings and their implications. Cari had observed the impact of customizations when she was in SaaS operations. Customizations increase risk, as they deviate from Sycamore's normal setup and can introduce unforeseen issues. But most teams argued that the ability to customize their software was a competitive difference and opposed any efforts to curtail them. Sycamore needed to find a way to enable this critical functionality while reducing risk.

Stephen and Cari decided to include the presence of customizations in their analysis, highlighting their NPS and ARR for customers with and without customizations. They also created special reports linking the results with the SI partner involved in the implementation.

Length of implementation was logged in Sycamore's project management software, but not in a way that was easy to capture. Now that Cari and Stephen knew it was a Moment of Truth, they needed to track the data, so they worked with the project management office to add this information to client records, enabling them to capture this in their CRM, which was already linked to their survey platform.

Once this ability to track data in the CRM was added, Cari's team created shared dashboards that centered on confidence as the primary sentiment and net revenue retention as the primary financial outcome, showing an overall number and breakdowns by each emotion. The dashboards were shared with senior leadership to create visibility to the customer experience as teams improved the results.

My Thoughts

While journey mapping is an excellent way to uncover the emotions in your experience, it can also help you determine which Customer Ecosystem Data are critical to evaluate the CX Loyalty Flywheel.

Change Makers use the results of journey mapping to identify which data are the most important, then focus on building the selected data into reporting. Readers of my first book know that I'm a huge believer in the power of journey mapping to diagnose the current experience. Journey mapping shows you how customers view their journeys and it should identify ways to track how those journeys progress without sending your customers a survey every two weeks.

Change Makers, such as Cari, recognize that surveys only give you part of the picture, so they extend the platform to include the Customer Ecosystem Data, allowing a nuanced approach to evaluate whether customers are having success.

CHAPTER 8

Do I See How Customer Ecosystem Data and Technology Drive the CX Journey?

CUSTOMERS COMMUNICATE WITH YOU REGULARLY THROUGH their behaviors; the business communicates back through its operations. Great programs discover the interplay between these two to identify how the true journey flows. This also serves as the baseline for measuring improvements to this journey, linking new operations to changed behaviors to improved financial outcomes.

How You Hurt Your Business by Oversimplifying Customer Journeys

When I give keynotes on Customer Experience Value, I use the following slide to get across the role of data. I call it "Every journey map you've ever seen, rolled up into one slide."

The journey begins when customers do something, such as searching for available products, putting in an order, or calling with a support question. Let's use that last interaction as an example, when customers call and ask for help logging in to your portal.

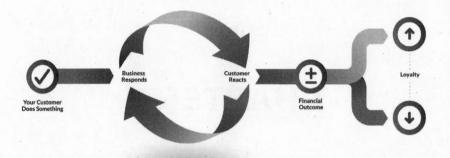

Figure 8-1: A conceptual customer journey.

Typically, a customer service agent takes the call and asks the caller for information, such as their login name and what URL they used. The customer provides the information requested, and the back-and-forth continues until the root cause is determined and the issue is resolved. There's a financial *outcome*—in this case, the cost of agents' time—and the quality of the interaction and outcome with the customer can either increase loyalty if the problem is resolved effectively or decrease loyalty if the customer is unhappy.

Once I've landed the concept of the journey, I move to discussing how Change Makers measure journeys differently. I build on the slide by adding surveys to show how most companies (superficially) measure this outcome (see figure 8-2).

The purpose of the follow-up survey is to ask the customer to assess their interaction with the customer service agent. And this is important because your organization needs to evaluate the quality of the call and track how customers feel about their interactions with you. But while this is important, it's insufficient. First, only a small percentage of customers answer the survey, so most of your clientele is unrepresented. Worse, those that do answer surveys tend to cluster to the extremes, meaning that respondents are more pleased or displeased than the average, which makes them less dependable as your only source of insight. Second, survey data miss

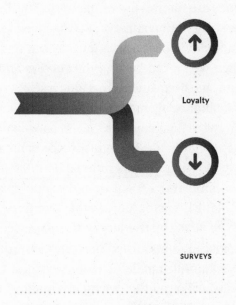

Loyalty

SURVEYS

Figure 8-2: Most organizations only use surveys to measure the success of journeys.

recording such critical data as how long it took to resolve the issue and whether customers had to call multiple times.[1] Third, surveys that take place at the end of the experience miss out on much of the true journey, especially for those journeys that take place over days, weeks, or months.

For example, we studied an independent agent's journey of working with an insurance company (not Hagerty) to sell a policy to her client. When we looked at the post-sales surveys, we had a number of verbatims that surfaced complaints about the experience but had a difficult time pinpointing what actually went wrong, as comments did not have a unified thread. This is a common issue. In his book *Thinking, Fast and Slow*, Daniel Kahneman showed how we live under the "tyranny of the remembering mind." Our brains can only remember a limited amount of information about an experience, and this recollection is heavily biased based on the peak point of emotion and the way the journey ended. Other parts of the experience are filtered out of memory. This limits the effectiveness of post-transaction surveys as a diagnostic tool. It helps to show how customers felt about the journey but not what actually happened. When we looked beyond the surveys and analyzed the operational data, we discovered something else.

First-time insurance agents need to be licensed to sell a policy, and we knew from the financial data that, in one segment, more than half of the agents never used this insurance company's products again! When we looked at the operational data, we discovered that the agents who complained about the sales journey also had a disproportionately long licensing journey that interfered with selling to their clients. By focusing on the survey, the insurance company was finding symptoms, not root causes. The operational data showed the root cause—the painful parallel *licensing* journey. Understanding the true root cause allowed the insurance company to address the problem of the extended licensing journey and reduce agent churn.

Change Makers measure more of the experience, as shown as the graphic builds out.

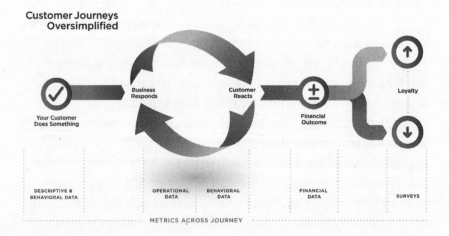

Figure 8-3: Customers' journeys from a Change Maker's view.

Surveys don't tell you what customers do. Data do. A Change Maker begins with the descriptive data, identifying whether the experience varies based on segment, region, or other features. Perhaps your top-tier customers get better service—and thus, better outcomes—or perhaps they have higher expectations and are more likely to be disappointed. The Change Maker also identifies the channel involved: Do they have different outcomes when they initiate contact via phone, email, chat, or through a sales rep, and how did that impact the outcomes? Descriptive data help diagnose whether problems are widespread or limited to a certain cohort of your customers.

Next, the Change Maker looks at the operational and behavioral data surrounding the issue. Are most issues resolved in one call, or do they linger, involving multiple calls? Do customers frequently shift channels, and does that frustrate or enable them? How long do issues persist, and how often do they escalate? All this gives context to your scores—and financial outcomes—that help you better diagnose both the root issue and its impact.

Finally, what were the financial outcomes? In this case, it's primarily the estimated cost to resolve the issue, although there may be canceled orders or other downstream costs.

Telling your operations team that "invoice issues have a low Customer Effort Score" is data. But sharing this—"Invoice issues that come in through chat have a much worse Customer Effort Score and typically require three sessions to resolve. As a result, even though it's using a low-cost channel, invoice issues typically cost us more through chat than when we move them to a phone call."—is more compelling, actionable information.

Discovering all of this gets you closer to the root cause, providing stronger impetus to change. Rather than simply using survey analysis to show that some customers are unhappy with their experiences, this deliberate approach to integrate the descriptive shows exactly which types of customers have issues that lead to lower future orders and/or higher costs.

Drive CX Impact through Technology

We talked earlier about the importance of establishing connections with finance. It's useful to spend time with your IT buddies as well.[2] Once the important data are discovered and integrated, technology puts the data to use in order to communicate and improve the customer experience. IT can help you not only build the technology but also integrate the data in a way that makes the technology useful. And this is a critical issue.

In Qualtrics XM Institute's 2019 report *The Global State of XM*,[3] the company broke experience management programs into three levels based on respondents' self-reporting: (1) considerably above industry average, (2) slightly above industry average, and (3) equal to or below the industry average. Technology limitations were the top issues for those "considerably above average" and were second for those "slightly above industry average." While average organizations had bigger issues, technology limitations still ranked fifth for them.

While nearly all of your company's technologies impact the experience, there are five distinct technologies that help measure and improve the customer experience, which we call the CX Tech Stack (see next page). Our survey of CX pros showed that Change Makers are far more likely to use these technologies than Hopeful programs. I could write a book just on these technologies, but for the sake of brevity, here's an overview. We will begin with a discussion of the voice of the customer.

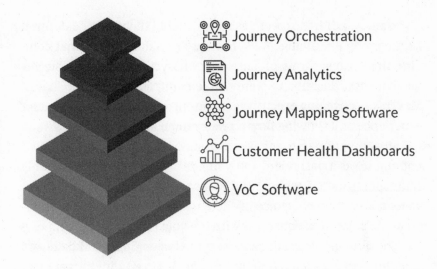

Journey Orchestration

Journey Analytics

Journey Mapping Software

Customer Health Dashboards

VoC Software

Figure 8-4: CX Tech Stack.

CAPTURE THE VOICE OF THE CUSTOMER AND INTEGRATE IT WITH THE VOICE OF THE BUSINESS

Listening to customers is a core competency of any CX program, and a voice of the customer (VoC) platform enables this. Our research shows that over 80 percent of companies with a CX program use VoC software to create surveys and report on the results. Advanced platforms also analyze text and voice data to complement survey scores with a more comprehensive analysis of sentiment, showing why the survey scores are what they are.

Having VoC software doesn't differentiate the success of CX programs. Success is far more about how the results are used. While reporting the current state of your customers' sentiment is obviously important, advanced platforms can integrate the results into the voice of the business by creating customer health dashboards that integrate the survey data with internal data, providing a comprehensive view of operational and customer results. Effective dashboards communicate how the customer experience impacts business and customer outcomes.

Frankly, I didn't expect dashboards to be such a big deal. But it kept coming up. Change Makers create rich dashboards that combine the various forms of Customer Ecosystem Data with survey results. These dashboards were visible examples of the work Change Makers do, engaging executives in the current state of the customer experience and showing how it relates to business outcomes.

Most programs either have no dashboards (no, PowerPoint does not qualify as a dashboard software) or have dashboards that only show survey data. Dashboards that display financial results are typically siloed from the voice of the customer. Change Makers integrate the voice of the business with the voice of the customer.

The different usage of dashboards between Change Makers and Hopeful companies is so extreme that, if I could investigate two items to determine whether you're a Change Maker, the second would be "Tell me about your dashboards." (You may remember that the first question is about how Change Makers assess and use data.) As with data, dashboards aren't the *cause* of a program or individual being a Change Maker. But they are highly correlated with programs driving change.

While advanced VoC platforms can create these dashboards, other companies use dedicated analytics and business intelligence (BI) tools, such as Tableau or Power BI. The specific technology used isn't what's important; it's the compelling integration of customer ecosystem and sentiment information that raises awareness of the current state of the customer experience.

Effective dashboards use what our CTO, Shawn Phillips, dubs the "sentiment sandwich," embedding sentiment data with the Customer Ecosystem Data that executives commonly see on their dashboards. As he explains, "Sentiment is like the peanut butter and jelly in the sandwich. It's yummy, just like happy customers. But it's squishy and messy, so it's important to surround it with items of more substance, like bread, or like financial, behavioral, and operational data. We put the sentiment in the middle, and surround it with the items that executives care about."

Paul Robinson, Senior Vice President of Customer Experience at Texas Capital Bank, offers more details about how he's able to use dashboards to provide much greater visibility to the customer experience:

A byproduct of our monitoring tool is that we are setting up the ability to provide near real-time monitoring for our journey owners. And obviously, we'll have all that reporting in our monitoring tool for our monitoring people. Still, I want everybody in the company to see the dashboard. Let's say I'm in charge of receivables in treasury services. I want to be able to give them a customized dashboard that says, "Here's how we're doing today on receivables in treasury services. Here's the volume of clients that are coming through our processes." And maybe emerging trends on problems that they're seeing, including some of the unstructured data, like the voice calls or social media. To push the data to our journey owners so they can react immediately.

Our approach at Heart of the Customer creates two types of dashboards. The first is an overall view of the customer experience, where we show the overall health incorporating the sentiment sandwich approach—showing the sentiment in the middle, the behavioral and operational data on the left, and the financial outcomes on the right.

The second is to create journey dashboards for the most critical journeys. In this case, the visualization changes to be based on the phase of the journey. We assign scores to the overall health of the journey, as well as to each phase. Within each phase, we include scores from at least two of the categories of Customer Ecosystem Data: sentiment, operational, behavioral, and financial. We use journey mapping to identify the most critical data, as well as to establish the score. Effective dashboarding is a skill. But learning this skill can accelerate your impact across the organization.

SHOW THE CUSTOMER JOURNEY AND CONNECT IT TO THE CUSTOMER ECOSYSTEM DATA

Customer journey mapping (CJM) software programs have been around for years but are now maturing to become more useful across the organization. Journey mapping software should show you the current state of the journey, consolidate information on all journeys, and tie in to your change efforts. If you had asked me about journey mapping software a few years ago, I would have told you not to waste your time and money. But then, in our survey, we found that while only one-quarter of standard programs used CJM software, more than half of the Change Makers relied on it to design their customers' experiences. Most CJM software only visualizes the customer journey. While that's helpful, advanced journey mapping software goes beyond visualization to include the Customer Ecosystem Data.

The traditional role of CJM software is to show the current state of the experience. I find that desktop publishing software is the best way to create highly visual journey maps. Because these maps are often printed out and used to communicate the current state of the journey, I refer to these as change management maps. Highly visual maps are very effective at communicating the state of the journey, motivating executives and staff alike to support the changes needed to improve customer results. My first book, *How Hard Is It to Be Your Customer? Using Journey Mapping to Drive Customer-Focused Change*, cowritten with Nicole Newton, goes into great detail into how to create these maps.

The one problem with a change management map is that the incorporated data doesn't change. Modern CJM software allows you to integrate the map with the Customer Ecosystem Data, creating a journey dashboard, or as I call it, a Living Journey Map. These Living Journey Maps communicate survey and business data specific to a journey. They can be updated regularly—even in real-time— showing the current state of the journey. This capability not only provides a dashboard on the health of the journey, it also provides feedback as improvements are made. This capability is particularly useful for a project team working to improve the journey. Having this data enables a test-and-learn approach, as teams can see the impact of their latest release in real time.

As of this writing in summer 2022, only a few CJM software providers have the ability to create a Living Journey Map.

JOURNEY ANALYTICS EVALUATES MAKE-OR-BREAK POINTS IN THE JOURNEY

Journey mapping is excellent at showing customers' behaviors and feelings as they go through their journeys. And that's important for change management. However, *journey analytics* takes it to a new level, applying machine learning to the journey in order to identify where issues occur at scale.

The category of software typically relies on a customer data platform (CDP) as the foundation for the analytics to work, tying the data together to create a complete customer record. The platform then creates recommended next actions to improve the journey.

This is a newer category of products that showed a big gap between Change Maker and Hopeful companies. Our survey showed that *only about one in four Hopeful programs* used journey analytics, compared to 81 percent of Change Makers—the biggest delta of any technology.

As its name suggests, journey analytics targets a specific customer journey, such as presales or customer support, and shows where customers are getting stuck. It can be used to identify leading causes of future support calls or typical reasons why prospective customers cancel orders. Organizations also use journey analytics to prioritize IT spend and agile efforts, focusing on where the analytics show the greatest return. This is clearly shown in Bill's case study that concludes chapter 9.

Research from Pointillist,[4] which specializes in journey analytics, illustrates the importance of this capability, showing 72 percent of high-performing companies analyze multiple customer interactions across channels and over time, compared to 28 percent of average performers, and 9 percent of underperformers.[5]

Of course, you can't apply analytics against big data if you only have a few customers, which is why journey analytics is more common in B2C or B2B2C organizations; they typically serve more customers. However, there are larger B2B organizations using this capability, and as familiarity with analytics platforms increase and costs of implementation decline, this will become more common in smaller companies.

Orchestrating an Improved Journey

Imagine that one of your key customers is experiencing a severity 1 issue. All hands are on deck working to resolve the issue, and it has gone on for a few weeks as your teams are identifying the root cause. In the middle of all this, marketing sends a mass email touting your platform's stability. How does your client react when he reads this? In the best case, he's mildly amused. In the worst case, he's frustrated and lets you know about it.

Most large organizations can't react in real time to prevent the marketing from going out to affected customers while the issue persists. Issues are tracked in one system, communications in another, and nothing connects the two. That's what journey orchestration is all about: sensing the signals from the customer ecosystem and creating interventions to create a smooth journey for your customers.

Journey orchestration platforms look at your data for signals from customers and the results of your analytics models to trigger interventions based on an individual customer's journey. The platform connects the data spread across multiple systems, such as logins or lack of response to a request for information. It then ties into your existing communications platforms to send messages, update workflow, or log a ticket. Most journey orchestration platforms sit on top of an analytics engine to guide the orchestration.[6]

This type of capability is new, and only one in twenty of the Hopeful programs in our survey used it. However, just about half of our Change Makers had used the technology in at least one aspect of their customer experience.

As an example of orchestrations potential, a company could use it for its customer-onboarding program, linking data from the company's website, the CRM platform, the marketing automation capability, and the ordering platform. If a customer creates a website login but never submits payment information to the ordering platform, the software can recognize this fact and link to the CRM and marketing automation platform to send an automated email after two days have passed. After an additional time period elapses, it can send a second message, or even a text. Finally, after a week has gone by, it can alert the sales rep or contact center to call the person. This was traditionally a manual process, where an employee would have to pay attention to each customer's individual journey or read reports to find out when a specific step hasn't occurred. The manual nature of this work meant that it often didn't happen.

Journey orchestration enables what I call a Journey of One, creating individual journeys, based on data, allowing each customer to accomplish his or her goals. By analyzing individual-level data, the systems can identify when an individual customer has issues and create interventions to resolve it. No more looking at a month's worth of data and sending a mass email. Instead, you can use the analytics to show where customers are frequently getting stuck. You can then create automated interventions that are triggered when the system determines an individual customer has run into a wall, and you can either send direct communications or alert an employee that action is required. It also enables A/B testing, so you can try out different interventions to see which best move the needle. You can set up a test for when customers miss a step in their onboarding journeys, testing an email versus a text. Perhaps you discover that the text drives more action but leads to more customers who opt out of your platform. You can then test different variations of the message to see if you can mitigate the opt-outs while keeping the improved outcomes.

While dedicated platforms exist for this capability, many companies use CRM platforms or other tools to accomplish this. This works well for the first orchestration activity, as it often requires only one or two new pieces of data that aren't already in the CRM. However, as more journeys are orchestrated, the CRM requires more and more data, making it difficult to coordinate updates. Also, as CRM isn't designed as an integration system, it doesn't allow for the easy updates found in most dedicated platforms.

This marketplace is quickly expanding. In the two years I've spent writing this book, the journey orchestration marketplace saw rapid change. During a six-month period starting in July 2021, the top four journey orchestration products—Kitewheel, Usermind, Pointillist, and Thunderhead—were all purchased to be integrated into other systems. The message from the market seems to be that journey orchestration is not a stand-alone capability but will be integrated into other capabilities. As I write this, organizations as diverse as VoC platforms, customer communications management, and call center systems are adding journey orchestration capabilities to their systems. So, while journey orchestration as a stand-alone platform may be dead, the capability of orchestrating journeys seems to be alive and well. I expect this to be a core capability for many companies by the middle of the decade.

Orchestrating Electrician Engagement

Schneider Electric is a global company headquartered in France that provides energy and automation digital solutions for efficiency and sustainability. The company has operations in more than one hundred countries and employs more than 128,000 people.

Christine Davis is the global business owner of Schneider Electric's journey orchestration capability,[7] working with the business units to apply the technology to improve the company's customer experience. Her goal is to make sure that partners and customers are actively engaged, which means that they are logging into its portal, mySchneider, and partaking in some sort of activity at least once a month. She tracks both an engagement metric and a revenue metric to make sure that Schneider earns a significant share of wallet for its customers, and that it is rewarding those customers' loyalty with targeted programs. Logins and revenue are two of Schneider Electric's "golden KPIs" that the organization tracks.

Schneider implemented a journey orchestration program to help improve engagement. As Christine explains:

> We purchased it because we needed to have visibility of things that we didn't already have, primarily on our partner registration process. We knew there were drop-offs, but we didn't have the visibility or understanding of where or when or how or why. We needed to reduce manual bottlenecks. Because it's one thing to be able to run a report and see something, but it's another thing to intercede while we're still top of mind for our customers, and not a week or a month later, when somebody analyzes the results and then finally gets the chance to contact them.
>
> Instituting this required change management because it's all about building the rapport with the business units. I still remember fondly the first time we introduced this type of a journey into a country. Their

first question always was "When is this email blast going to be sent?" And I had to explain that it's not really an email blast. The communication will be sent at the moment that the customer actually needs it. It might be one email today, two hundred tomorrow, fifty the next day, just depending on when it makes sense for our customers. This was an absolute mindset shift.

Christine started as a US employee, implementing journey orchestration domestically before moving to a global role. She walks through how she implemented journey orchestration across the globe:

I went to our top countries and identified our digital customer experience leaders and marketing managers, and introduced the topic, telling them, "This is our Active 30." We call it Active 30 because we want our customers to be active within thirty days. And so, after thirty days of inactivity, we send an email notification and another one after sixty days of inactivity. You can almost call it an elementary journey. But it's one of the most impactful that we still have today, where our hit rates are super high to be able to keep somebody engaged. And it really helps people to see that, at the point of this individual person being thirty days inactive, we want to say, "We miss you." After sixty days of inactivity, we want to say, "We *really miss you*," and at ninety days, we want to tell them that we're crying. We tell that kind of a story to get them on board with what exactly our platform is, and how we want to treat those people as individuals and want to talk to them exactly when we meet them and to get them back into our digital experience.

Orchestration is not a replacement for marketing campaigns. It is an enhancement, preventing churn. We've seen tremendous response. The email response rate is higher than any other. We're able to measure the engagement rate and activity, and it's so high because it's delivered to the right person at the right time with the right message. This has a much better impact than telling somebody what we want to tell them about.

Schneider's KPIs regarding its portal have changed as adoption increases. Initially, KPIs focused on registrations to the company's partner portal. As adoption increased, the focus became more about active users, and now it's *returning* active users. A significant KPI is that logging in at least once a month is an indicator of engagement with the company, which translates to a higher share of wallet.

Implementing an orchestration platform is not a quick-and-easy fix, requiring efforts across the enterprise. Simply identifying the right data can take weeks or months, followed by gaining access in a secure way. Christine gives us a look into what it was like to implement the journey orchestration:

> It's better for this orchestration system to have visibility of everything, so we can determine, "Is this person registering? Do we know them or not?" And the only way we can determine if we know them is to compare it against the data that we already have. That was a lot of learning, figuring out what access to give, and then how to map the information together.
>
> I also have an analyst background, so that helps, as I understand the structure of our data to begin with. You take a web hook, and that web hook offers an email address. And then you look at our CRM system, where there's not just one field that has an email address. And then also sifting through the garbage and cleanly mapping what data is supposed to look like. And acknowledging that there is room for error—how can we mitigate that error in the best possible way?

This process took nine months as Christine and her team worked across the organization. Then, once the data was integrated, further time was required for testing the message to ensure it resonated with customers, looking through the journey analytics to ensure that this new process was encouraging the engagement the team sought. Christine continues:

Engagement was one of the hardest things to measure. That's why I chose to be the business service owner of opportunities because I wanted to see the actual sales growth. We started by hypothesizing that an engaged partner is an emotionally engaged partner.[8] And we discovered that, within certain personas, this system allowed us to measure engagement better. Tracking sales data with our IT solution providers is easier because they buy directly from us. But for electricians, it's harder because they purchase from our distribution partners. We know from our personas that buy from us directly that engagement creates more revenue, so we can infer that for the other personas, it's working as well.

Schneider Electric presents an excellent example of using journey orchestration to create improved outcomes for the company and its customers. And I especially enjoy how Christine discusses how technology can actually create a more human experience. While technology is great when it automates a manual experience—especially one that often isn't done in a timely way—it's even better when it is targeted to creating the emotional connection required to create long-term loyalty.

Dow Combines Data and Tech to Engage Leaders

Dow does not lack for data and measurements. If anything, the company (like most its size) has too many measurements, making it harder to align on what most matters to improve the customer experience. To cut through the noise, Jen Zamora worked with the data science team to determine which metrics most impacted the survey scores. After eighteen months of improved access to data, more survey results, and model refinement, they were able to identify the linkages between the behavioral, operational, and sentiment data and financial outcomes. For example, Dow can show that a severity

1 issue that extends past a certain time limit for a critical customer leads to reduced order margin in the future. In this situation, Dow doesn't need a survey score to act, although it does help to provide context to the issue.

One of Dow's critical journeys is product availability and delivery—going from the forecast to the order to delivering the product to a customer site. For this journey, Dow focuses on two operational metrics: on-time delivery and Get It Right (GIR). GIR is a summary metric that combines the incidence that the delivery is on time with the right product and no defects. From its analysis and journey mapping work, Dow knows that when these metrics demonstrate a high degree of execution, customer survey scores will be high for product-availability effectiveness and the outcome metrics of effectiveness, ease, and enjoyability. These metrics in turn predict future product margin and order velocity. It is this linkage that proved the importance of focusing on customer experience. Effectively understanding your data and its linkage to customer outcomes reinforces your change management, showing executives how focusing on the experience will help them accomplish their KPIs.

Dow's dashboards integrate the operational data with the results of multiple surveys. While we can't show the company's proprietary data, the next page shows a wireframe for its product delivery and availability dashboard.

The first section contains the Customer Experience Index (CXi)[9] scores of effectiveness, ease, and enjoyability, created by Forrester. The CXi is used by companies around the world, and Dow uses it for its relationship scores. The next section contains the operational data showing the on-time delivery and its related GIR score and on-time delivery. The CXi scores and operational scores are easily compared. Next, the wireframe shows the supply chain's individual customer experience goals for the current year, allowing executives to see a full picture of the customer experience in one view. Information from the top three quadrants is complemented with results from multiple transactional surveys related to this core journey.

CXi Scores	Get It Right (GIR) and On-Time Delivery (OTD)	2020 CX Priorities for Integrated Supply Chain
Chart showing survey results over time	Chart showing results over time (Business KPIs) GIR = OTD plus right quantity, right product, etc.	Product availability and delivery Customer complaints List of key enablers/ projects

On-Time Delivery Confidence Score	Product Availability Confidence Score	Complaint Satisfaction Score	Complaint Experience Score
Chart showing survey results over time, broken down by overall, key, and priority clients	Chart showing survey results over time, broken down by overall, key, and priority clients	From relationship survey: % satisfied, chart showing survey results over time, broken down by overall vs. top priority clients	From complaints survey; score on 5-point scale, broken down by overall vs. top priority clients

Figure 8-5: Wireframe for Dow product and delivery dashboard.

This highly accessible and informative dashboard reinforces the communications and other change management tools Jen's team uses to share the current customer experience and to encourage leaders to keep improving these outcomes.

I vividly remember when I joined Jen for her cross-functional customer experience update meeting, and she walked the team through the dashboard. The information was so compelling that I immediately thought, "This is how it's done!" I loved the integration of the Customer Ecosystem Data with the sentiment in such an actionable format.

That reaction was validated as the meeting went on, and Jen shared *my very favorite CX business problem*—ever! Her dashboards were so engaging that executives from throughout the organization were regularly logging in to see the results. So many, in fact, that even though Dow had purchased one thousand dashboard licenses, *they ran out*! The team was forced to rationalize which leaders could see it, until they negotiated with Qualtrics for unlimited licenses. I told Jen—and I repeat this to others—that *this* is the CX business problem I want all of our clients to have!

Hagerty Can Predict Retention

Being a B2B2C organization adds complexity to journeys, as Hagerty interacts with both agents and policyholders, who also interact with each other. However, having insurance as a lead product also offers some benefits. As Nancy Flowers explains, "One advantage is that we have actuarial scientists who can do predictive modeling. For example, we can use the number of calls and the cost of those calls. We bring all of this into the modeling when we are building a case for change." She can lean on her partners to determine how the Customer Ecosystem Data impact retention and additional products.

She applies similar work to the B2B portion of her experience:

> We segment our agencies by productivity in a model. But it does have to do with policyholders because, for example, when we take on an agent, we may roll over their entire book of business. So, let's say that the agency came from a competitor of ours; we may move all of its book of business to Hagerty. So, we look at the last date of production, as well as [the agent's] overall book of business with us. It's like a little magic box. The other thing with us in the agent world is we have captive agents.[10] It's a little different when you're looking at captive agents who are at a partner versus like an independent agent that has market choice. An independent agent could place one piece of business with a competitor and one piece of business with us, so we measure different things in captive agents versus independent agents.

One area where Hagerty is mature is combining journey mapping with internal KPIs, something many organizations never consider. The company is bringing in new journey mapping software to automate those links, allowing them to create Living Journey Maps—maps tied to the data that serve as dashboards on the current state of the journey. Nancy goes into more detail:

We have a Top Gear agent program, and it shows the importance of segmenting your data as you analyze it. When we look at agents who sell our premium membership product, their clients have a higher NPS and retention. Another example: We have a program where we have great automotive content because we're really an entertainment and automotive lifestyle company rather than just another insurance company. We have this program for agents with content they can share. The content is ours, but they can send it to their customers. And it really helps with their reputation. So, when we look at NPS and "likelihood to bring us business next year" by segment, there's so many more insights when we incorporate the segments.

UKG Links Everything Together

Roxie Strohmenger is a data hound, and so she ties her efforts to the business data in every way she can. She creates specific dashboards for each of her journeys, integrating descriptive and operational data—such as account type, market segment, and how long it takes to close a support issue with customers' survey scores for the support experience.

She started her program in 2019, which she entitled, "The Year of Foundations." That was when she brought in a new voice of the customer (VoC) platform and focused on integrating the information from the data warehouse that she needed, as well as the value chain metrics CLV and ARR.[11] The data were spread across multiple data lakes but weren't linked, so she began by tying all the various sources of data in to the VoC platform, so she could use that tool to do her full analysis. She even tied the data from focus groups and interviewed participants to create a broader profile of her customers.

A common approach in surveys is to do a driver analysis. In this type of research, you have a dependent variable, which is typically a top-level score such as NPS, then you look at which underlying questions most drive that top-level score. It's a pretty common survey tactic, but Roxie does this same thing with data, showing which data most tie to the financial outcomes she's interested in, such as CLV or cost to serve. As she explains, "We get them to talk about emotion. You're not predicting a 'likely to recommend' outcome, but rather, you're predicting a business outcome." She goes into more detail:

> I look at OSAT [overall satisfaction] and CSAT [customer satisfaction] for interactions with a team member, and those are great. But what really moves behavior is when you bring it down a notch to the quality dimension level and map that into behaviors.
>
> Take, for example, the knowledgeable staff member, which was something we hadn't looked at before our work with Heart of the Customer. I sat there and said, "All we have is commentary. We don't have a number. We don't know how bad or good or how okay it is." So, we added expectations as a metric to the transactional metric, and now we know if we didn't meet the expectation level of the customer. Now we look and we can see that knowledge is a critical driver. Their manager can say, "Okay, now we need to make sure that we have you go through courses, additional retraining, recertification, whatever that is." Now let's monitor. Now let's have scorecards. And to be able to sort of say, like, "How are you doing at the overall level?" We never had that before.
>
> So, as a result of our journey mapping, we now have a battery of questions like "Are they knowledgeable?," "Was it easy to track the situation?," "Was there clear communication?," "Did they display empathy?" All of those factors that we know are a CX best practice, or through the benchmarking that we did are drivers that differentiate us relative to our competitors because we quantified it. So, we can say

this is what we need to focus on. Before, a lot of the data wasn't merged with behavioral data, outcome data, descriptive data. So, we didn't have that.

That was one of the things that, when I came on board, I was up front and adamant that not only do I need the ability to measure with perception metrics, the quality of the experience, but it was fundamental that we would have those perception metrics automatically tethered to a host of descriptive metrics. This can be at the customer level or the account level. For us, employee size is a big deal, how long is their tenure, how long they've been live with our solution, all the descriptive metrics, as well as data about the event, the time to resolve a support case, or anything along those lines, but then the sexier metrics are tethered automatically to the outcomes. So, this gets into financial. This is annual recurring revenue and customer lifetime value. Did they renew, or did they not renew? Did they increase their wallet share with us? We have everything automatically integrated so that every time we capture feedback, all of those variables are automatically tethered for us to be able to look at that and see what the relationship is. So, you can run the regression models, you can sit there and say that there's an increase in confidence or decrease in frustration.

We feed about two hundred pieces of data into our VoC platform, from implementation data such as time to engage, which is how long it takes from contract to when they started implementation. Time to [go] live, which is how long it took from when they started to launch UKG Pro and run payrolls. TTR, time to resolve, number of cases that a person submitted within a set time period, number of escalations, all of those behavioral context variables.

Bringing all this data together enables Roxie to understand how the data connects. She can see how prolonged support issues impact not only the cost to serve but also likelihood to purchase new products, a critical component to ARR. Then she can see common points of friction, such as how long an issue can go on before it impacts customers' overall satisfaction. Roxie goes into more detail about how she analyzes the customer experience compared to loyalty:

I want to know if our customer experience is protecting revenue, but then there's also the cost-to-serve element. Are we starting to see that customers are executing on the behaviors we want? Which are things like they're not raising their hand [calling in service issues] as often? I'm not saying, "We don't want them to raise their hand." But are they repeatedly raising their hand for the same thing? Because then it means we haven't enabled them appropriately. And that's where the confidence is not activated in the right manner.

Now we analyze, and we automate all of that so it's always integrated. And then we have our dashboards set up in a manner that looks at things through the lens of not only perception metrics but also descriptive and outcome metrics. And then anything that is of an advanced analytic nature—regressions, structural equation models, all that type of stuff—that is done on the side because current dashboards don't execute on that as well.

Most programs rely solely on survey data, but through integrating the business data, Roxie can go much deeper in understanding how activities also impact sentiment, and eventually financial outcomes.

■ ■ ■

It is clear in the stories you have just read how operational data informs the customer journey. The focus of the next chapter is taking information to build an effective dashboard strategy. The big takeaway is that you can orchestrate the customer journey. Consider the time and cost savings, ability to sell more products and services, and generally happier customers—and employees. It's all possible.

Cari's Story

As Cari worked to improve the implementation experience, she and Stephen discussed the need to show progress with the teams at their weekly one-on-one. "It's great how you've been able to jump in on the implementation working team," Stephen shared. "I don't know how you do it—that's a lot on your plate."

"Yeah, it's certainly been more work than I expected," Cari responded. "It's not a surprise how much impact implementation has. It's really complex, involving a bunch of teams on our side. But it's our most critical journey.

"What we're missing, though, is a way to show the impact of our work when we're done. I love the CX dashboard you created, showing the overall engagement and the net revenue retention based on customers and their emotions. Incorporating the new widget that showed the breakdown by implementation length was also a huge win—Patricia [Sycamore's COO] asked me about that linkage last week. And even Yolanda asked if we could look at NRR by implementation length! Implementation is so important that I'd like to see if we can't create a dedicated dashboard for it."

Stephen thought about it. "Yeah, I could see that. Maybe we can even create a link to it from the main dashboard, since so many people are looking at that. We might even repeat the section on how the length of implementation leads to different survey results, but also tie it right to NRR," he said. "Exposing the current length of implementations and its impact will provide a ton of visibility. Cari, maybe you'd better check with the new senior director of implementations, Mikkel, before providing that kind of exposure. People will be looking at the dashboards pretty regularly, and for some, the dashboards could be a nasty surprise. Let me put together a wireframe of a dashboard layout, and you can run it by them to see if they have any feedback on what we're showing and how it's delayed."

My Thoughts

This is where your hard work in getting access to the data pays off! Successful dashboards are the hallmark of a strong CX program, but they only happen after months of hard work, identifying what data matters, crafting the story, and then displaying it in a compelling way.

The good news is that once they're created, dashboards do some of the heavy lifting for you, communicating the current state of the experience and its impact on the business—which makes it worth the time to get it right!

CHAPTER 9

Do I Have a Dashboard Strategy That Works?

SUCCESSFUL DASHBOARDS ARE ONE OF THE MOST VISIBLE components of a great customer experience program. I emphasize *successful* because most programs either don't have dashboards or have dashboards that are only viewed by the customer experience team. Identifying the most compelling data and sharing it in a consumable manner are critical skills to ensure your program has continuing impact.

Measure the Customer Experience against Business Outcomes

Getting access to all the data needed to inform your customer experience isn't easy. We learned in the last chapter how Roxie Strohmenger required this as a condition to starting her role, but that approach doesn't work if you're an existing CX leader. The results from getting the access are worth it, as it enables you to show your value, as well as to communicate using language—data—that your internal customers also use. So, take the time to make the relationships and build the business case. You'll be glad you did.

To show how mature organizations operate, I've brought in two case studies. The first profiles Bill Staikos, who until recently led customer experience at a large B2B financial services institution, and the second profiles Natasha from XYZ Software.

Using Data—and Dashboards—to Drive CX Success

Bill's organization had progressed to the point where it had data and technology to show the customer journey, then used dashboard tools to present the information to functions across the company. Creating a game-changing customer experience necessitates alignment between silos, and one aspect of that alignment is shared data and interpretation. (One client originally had eight contradictory ways to measure on-time delivery.) It's pretty difficult to agree on the current state of the customer experience when your teams are working with different "facts." Creating a shared view of the data behind the experience breaks down silos that hold back transformation. Our stories illustrate this very point.

START WITH MEASUREMENT

Creating a game-changing experience requires the technology to analyze the current customer experience and the data surrounding it. That technology calls for access to data, so start here. This access requires gaining leadership support (which we'll discuss in Action 4), then building relationships with your analytics and IT colleagues.

Bill is a big believer in customer experience. In addition to his day job, he's a frequent commenter on LinkedIn, hosts a podcast, and leads a private group for those newer to CX, helping them to learn CX best practices from speakers within the discipline. I had the chance to speak to his group, and the questions asked by the participants suggest that he's done a solid job at accelerating their knowledge.

He had been at the organization for almost two years when I conducted our interview,[1] quickly accelerating the organization's focus on customer experience. Progressing that quickly as a new hire is a laudable accomplishment, but those who know Bill aren't surprised. I first met him years ago, stopping to see him while I was in New York, and was impressed with his disciplined approach to driving change.

One key to his success is using data to guide his organization's teams to focus on what matters most to customers. Bill knows that the way to financial services executives' hearts is through their heads,[2] so he focuses his team on providing the information needed for his company's product owners to make smart decisions. When I asked how he proves he's adding value, he gave me multiple examples for how he proved ROI. One compelling example, though it wasn't from changing the experience, illustrates his approach. When he brought in a VoC platform, he saw a return on investment in the first year, through improved decision-making of his agile project management teams resulting in less technical debt.[3] As he explains:

> For our measurement platform, we were net neutral on year-one costs, which was a seven-figure sum. For one thing, we were able to avoid hiring one person because a lot of the work is automated, and we were also able to identify new areas of opportunity for efficiency gains in places like the call center. So, that's one piece.
>
> The one way that we really try and execute against how we're delivering value is in our agile teams. We train developers, scrum masters, and other team members on a human-centered design toolkit, helping them set up persistent feedback channels, helping them analyze and look at their backlog. When analyzing our impact, we look at changes in what they deliver in a two-week sprint. Then, on a quarterly perspective, we look at changes to customers from a financial perspective.[4] And we look at technical debt and how much we've removed.
>
> We give our agile teams journey dashboards, and you can light up the journey as red, amber, or green. If you're a

product owner, you can look at that and say, "I have a thousand things in my backlog. Where do I focus?" Now we're able to tell them that the highest impact item out of those thousand is number 854. Not the first one in the backlog. So, now we're creating massive optimization and efficiency gains, and those leaders are able to direct their resources in the right place. We can identify and see the impact over time, and we quantify value that way as well.

In the journey dashboard for underwriting, we've built in predictive analytics, to say, if we change X, Y, and Z, we will increase by 20 percent more loans coming from this client. So, go fix X, Y, and Z. We all want people looking at data in a dashboard . . . and saying, "I'm going to start here, even though the problem might be bigger somewhere else because that is a symptom, as opposed to the core problem."

Bill's focus is to make his organization's agile teams more effective through embedding the VoC into their design work, and he can evaluate his success based on how much business those teams' customers send to his company. His organization has more teams than he can effectively service, creating a natural experiment that enables him to show how the teams he can serve are more effective than the rest. Which then leads him to receive more resources, accelerating his impact.

NEXT STEP: PARTNER WITH ANALYTICS

Expect to spend a significant amount of time with your analytics and IT partners as you begin to assess your business's measurement infrastructure. While some Change Makers have the analytic talent and resources on their teams, most partner with their organization's analytics function for more advanced analysis.

You may face a challenge convincing these teams that sentiment data are relevant in predicting business outcomes. Sentiment data feel "softer" than behavioral data. Another challenge is that many—perhaps most—of your customers won't have survey scores, and each individual at your client company will have different scores.[5] This increases the analytics challenge, as they have to work with incomplete and contradictory data sets. Change management is critical here (hold on—we'll get to that in Action 4: Grease the Flywheel with Change Management). Once you've successfully created the partnership, your analytics team can help create your models to show which aspects of the customer experience most impact those critical financial outcomes, such as reduced churn or increased ordering velocity.

Most Change Makers started with measuring the overall experience, then selected a specific journey to analyze. This relates to the research I shared earlier: Successful organizations first map the end-to-end experience, then come back and work on subjourneys. Starting broad allows you to take a step back and view the entire experience, enabling you to target your next steps appropriately. This is the best long-term approach. However, sometimes you need to show impact immediately, and trying to get all the data required can feel daunting. In that case, you may wish to start by looking at one critical journey first, show the impact, and then move on to the next journey. This allows you to start small, but it does mean you'll have to go back and ask for access to data multiple times as you add more journeys.

Journey mapping provides a practical framework to get a clear line of sight on the critical data that impact customer outcomes. By starting with customers' views of their experiences, you can identify which teams are involved and the type of behavioral and operational data that may be related to their experience, such as Dow identified in its Get It Right metric. All this can be used to create what I call a Journey Health Score, which combines sentiment, behavioral, operational, and financial data to show the health of the journey, as well as specific phases. You may remember this concept from Olga's case study back in chapter 1, although she didn't use this exact term. This score helps executives and teams quickly evaluate where they are doing well and where they struggle.

To return to our story, Bill's team speaks in data, something that I found true in most of our Change Makers.[6] Bill certainly epitomizes this, as he says:

> The problem is not data. And it hasn't been for years. The problem is getting good data, so that you can use it, or you can combine it with other data sets. You need to have an approach where you start with thinking about the data that exist and incorporating that in your approach, because if you don't have that mindset, nothing happens. You need data architects to start having that conversation. And not a lot of CX teams have data architects, let alone data scientists.

So, Bill needed data architects. But, of course, the notion of creating silos is anathema to him. He needed his data architects and analysts to be sitting next to others doing similar work. Rather than creating a redundant department, Bill funded two headcounts in the data analytics team, saying, "They're your people, but they can only work on my CX projects."

BUILD THE TEAMS AND CREATE THE TOOLS TO MEET YOUR NEEDS

Bill's comments reflect a change I'm seeing to customer experience. Traditionally, you could get by through a focus on the sentiment data captured in surveys and perhaps speech or text analytics. Those days are going away.

The Change Maker of the future will measure the customer experience not only through surveys and voice/text analytics but also by using the same data their internal customers review—the descriptive, behavioral, operational, and financial data (i.e., the Customer Ecosystem Data) that show who the customer is, what they do, what the business does around them, and then the impact of that experience.

Once you've determined the most critical data to track the experience, find out which dashboards already exist. In my experience, you will have more success integrating new metrics and business intelligence into existing dashboards than creating your own—and perhaps competing—tools and hoping executives use them. Success will require proving that adding your new data can better answer their questions than the current dashboards.

For example, we worked with the sales leader of an $8 billion division. When I asked him what might be missing from his dashboard strategy and tools, he told me, "You know what I'd like to know? When we lose a customer. I don't know that. Ideally, I'd like to know a few things: how many customers we've landed and their value; the annual value of our average existing customer; and then, how many customers we've lost and how much value they had on average."

We create dashboards to keep the state of the customer experience top of mind for executives, helping them to prioritize customer outcomes in their day-to-day work. To build this desire to use your dashboards, discover what critical questions with CX implications are not being answered and build dashboards to answer these questions. The ultimate dashboard strategy may take multiple iterations and years to implement, as you learn about what data matter and incorporate change management. But it's worth it. The way an effective dashboard can convey critical and current information is powerful proof of the impact your CX program is making.

When creating dashboards, apply the same skills you use with your customers—watching the data and measuring the journey—to internal teams as you monitor how they engage with your dashboards. This is a principle that Bill follows rigorously.

The more impact Bill creates, the larger his department becomes. His CX program includes four teams, including human-centered design, insights and analytics, client solutions (providing direct support to client-facing teams), and a CX strategy and operations group, with two members solely focused on change management. All told, when you add in his thirty-five-person CRM team, he has eighty people reporting to him, which grew substantially during his tenure.

One thing that separates Bill from just another technology- and data-focused person is his approach to change management, specifically the ADKAR model,[7] discussed in Action 4. Discussing one particular piece of data and technology his team created, Bill explains:

> We're building these journey dashboards with data flowing through them, but no one's going to use them unless we actually have a formal change-management strategy in place run by someone who has this as their day job. I created a CX strategy and operations team to connect all the dots for us and help people adopt all these tools.
>
> We created the change strategy, starting with communications to drive awareness. We started with a Gartner assessment, which we just finished. When I began, we were at level one, and now we ranked three out of five, which is in the top 15 percent of all B2B organizations. That is a pretty awesome achievement, frankly, with eighteen months of work.
>
> We have started everything from small roundtables and interviews. We're setting up a CX week; we've created a CX playbook. We're actually wrapping that up in the next two weeks. So, our agile teams know the tools they have access to and who they need to go to. Even with over forty people, we can't directly impact our thousands of employees, so we're creating tools to give us a little bit of scale.
>
> Another thing we've created is one-pagers. On the front, it talks about what's happening from a CX perspective in our organization. The back page is specific to that part of the organization. And at the bottom of that is, here's what our ask is for this quarter, which can be anything from "Go out and talk about this topic in your town hall" to "We have

five policies that are fundamentally broken that we need to go fix, you really need to get people on this." So, that's quarterly communication and engagement.

Orchestrate the Customer Experience to Align with Business Outcomes

I am convinced that journey orchestration will be a core CX capability in a short time. Like many capabilities, it will begin in B2C before it migrates to the B2B world.

Measurement and orchestration have different outcomes. Measurement provides your organization with business intelligence by analyzing the state of the customer experience, enabling your organization to act on this knowledge. Orchestration changes the journey based on individual customer needs. Both require that critical data be identified and exposed.

One common use case for orchestration is providing operational transparency on where customers are in their journeys. It's difficult to offer a positive customer experience if your customers don't know where they are in the experience! It's also important to provide employees with this same visibility. Building an internal view of how the journey is progressing allows your service employees to share progress with customers, which is table stakes for a great customer experience. Sharing that view with customers can provide them the control and also build their confidence. Individual customers have different needs. Some want to have status updates pushed to them, others want to be able to go to your tools, and still, others will never look, will ignore your emails, but will be frustrated if your organization doesn't manually contact them when delays happen. That's why it's critical to start with customer research to better understand their needs *before* you create your operational transparency.

Analyze the CX Journey

Journey analysis is required for B2B organizations of any size. Understanding the points where customers drop off and identifying their root causes is critical. That said, a journey analytics *platform* only makes sense for larger B2B organizations with many customers.[8]

B2B2C organizations are typically better candidates for journey analytics and orchestration platforms, as they typically have more customers, and much of the experience happens within internal systems. For example, while insurance organizations often sell through independent distribution, much of the journey, including sales, claims, and ongoing engagement, happens in the insurance company's systems, enabling the analytics.

Having the right analytics may arguably be more important for a large financial organization than in some other sectors. Bill has found that, in addition to democratizing the data and emphasizing change management, technology is critical to analyze and communicate the experience. He takes a "less is more" approach, using fewer platforms to deliver greater impact, but fully utilizing those ecosystems. He says:

It's not just about surveys. We have text and speech analytics baked in, including our platform's AI capability and text and voice analytics. We're also looking to bring on a journey orchestration product, and [our CRM] is a big part of that—that's where we close the loop. That's where the insights actually get funneled, so there's not the "swivel chair" effect for client-facing staff. Like what can happen to contact center staff who get rated in [our VoC software provider] but then have to switch to the CRM when they're talking to clients. My approach to software is to use the tools that people are using and consolidate everywhere else.

Pushing tools into decision-makers' hands, including middle management, means they can use the tools to educate and inform their teams about what's happening with the customer. Now, understand that not everybody can connect the dots. And I think, for CX teams, that's probably one of the hardest things because there's no great scalable way to change people's minds. You just have to keep on communicating, keep on connecting the dots for people, and hopefully, it clicks. And for those that it doesn't [click], hopefully, they self-select and realize they're not a fit for our culture and move on from the organization. But that takes a lot of time. I mean, at my previous organization, we got to a really great place culturally. But it took two and a half years.

Bill is one of the most data-focused CX leaders I've met, and he provides a vision of what customer experience may become in the future. A comprehensive view of the customer journey allows your organization to better target projects against customer needs. According to the Genesys report mentioned earlier, 41 percent of organizations can't explain why customer experience metrics go up or down.[9] If you don't know why they're changing, then you certainly can't target the right interventions to improve them.

Let's close this chapter with a case study—in this case, Natasha at XYZ—to show what another mature program looks like.

XYZ: Tie Data to Business Outcomes

While B2B companies typically have fewer customers than B2C, XYZ is one of the world's largest SaaS companies. This size enables them analytics capabilities not available to smaller B2B organizations, creating a customer lifetime value score (CLV), which many track, but also enabling more detailed journey analytics and orchestration.

To ensure its experience remains strong, the company surrounds CLV with a host of operational metrics, such as usage, knowing that increased usage is a strong predictor of retention, and complement this with NPS as a relationship metric, as well as customer satisfaction at individual touchpoints. As Natasha explains:

We capture the customer's experience wherever they are in their life cycle, looking at their perception of us, their emotions, their satisfaction, and their perception of value of the investment with us. More importantly, we also look at their engagement because sometimes what people say and what they do are two very different things. Analyzing behaviors is crucial. Are they engaging with our content? Are they attending our events, our webinars? What do they read? How are they engaging on our website? How are they engaging our communities? And then, of course, how are they engaging in our product? Are they using it? What features and functions do they use? We look at engagement as one of the key metrics for understanding CX.

And then, ultimately, we look at the outcomes along that journey to see if they are converting from prospect to customer. Are they growing? Are they staying longer? What's the retention; what's the renewal? We look at those types of metrics to understand our customer experience. We capture that feedback in our CRM system, even our survey goes back into our CRM system. We do a scorecard every quarter that we share with our executive team.

We've developed models tying NPS scores to customer lifetime value, so we can connect the dots internally. This allows us to also understand key drivers of customer loyalty and its impact on our financials. With models like these, we can make investment decisions on where to improve.

When I asked Natasha how she came to have such a data-focused approach, she shared the story of how she came to lead XYZ's customer experience program:

> My background is in consulting and finance. I used to generate CEO scorecards of company performance metrics, and I always believe in the balanced score-card. Sometimes we get so obsessed over one metric like NPS, but that's just one indicator. Think of it as a balanced scorecard, because, by focusing only on NPS, you could unintentionally make something worse. So, we have to look at perception, but we also have to look at the engagement. Sometimes you have to ask yourself: "If the customer is not happy, but is using our product, is that okay?" I want to make sure our customers are happy. It's not just a matter of growth, because I think long term, three to five to ten years. That's how we keep them loyal.
>
> Customer experience is tough to measure, because it's about emotion. But at the end of the day, *you have to tie it to your business outcome*. You have to do both. So, we developed a number of metrics to tie these together. First, our marketing team has created an engagement score, based on over fifty metrics, such as whether our customers download an article. Based on the algorithm, the team comes up with a score at an account level. Every customer has an engagement score from the journey stage. We've done some analy-sis that shows that customers who are more engaged with us tend to have higher NPS and CSAT scores, so we know that these are key drivers for these customer experience metrics. Having it at the account level allows our account teams to work and prioritize what accounts they focus on to encourage engagement.
>
> Then we have a Net Adoption Score developed by the data science team, where it looks at features and functions, depending on our product, because not all products are the same. You have the healthy versus

unhealthy usage, where customers are not spending time with certain features or functions. The algorithm comes up with a score based on an index of 100. We look at the adoption and engagement metrics from a product standpoint. And then we also have an engagement score from a customer success standpoint, which looks at the same concept as marketing.

Our teams in customer success created early warning system scores, where they look at the account health, analyzing over 150 factors, and that's where our Customer Success Managers come in. This helps them prioritize what accounts they focus on to make them successful. So, we do have a very robust system from presales to post sales.

Most of our data is in our CRM system. But text analytics sits in our data lake. We bring it together through our analytics tool, Tableau, which we then share with our executive team in the overarching CX dashboard. However, within each of those metrics, there are teams that do so much more analysis.

For example, in the CX scorecard dashboard, where we show the usage and adoption of our product, we use Net Adoption, but our data science team has supporting dashboards that go into that data set much further. Think of it as an overarching scorecard, but then you can dig deeper into each of the areas that has its own set of dashboards that slice and dice the data based on product line, based on customer segmentation, or based on region. So, those teams own that, and then you can even go down into specific accounts if you want to. It's like a cascade of dashboards that we use, and we link them together. All the data sources, ultimately, are the same. But the views are flexible because you have different audiences.

Instead of a separate journey analytics and orchestration platform, XYZ uses its CRM to orchestrate customer journeys. As Natasha explains:

In our Customer Success Group, we create the journey that we want our customers to go through. For example, day one when the contract is signed, provision flips on, and this is the email that they get. Here's the link to get started, so they curate content that would help the customer get started faster. Time to value is really important for us. So, they orchestrate the onboarding journey, which lasts from day one all the way to the first anniversary, providing guided content. As we strive to continually improve, the marketing team is putting in journey analytics to better understand the customer journey and to develop newer ways to help our customers be more successful.

What I love about CX is that it is both an art and a science—that perfect combination. And so, that's how I landed in this role and have loved it ever since. My goal is this: How do I make XYZ be the best from a B2B standpoint, using technology and using design? It's just such a perfect combination, in terms of this role. And I think there's a lot more that we can do.

Natasha's story is a great example of bringing everything together. The company started by identifying the most critical Customer Ecosystem Data, then used technology to communicate the data across the organization in an actionable way. Like our other Change Makers, Natasha has demonstrated the CX Loyalty Flywheel, connecting behavioral data to NPS to CLV, the ultimate outcome. XYZ knows that it has to earn the right for customers to want to work more with it and purchase additional products, so it creates systems to determine whether the company is creating that value in individual accounts. The company also uses technology—notably journey orchestration—to craft an individual journey and react in real time when it doesn't go according to plan.

Another note: Let's compare the comments Noah had in chapter 2 to Natasha's. Although they are in very different industries—banking and SaaS software—both found that interaction predicts emotional engagement, which in turn predicts financial outcomes. That may not be true for every type of experience, but it's something to consider. Rather than focusing on reducing ease, does it make more sense to encourage more activity? Only by analyzing the Customer Ecosystem Data and tying it to financial outcomes can you know for certain.

■ ■ ■

Action 3 focuses on extending how you analyze customer experience to go beyond traditional sentiment-only approaches to use the Customer Ecosystem Data to gain a more comprehensive view of what is happening with the customer and in your company, as well as to use technology to share those learnings—and perhaps to improve the outcomes. Once the data are identified, the next step is to create a dashboard strategy to share the results. Once that dashboard strategy is in place, acknowledging that it will undergo continual development because business is never static, the next stage is to use those results to motivate your teams to work together to improve the customer experience.

Cari's Story

Cari checked with Mikkel, the team lead, about sharing the length and status of current implementations with leadership, and initially, both thought it was a good idea. But that sentiment soon backfired. The knowledge that implementation delays were a key source of frustration led to pointed questions from the senior executives about what was causing the delays.

Mikkel reached out to Cari for help. "I thought exposing implementation data to senior leadership might help us get more resources," he said. "But instead, I'm constantly fielding questions about implementations, and I don't always have answers. We have a weekly review where teams share what's happening, but I'm at the mercy of what they report. Is there any way you can give me more data on what's happening, so I can help the teams identify common roadblocks?"

Cari considered it. "Well, in our journey map, we identified some of the common issues that can cause delay, such as resources not being available at Sycamore, the SIs, and the end client," she said. "These constraints create delays in a number of areas, such as starting our testing. I know of some software that allows us to integrate the data into the journey map, so you'll be able to monitor it and get a bit of an early warning. This data is more granular than what leadership sees and should help you identify issues before they bubble up to the executives. Would that help?"

"Definitely," Mikkel replied. "I've always been at the mercy of weekly status reports. If I can get more visibility to this data, I can reach out to my teams before the issues cause major delays. Can I compare the results across teams?"

"I think we can do that. Will that help?"

"Oh, yeah. Right now, I can only see what's happening at a high level. I know that some of my teams seem to finish their implementations faster, but I don't know why. I suspect that if I can get down to a lower level of data, I'll have a better baseline we can use to drive improvements. What do you call this?" Mikkel asked.

Cari went into the details. "It's a Living Journey Map. You know that journey map we created a few months back? This software attaches the live data to the map. In your case, delays in testing, identified errors, and rework, assuming that the data exists and is accessible, which I believe it does. And we can also make it available to your project managers, so they can see how their data compares with others. So, hopefully, they can manage the issues themselves, without you having to call it out."

"Great, let's make that happen," Mikkel said. "I'd love to have the answers ready next time our COO calls. Or, hopefully, I can actually let Patricia know ahead of time—before the questions come."

My Thoughts

Before working to change a journey, it's critical to understand what the journey truly looks like, which is where the Customer Ecosystem Data comes in. Sharing it on dashboards and Living Journey Maps also creates visibility and accountability to the organization. This will create interest and support in the change—assuming you can successfully pull it off!

Change management, which we'll move into next, isn't a traditional customer experience capability. Few CX maturity models specifically call it out. But it's one of the defining characteristics of a Change Maker—moving beyond reporting to driving change.

Getting the data to monitor the CX Loyalty Flywheel is the first step. The next is to build change management to grease it, accelerating impact.

Takeaways

Identifying Sources of Value in the CX Loyalty Flywheel

Please use the workbook that you can download from DoB2BBetter .com/workbook to complete the exercises and activities. Completing this work will result in a playbook that will help you plan your CX program and provide insight into questions and challenges that your fellow CX colleagues everywhere are facing. We will continue on with Cari's discussion from Action 2 and imagine what I'd ask her about the Customer Ecosystem Data.

In Action 1, we identified calculations of revenue-based financial outcomes. For those calculations, where can you find the data and who owns the data?

CARI: Annual recurring revenue, or ARR, is in the existing executive dashboard at a consolidated level. We can calculate it based on this year's software revenue, using the data in our CRM. Sales operations owns the CRM version; finance owns the calculation.

Net revenue retention is not currently reported. We calculate it based on this year's and last year's software revenue, using the data in our CRM. Sales operations owns the CRM version; we'll work with finance on the calculation.

In Action 1, we also identified calculations of cost-based financial outcomes. For those calculations, where can you find the data and who owns the data?

CARI: Length of implementations can be found in our project management software handled by the project management office. Issue resolution is in our workflow system, but we do not have the means to calculate the costs. For the costs of extended implementations, I'm hoping we can work with our project management office to get the length, and HR to get the costs.

What are the most critical journeys for which you will need dashboarding data?

CARI: Based on our journey mapping and survey work, implementations and service resolution are at the top of the list. Upgrades are a specific type of implementation that deserves its own dedicated dashboard. And, given the focus on growth, it probably makes sense to build a presales dashboard as well, although I don't yet know enough about the journey to build one.

Well, let's dive into one of them first. Where do you want to start, and are there more granular cost-based sources of data that will be useful? Where will you find that data?

CARI: It makes the most sense to focus on upgrades, since we do more of these than new implementations. We'll need to understand the resources attached to the upgrade and an estimate of salary plus benefits plus how long the implementation team spends on the project. We can get the length of time from our project management system, and I can work with HR to make some estimates on costs for the people. Of course, I won't have a live feed for salaries—we'll have to work with assumptions for that—but I should be able to get something for the length of implementation, and we can combine these two for a cost per upgrade.

On this same journey, what qualitative data do you have in order to understand customers' behaviors? What are the key behaviors that you need to track?

CARI: Our journey mapping identified that the key behaviors we can track include opening tickets (a big one), changing project managers (although we can't really track that), and escalating issues to leadership.

Which data track to each of these behaviors?

CARI: We can get the number of open tickets per client, the number of severity 1 tickets per client, and the number of tickets that are reopened after being closed prematurely from our workflow software, which my old department, SaaS operations, manages.

We can't yet track escalations to leadership or when a project manager is replaced. These are a big deal, but aren't tracked anywhere.

What operations impact this journey, and where can you find that data?

CARI: We can see delays in implementation when a project is marked red in our project management software, but I'm not yet sure how to integrate that. Changes to the project team members is in our project management software but not in a form we can report on. So, we have some work here.

Where is sentiment captured based on this journey, and where can you find that data?

CARI: We own this data. We currently have a relationship survey, an implementation survey, and an issue-resolution survey. These are in our VoC software platform, although we will have to manually analyze which customers are currently in an implementation, since that's not a field that we have.

What descriptive data can be used for drilling down, and where can you find that data?

CARI: The key five items we want to drill down into are the system integrator, the Customer Success Manager, the product(s) being upgraded, the customer segment, and the individual customer. All of this is in the CRM, managed by sales operations.

As your CX team designs these dashboards, who are your most critical audiences? And what information do they need to see?

CARI: The executive committee is our most critical audience. The committee members need to see that we're tying our CX results to finances. Those results are featured in the first-level dashboard, and that will hopefully interest them enough to click into the implementation dashboard.

Has the CX team thought about permissions that need to be granted? This is a necessary step to take before publishing any data. Is there anybody your team needs to align with?

CARI: We'll need to check with our finance resource to ensure she agrees with our ARR and NRR calculations. We'll also need to tell our implementation leaders that this data will be visible to the executives, so they don't get surprised.

Have the analysts on the CX team thought through the presentation of the data?

CARI: Yes, we use the sentiment sandwich approach to show how customers feel and to show the operational and financial impacts to the business. We didn't want to clutter up the presentation with too many metrics, but we wanted to make sure we included all three categories.

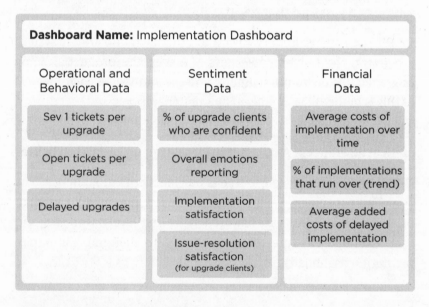

Dashboard Name: Implementation Dashboard		
Operational and Behavioral Data	**Sentiment Data**	**Financial Data**
Sev 1 tickets per upgrade	% of upgrade clients who are confident	Average costs of implementation over time
Open tickets per upgrade	Overall emotions reporting	% of implementations that run over (trend)
Delayed upgrades	Implementation satisfaction	Average added costs of delayed implementation
	Issue-resolution satisfaction (for upgrade clients)	

Figure 9-1: Implementation dashboard.

ACTION 4

GREASE THE FLYWHEEL WITH CHANGE MANAGEMENT

CHANGE WITHOUT CHANGE MANAGEMENT
IS JUST TALKING.

"You can't transform the customer experience in a haphazard or siloed way. You need to embed a customer-centric mindset and CX discipline into the very DNA of your organization. The exact paths will vary, but successful CX organizations do this through very intentional means: shifting from an inside-out to an outside-in focus, connecting every employee and their day-to-day actions to the customer's success (and business growth) so each individual can see the impact and ownership."

—Andrea Krohnberg, CCXP, Global Director, Customer Insights and Experience, Kelly Services, Inc.

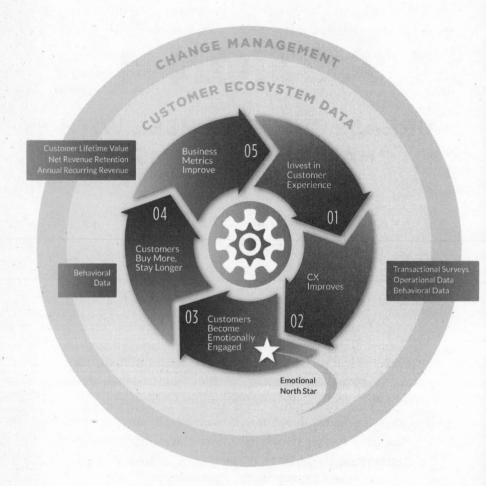

Figure 10-1: The CX Loyalty Flywheel in action.

LINKING YOUR WORK TO FINANCIAL OUTCOMES, MEASURING and managing emotions, and displaying the Customer Ecosystem Data are all critical to build an effective customer experience program. But they won't accomplish anything if your employees don't know about them. Or, even worse, if they don't care.

Participants in our survey of CX professionals cited their top three barriers as organizational complexity, not having enough or the right staff, and leadership buy-in. Change management helps overcome these barriers, engaging teams throughout the organization to work through the complexity, providing extra hands in the effort, and aligning leadership on the importance of customer focus.

That's the topic of our fourth and final action: using change management to rally your organization to use all the infrastructure you've put in place to grease the CX Loyalty Flywheel, improving outcomes for both the business and your customers.

We'll start with an overview of change management in chapter 10, including two of the leading models. Next, we'll zero in on applying the concepts to leadership in chapter 11. Finally, we'll show how to use change management practices to involve frontline employees in an improved customer experience.

CHAPTER 10

How Can My Small Team Influence Our Thousands of Employees?

SUCCESSFUL CUSTOMER EXPERIENCE LEADERS CHANGE THE organization. While some are trained in classical change management techniques, others have found their own ways to change the organization. But one theme holds true: without finding ways to engage executives and frontline staff, all the rest of the work is for naught. Let's hear from a great B2B case study on changing the culture at Wolters Kluwer.

"Every Single Person Has a Mission"

I introduced Darin Byrne, Vice President of Client Experience and Delivery at Wolters Kluwer Compliance Solutions in Action 2.[1] You may remember that his organization creates products and services to help banks stay compliant on mortgages and other loans. Darin has a strong focus in customer experience, and especially in change management. Prior to his current role, he was the Senior Director of Services, where he brought the notion of customer experience to the firm.

One of my favorite examples of his approach emerges when I contrast how he and his manager, Steve Meirink, Executive Vice

President and General Manager of Wolters Kluwer Compliance Solutions, talk about how he came to be such an effective Change Maker. When I interviewed Steve, he summarized Darin's background by saying, "He didn't, in my opinion, grow up in customer experience. He grew up from an operations and Lean Six Sigma perspective, so he had a bias to look at data. And he had a bias to just implement. When I speak to other customer experience professionals, they don't come from similar backgrounds. And I think that's what makes Darin so unique."

This is a compelling example, and one that we've found elsewhere: Change Makers cut their teeth in another department and learn the business before migrating to customer experience. This provides them a more holistic view of the business, which they then apply to their role in CX. But when I shared this with Darin, he chuckled and explained that Steve's description of his background was incomplete:

> I know Steve told you I had an operations background, but I wouldn't say that. Let me tell you the story to explain my background.
>
> My first job at fourteen years old was a summer camp counselor at a Boy Scout camp. This camp was run by a few pretty remarkable people who were big mentors in my life at a very young age. Our mission at the summer camp— the well-stated number one mission—was that for every scout that comes through there, this will be the best week of their life.
>
> There's a lot of discipline and a focus on cleanliness and making sure everything is safe and in order. And then, throughout the week, we're going to have fun. We're going to create experiences for them from every meal and have songs and fun and games. And that's going to be a blast. And then they're going to go off and do their merit badge classes, and they're going to be treated with respect and cared for.

The whole week is this great customer experience, and we all had a part to play in that.

But what made an impression on me from an early age was that every summer the staff would take a weekend trip down to the Opryland theme park. It was a treat for the staff, but it was also a learning experience because, when we got to the park, the camp leader said, "Okay, you're going to have fun today, but here's your assignment. Pay attention to every single person who works at this park. Pay attention to the people who start the rides, pay attention to the people who serve the food, pay attention to the performers. Pay attention to the guy who's sweeping and picking up the trash. You'll see that when you're riding on the train around the park and come to an intersection, the guys sweeping will stop sweeping and wave at all the people on the train. Watch this, watch what they do. These people at this park have been trained to make that a great experience for you as a guest. Every single person has a mission, and that is to make your day at the park the best day of your life. And that's our point in the camp: this is going to be the best week of the campers' lives."

So, that was my start from when I was fourteen years old until I was a twenty-year-old working at summer camp, and the importance of experience is totally ingrained in me. Just out of college, I started with Cincinnati Bell, which later became Convergys and now Concentrix. I got training very early on through the Cincinnati Bell/Convergys mindset of customer experience. And so, when I came to Wolters Kluwer Compliance Solutions, I brought that approach into the business. And you know, especially when I took over the professional services team, I started to deliver that same customer experience service excellence program to the people here. I don't think Steve and I have ever had that conversation. But the importance of a great customer experience has been ingrained in me from the beginning, which informed my operations approach—not the other way around.

Whichever you credit—his time in operations or at the summer camp—Darin works hard to create a great experience for his customers, who are primarily employees at banks. And this has driven growth for his program. **And much of that growth is the outcome of his focus on change management**—an essential aspect of driving customer-focused change. Unlike most customer experience leaders, Darin isn't responsible for his organization's surveys—his market research team does that. This accomplishes two things: it's one less responsibility he has to manage, freeing up his time to think about how to move an organization. Second, unlike most CX leaders, there's no risk that he'll be considered the "survey person." This is a label that Change Makers avoid. They're fine with using the survey to drive change. But, like Nancy Flowers told us in Action 1, they prefer to talk about business outcomes than survey results. Darin doesn't have this risk.

Bringing the Client Experience to Life: Engage from Within

Let's start by looking at how Darin works with his fellow leaders. While Wolters Kluwer executives believe in customer experience, they have a lot on their plates and often need to direct their energy elsewhere. One way he brings the client experience to life for his fellow executives is by assigning each an important client to sponsor, which effectively captures their attention. As Darin explains:

Most of our executives are engaged with customers anyway. But this program requires them to have a different level of engagement. Instead of the relationship being small talk over dinner, now the executives need to thoroughly understand the survey results our customers shared with us over the last quarter. And what work we've been doing to drive improvements, specifically in the areas where our customers told us we weren't doing well. It gives that executive the ownership mentality to say, "Okay, I have a stake in this now. Not only am I supposed to be talking about it so that everybody else buys in, but now I've got to be aware of what the customers are saying, and engaging in the collaboration with the customers as well."

A common best practice for early-stage customer experience programs is to create a governance committee. As the CX program builds, executives meet to review the current state of the customer experience, including assessing the outcomes of surveys and new research, and approve changes to the journey, something we'll discuss later in this chapter. In the early days of Wolters Kluwer's client experience program, this was crucial to gaining organizational buy-in. Including senior leaders in the decision-making gave everyone a sense of ownership and helped create awareness of the program. But after a few years, Darin came to realize that it was no longer needed. As he explains:

In the early days, we didn't have the buy-in on the importance of client experience, so I had to build a guiding coalition of peers who believed in this and who came to realize that this was not a strength of ours because we were focused on short-term financial results. The CX council I started was a grassroots effort of getting other leaders in the organization to do something to drive improvements. Not necessarily under the radar of the senior executive, but more like building strength in numbers by expanding awareness of our program. We were clear: "No, we're not going to ignore that we have to earn financial results. It's just that if we focus first on the voice of the customer and the customer experience, everything else can flow from that. We should do these initiatives to make the customer experience better, not *just* to improve our bottom line. If we make customer experience better, then we improve the bottom line as well." That lasted through the transition from our old leadership to the new leadership.

And then Steve came in, and he and I were able to connect more. He valued customer experience from the very beginning, and he brought that into the senior leadership team. As a result of his leadership, we didn't really need a CX council anymore for oversight or to provide governance because now the senior leadership team was providing that governance. In essence, that whole thought behind the CX council has evolved to just being the way that our senior leadership team operates.

One of Wolters Kluwer's products is software, and one problem I frequently see at software companies is when the product team loses connection to customers' needs. While Wolters Kluwer uses journey mapping to get product leaders to hear the voice of the customer, the company supplemented this effort (prepandemic) with another unique program: *an externship*. Darin shares:

It's the opposite of an internship. We take an internal person and place them in a services team to visit a customer, essentially a ride along. The requirement is that when you go on the externship, you have to write up a summary. And one gentleman who did this, one of the best ones I saw, wrote a ten-page summary. He was a great storyteller, so it was just a fun read. But you can see the light bulbs going off, like "I didn't realize that this is what that other team did when they go out and talk to customers. And then the biggest thing was I didn't realize that when we do X, Y, and Z, what it means to the customer or the services team to have to work around that."

It's really neat. It's powerful when you give someone who's buried inside the company the opportunity to ride along with people who go out and visit customers, live a day in the life with someone who interacts with customers.

Lisa Hagen is on Darin's team.[2] She shared with me a road show she built that has become a powerful teaching tool for employees about assessing and improving customer experience. What she does is an excellent example of how change management can change the culture of an organization, team by team. The goal of the road show is to have employees look at their business and interactions with customers through a customer mindset. Every year, Lisa hosts twenty road shows in different parts of the country.

She first engages with leaders to identify employees who should attend the road shows. She then joins team meetings to better understand what the team does and how the team members engage with customers, which enables her to customize content. At the road show, her focus is to challenge the participants on how they can act based on what they learn about their customers or identify areas where more work is needed to assess the customer experience. Lisa says:

Of course, our teams know what it feels like to be a customer in their personal life and how they want to be treated there. But that's not enough to know how *our* customers want to be treated. Our employees know too much of what it's like at Wolters Kluwer, and it can be hard to think about what it's like to be a customer. So, our road show educates our people on understanding what the customer experience is. The road show is a big success. It helped start turning our culture toward the direction and the vision of what our leaders really wanted it to be.

A change management concept we'll discuss later in this chapter is creating the *ability* to provide an improved experience. Employees don't natively have all the skills required to create better customer outcomes. To help teams provide a better experience, Lisa offers active listening training that's part of Wolters Kluwer's Service Excellence program. You may remember the Hagerty case study where its new towing provider had strong operational results but lower survey scores. That company clearly could have used Lisa and her active listening program, as this skill communicates empathy and helps customers to feel heard.

As Darin explains, "We want to continuously improve our active listening skills in product support in the hopes of understanding the pain behind the issue or a bigger issue that we might be able to solve."

CX Won't Stick without Change Management

Let's recall what Wolters Kluwer's CX council agreed as its path forward: "If we focus first on the voice of the customer and the customer experience, everything else can flow from that. We should do these initiatives to make the customer experience better, not *just* to improve our bottom line. If we make customer experience better, then we improve the bottom line as well."

Transition means change, and this goes to the heart of our focus in this chapter: customer experience initiatives will not stick without change management.

No matter how well intended, customer experience efforts are at high risk for being just another flavor-of-the-month program. I met with the president of a billion-dollar retail company, and he shared: "I'm concerned about bringing in a customer experience initiative, and everybody then asking, 'Okay, how long will this last? If I just wait, I'm sure it will blow over.' How can I overcome resistance and then how do I make sure that the customer focus continues?"

This is a risk for companies of all sizes. Changes in personnel, reallocation of resources, and leaders who have to deal with "more urgent" matters can all cause the organization to forget its focus on customers. For years, when Qualtrics XM Institute surveyed customer experience leaders, it found that the biggest challenge cited by the leaders was dealing with "other competing priorities" in their organization.[3] Long-term success requires a focused effort with planning, resources, and confidence in the long-term benefits of CX.

It takes *change management*. Without an effective change management approach, there is a high risk of customer experience becoming just another short-term initiative. Linking CX to organizational value is necessary and can provide insight into the potential of CX, but a deliberate change-management approach ensures value is realized.

As an example of this risk, look to digital transformation efforts. The authors of a McKinsey report found that 70 percent of digital transformations fail, most often due to employee resistance.[4] If it can happen to digital transformation, which typically has the attention of every leader in the organization, it can happen to your customer experience efforts. Change management ensures employees receive the necessary resources and support as CX is implemented and becomes ingrained in the culture, so that behaviors change to better support customer needs.

Participants in our survey of CX professionals cited their top three barriers as organizational complexity, not having enough or the right staff, and leadership buy-in. Change management helps overcome these barriers, engaging teams throughout the organization to work through the complexity, providing extra hands in the effort, and aligning leadership on the importance of customer focus.

Change management requires leadership support. While it's fun to share bottom-up stories of CX programs creating such a groundswell of support that the executives *have* to pay attention, they're not realistic. As you've read, many of our Change Makers report directly to senior leaders, as it's almost impossible to drive an improved customer experience at lower levels. I know of one organization that created a part-time manager role to lead customer experience. It's no surprise that little changed after three years. However, reporting to senior leadership isn't enough to guarantee success. We interviewed plenty of customer experience executives who failed to drive change. The Qualtrics XM Institute report *The Global State of XM* found that those organizations that self-assessed at or below the industry average for experience management cited "lack of leadership for these efforts," second only to "lack of clear strategy" as reasons why they weren't able to drive progress.

My important message to you is this: You can link your work to value, create an Emotional North Star, and measure the Customer Ecosystem Data. But unless you create a deliberate strategy to engage leadership and employees to change their behaviors, it will be for naught. The strategy requires an effective leader who applies change management practices.

HIRING A CUSTOMER EXPERIENCE LEADER

If you're an executive who is looking to bring this focus on customers into your organization, you may be tempted to hire somebody from the outside, as this person already has a track record of success in customer experience. I suggest you rethink that approach.

While Roxie Strohmenger is a great example of somebody brought in from the outside who can immediately create impact, she appears to be an outlier. If we look at our Change Makers, only Roxie, Bill from chapter 9, and Stacy Sherman (we tell her story in chapter 12) were new to their organizations. And Bill came from a competitor, so at least he knew the drivers of success.

Look at the rest of our Change Makers, and you'll have a hard time finding somebody with a traditional CX background. Jen Zamora was at Dow for nineteen years before moving into customer experience, Natasha was at XYZ Software for eight, and Nancy Flowers was at Hagerty for six. Darin ran the services team, Dave was a programmer and an operations lead for nThrive, Olga was an engineer, Phil ran operations at the MAC, Laurie (who we'll meet in this chapter) led marketing at Chief and its successor Milestone, Ben led digital transformation at Compassion, and Barbara ran management, planning, and analysis at the VA. It's not that it's impossible to be successful coming from the outside—it's just that it's harder, as you have to learn not only the culture but also the measurements of success. It is possible to be successful coming from the outside. In fact, I've successfully helped in hiring a CX leader from the outside. But it does require a much more extensive onboarding plan to ensure they have the support they need.

This isn't just my opinion. There is significant research that shows that experts who move to different organizations often flounder. It's the result of cognitive entrenchment, the tendency to use the same approach that served the experts well in their former organizations, only to discover that these same approaches don't work in the new context. This is even true in roles where you wouldn't expect it, like stock analysts.[5] In *Thinking, Fast and Slow*, Daniel Kahneman shared that experience has very little to do with expertise in many domains. For example, experienced managers were no better at guessing who would be a good employee than a chimpanzee throwing darts. The fact is, the expertise of even accomplished professionals might only apply to certain, specific situations. Their knowledge is near useless for broad application.

That's what we found in our interviews. While there are rock stars who were successful in new organizations, those Change Makers almost always had consulting experience, which taught them how to adapt. So, as you're looking to add a new leader, tread carefully. My CX friends won't like this, but my recommendation is to look internally first.

TWO CHANGE MANAGEMENT MODELS

Once you have your leader, the next step is to build a change management approach. The change management field offers two leading models: the Prosci ADKAR model and John Kotter's 8-step change model. But you don't have to choose one over the other; I find that they're compatible. ADKAR speaks to the broader context of change management, while Kotter is more focused on the process.

I typically lead with ADKAR[6] because it's a relatively simple, but not simplistic, model. I can explain it in one slide so that anybody from the frontlines to the executive suite can understand it and how to apply it. ADKAR stands for the following:

- **Awareness** of the need for change
- **Desire** to support the change
- **Knowledge** of how to change
- **Ability** to demonstrate the skills and behaviors
- **Reinforcement** to make the change stick

ADKAR speaks to the content of messaging. The first step is to make employees **Aware** of the customer experience effort, why you're doing it, and what's expected of them. The next is to build the **Desire** to change behavior and adopt new behaviors needed to improve the experience. Employees then need to **Know** how to improve the experience, and be **Able** to do that, whether through training or improved tools or technology. Lastly, if leadership fails to **Reinforce** the need for change, employees will revert to their old behavior.

In contrast, John Kotter's 8-step change model speaks more to change processes.[7] His eight steps are as follows:

1. Create a sense of urgency.
2. Build a guiding coalition.
3. Form a strategic vision.
4. Enlist a volunteer army.
5. Enable action by removing barriers.

6. Generate short-term wins.
7. Sustain acceleration.
8. Institute change.

Kotter's model speaks to the requirement to *show what needs to be done* (a combination of Awareness and Desire), *engage leadership* (Desire and Reinforcement), and *take specific steps to enable the change* (Knowledge and Ability).

In our interviews, nearly every leader we interviewed acknowledged the importance of change management, but few had even basic knowledge of models and their applications. Their primary change management tool was email. Compare this to the Change Maker's approach to communication described in chapter 9, in which Bill created monthly communications that updated the organization about the current state of the customer experience and what was needed from them, or Darin's initiative, in which he assigned executives to specific customers to ensure they kept the customer experience top of mind.

Mass communications are obviously part of change management. But alone, they aren't sufficient to grease the CX Loyalty Flywheel or sustain the new behaviors required to create the emotional connections needed for improved customer loyalty and organizational support across the many silos.

Hopeful programs (those who cannot show that they're driving change) primarily focus on building Awareness (what customer experience is) and gaining Knowledge of the current customer experience efforts—and sometimes adding training to create Ability—but stop there. Change Makers add a focus on creating Desire and work with executives to Reinforce the need for customer-focused improvement. Showing a financial return for your help will also help Reinforce the importance of your work with executives.

As we walk through these efforts in the following chapters, I'll use ADKAR for reference, but it's not too hard to see Kotter's influence in this as well.

Legrand | AV: Engaging the Entire Company in Customer Experience

Laurie Englert is the Vice President of Customer Experience for Legrand | AV, a division of Legrand, a global company based in France that provides electrical and digital building infrastructures. The AV division focuses on selling mounting, camera, and display solutions for various audiovisual technologies. Or, as the website states, "Legrand | AV brands create amazing AV experiences through innovative solutions and exceptional service." So, even its tagline talks about experience!

Laurie started as the Director of Marketing at Chief, a $50 million company that created commercial mounts for televisions. From there, the company grew and acquired additional brands, rebranding to Milestone AV Technologies. Laurie was the Vice President of Marketing until 2014, when the company set out to improve its level of service. Using Stanford's Design Thinking Innovation Framework, Laurie and her team interviewed customers and found the company needed to up its game in the "less manual, more digital" world. As a result of this project, Laurie assumed the vice president of customer experience role, while still retaining marketing responsibilities. The company continued to grow, until it was a close-to-$800-million organization that was acquired by Legrand. As Laurie explains, "One of the many reasons Legrand bought us was that we had a focus on CX, and [Legrand] wanted to do CX right."

When we interviewed the Legrand | AV teams for this book, I didn't have a clear picture of the company's culture, although I've known Laurie for years. During a break in the interviews, I turned to my colleague Diane Schnitker,[8] who accompanied me, and told her, "There's something different here, and I can't quite put my finger on it." She replied, "Oh, I know. Every single person has talked about how he or she recently talked with a customer. I don't think we've ever seen that before."

And she's right. As a culture, it was impressive how many people talk with customers frequently. What's even more impressive is that no one thinks this is unusual. But very few of the "customer experience" people we interviewed at other companies actually spend much time with customers! Laurie explains the seminal event that led to this focus on regularly talking with customers:

> I used to run all of marketing. And every year, my boss would come to me and ask, "What big ideas do you have?" I'd go back to my desk and do research on the net, talk to my coworkers, and come up with ideas. Yet, we never asked customers what they thought. Crazy, right? One year, we decided to do a complete rack builder[9] tool to help customers create their own AV racks online. Brilliant, right? This project enabled customers to build a system and order it. It was a complex project that used a lot of resources to create! A year later, we realized the usage was really low, so I decided to visit customers and ask why. One rack builder guy summed up all the comments: "I don't need a tool. I want to build that myself. That's what I do. I like your tool, but I just use it to check my work. I'm not going to order through your site because I often make changes on the fly." Whoa! Imagine how much money I would have saved if I would have asked customers first. And so, our empathy journey began. We started asking customers lots of "what would you want to do" kind of questions and realized you don't have to sit in front of your computer and come up with a plan because it builds itself just by talking to customers. Why would you ever do anything different?

And she doesn't. Laurie is always talking with customers. And it's not just her. When I interviewed her divisional president, he regretted that, as his role grew, it reduced how frequently he could talk with customers, now only about once a month, which is actually more than many of the CX leaders we interviewed! He also requires that anybody asking for investment shows him customer feedback to make sure any investment is based on the voice of the customer.

Training is a core component of Legrand | AV's customer experience toolbox. For years, Laurie has offered design thinking classes, both on her own and with Legrand | AV's preferred vendor. She also reaches out to partners and customers and teaches them design thinking. She even conducted design thinking exercises with an accounting team who couldn't get along! Legrand now offers employees regular CX Essentials classes, design thinking (both in person and online) classes, and CX courses targeted to executives, ensuring that all staff understand the core concepts.

Personal ownership is integral to how Laurie helps divisions adopt CX. As she explains:

> We do design thinking projects throughout the whole company to get even more buy-in. For example, we did employee interviews, asking, "How might we be the healthiest company ever?" They came back with great ideas. We listened, bucketed the themes, brainstormed, built prototypes, and tested them with employees. And then we implemented a healthy, affordable café option, yoga classes, and a bike club. And then employees knew we were serious. We listened, and we followed through. They were hooked. And they wanted to be part of what some called the design thinking movement.
>
> Many employees asked when they would get interviewed and how they could help on a customer prototype. Empathy works everywhere! Embedding it "physically" in the culture is equally as important. We have a room called the Nook where you see all our journey maps and all our personas. I take employees and customers through it all the time; we see products that we made through the design thinking framework, and we show the customer empathy interviews, themes created, and results. You see employees getting comfortable enough to say, "This is a real thing. And I believe in it." More importantly, they want to know how to get involved. So, now they're hooked, and they search for more information.

Legrand has established a three-phase approach toward designing its customer experience: Is it effortless? Does it build trust? And is there partnership? Laurie applied it to a project she recently ran: "We had some issues with invoicing. So, when we looked at it, we asked, 'Is the process effortless? Is there trust? Is there partnership?' And we worked to get it mapped out. It's essential we embed these three attributes into our company."

What I enjoyed about Laurie's work at Legrand is how she uses her personal passion to create organizational impact. Laurie isn't a numbers person, so she surrounds herself with those who are. But she's absolutely a customer-focused leader and has changed the dynamic so that employees throughout the company know it's useless to pitch ideas before getting customer feedback. This helps to validate ideas, and the constant persona interaction with customers helps employees develop new ideas regularly and prioritize based on how often a customer complains!

MANAGING CUSTOMER JOURNEYS

Our research showed that organizational complexity is one of the biggest challenges in improving journeys, and a big part of this is decision rights. Most journeys make their way across departments, and a common cause for customer friction is the handoffs across these departments.

For example, if we look at the journey of shipping manufacturing inputs to a customer, the departments involved include inside sales for receiving the order, shipping for gathering inventory and sending it out, logistics/transportation for managing the delivery, and a third-party shipping firm for handling the delivery, plus customer service for managing any issues that occur. The journey may also involve account management for bigger issues, manufacturing to make sure there is sufficient inventory, and other teams. Each department has its own reporting structure and KPIs, and the risk is that any updates to the journey can degrade an individual department's performance on its KPIs. For example, adding communication to create transparency requires more of the department doing that communication, which will interfere with its other activities.

Properly managing customer journeys requires dedicated resources, which are seldom a priority for organizations, and accountability, which is another issue. For example, an "ownerless" journey that crosses organizational boundaries typically faces a lack of accountability. A common example is onboarding—one of the most important journeys in a B2B customer life cycle—where there is frequently no single individual responsible for managing the experience. I have noted that the journey manager role is taking hold among European companies and starting to spread to the United States. The journey manager is accountable for working across departments to ensure the successful engagement of the customer.

Our survey told us that Change Makers were more likely to have journey managers on their teams (by a margin of two-to-one over Hopefuls), and Change Maker journey managers typically had more authority than Hopeful journey managers. (At Hopeful companies, 78 percent of journey managers could only advise those who had control over operational processes, whereas 75 percent of journey managers reporting to a Change Maker had at least some operational authority.)

Pointillist's research found almost the exact same outcome, citing that "68 percent of high performers have a dedicated role or team for customer journey management or analytics, versus only 31 percent of underperformers."[10]

In the summer of 2021, I asked my LinkedIn community about journey managers: "The concept of journey managers received a ton of buzz two years ago, but I haven't heard much lately. I'd love to hear from #CX practitioners whether you have assigned journey managers, and how that is working."[11]

Gary Batroff of Thunderhead reported, "I did a LinkedIn search of journey managers a couple days ago and it turned up ~230 in the

US. In looking at CX leaders building CX programs and teams, this is often one of the first roles filled."

Nicki Phillips-Lord, senior customer experience manager at M&G plc shared:

> I'm a huge advocate of journey managers and have seen it become a well-established and critical role within two different CX functions now. They worked really well in my previous organization where our team of journey managers, who sat in a centralized CX function, were assigned specific journeys. We also assigned journey owners; these were senior leaders in the operational or marketing team responsible for KPIs that the journey needed to hit.
>
> Together they, along with a cross-functional working group, worked to monitor customer and business metrics and ensure the right change was implemented. The journey manager was responsible for working with insight teams to collate reporting packs, drawing out key discussion points for monthly reviews and most importantly driving the core initiatives. The journey owner held accountability for the journey improvement and was the key decision-maker.

Andrew McInnes of Pointillist shared, "I'm seeing these roles a lot recently, particularly in large and complex orgs. . . . Some are dedicated roles. Some owners and managers have these responsibilities overlaid on top of their existing roles. Some of these folks have direct responsibility for experiences (e.g., they can drive redesign projects). Others are in more of an analytics and enablement position."

WHAT THE DATA SAY ABOUT JOURNEY OWNERSHIP

Our survey discovered that Change Makers were significantly more likely to assign journey managers to drive progress. A typical

CX leader tries to influence the entire customer life cycle, meaning that responsibilities are a mile wide and an inch deep. A journey manager is the opposite. They focus on one journey, such as onboarding, working across the organization to create a consistent outcome. Our survey showed that journey managers at Hopeful organizations primarily aggregate reporting data. Journey managers at Change Makers are more likely to have direct access to decision-makers and are thus able to lead the trade-off decisions required to create a successful journey. Journey managers are often existing staff members who are familiar with the journey, elevated to a more visible role that is responsible for driving improvements.

I define a journey manager as someone working directly with the teams to create outcomes. Like most customer experience roles, this person has tons of responsibility but no authority so must use change management to bring other teams around to creating an improved journey. I define a journey owner as a leader who takes responsibility for a specific cross-silo journey.

Looking again at onboarding, the journey owner may be a customer success executive who works with a member of operations (the journey manager) to improve the outcome. The journey manager does the day-to-day work, and the journey owner provides the oversight to help make the improvements a success. This may feel unnecessarily complicated, but unless your organization creates a dedicated onboarding function, it's often the best way to align teams to create a better journey.

If value results from the CX Loyalty Flywheel, emotions accelerate it, data show you how it works, then change management lubricates the flywheel. When all your teams are aligned on what customers need and understand their roles in creating those outcomes, it ensures the flywheel doesn't get stuck. Without it, you may invest in customer experience, but the teams may not do what it takes for that investment to stick. You can communicate that trust is your Emotional North Star, but if employees don't know or care, then that trust will never be created. Change management is the skill that ensures the flywheel keeps spinning.

■■■

The first three parts of this book focus on how to build the infrastructure needed to create great customer experiences. But, once that's done, what does a customer experience leader need to do to launch CX and make it sustainable? Getting buy-in is a starting point. There are four critical steps the leader needs to take:

1. Create a compelling case for change.
2. Activate executives.
3. Move middle management.
4. Engage employees.

In chapters 11 and 12, we will examine these steps in depth and provide you with a game plan to implement your own CX strategy, with support from across the organization and with the resources you need.

Cari's Story

Dale and Cari continued to prepare for their CX council. Over their first six months, they established a common agenda:

1. Share new information on the customer experience—relationship survey scores, research, and the latest transactional survey scores.
2. Focus on the Dirty Dozen—the top twelve issues facing customers.
3. Report on initiatives to solve the Dirty Dozen challenges.
4. Highlight new entrants to the Dirty Dozen.
5. Assign ownership to new Dirty Dozen issues.

As she established the program, Cari explained the process to Stephen. "Sharing the updates—like the latest survey results you put together—can be covered in two to three minutes, or take as much as fifteen minutes to cover when major items come in," she said. "We email the Dirty Dozen list in advance, so we don't have to spend much time reviewing old items. As you know, we created the Dirty Dozen list based on a combination of surveys and issue-resolution data. I really want our executives to get uncomfortable seeing the same issues show up for multiple months, so they feel a push to resolve them.

"The CX council then assigns each new issue to one executive. They can't send delegates to the meeting—if they are unavailable, their team goes unrepresented—and those who don't attend seem to receive more action items! We have each leader share the items they're assigned to.

"When we get new items, it's typically because old ones were retired, but major issues can reshuffle the list. The team discusses which leader is best to own it, and that leader reports on progress at next month's meeting. We share copies of the notes with Shirley [Sycamore's CEO], which helps drive progress, as she's known to ask her direct reports about progress on resolving the Dirty Dozen challenges assigned to them. This support is so crucial at keeping executive engagement—no one wants to be unprepared when she asks the questions!"

My Thoughts

Executive engagement is critical to a successful CX program. When I was with the health insurance organization, my boss's boss felt that customer experience was a waste of time. Instead of trying to fight that battle, I decided to drive a bottom-up approach. It failed, and it shouldn't have been a surprise. While everybody loves the story of a bottom-up initiative, ADKAR reminds us that change dies without executive reinforcement, and Kotter shows the importance of a strong change coalition. Too many programs die a slow death because executives don't have a role. As a result, while they give lip service to the importance of CX, they don't prioritize actions that will drive it forward. As we analyzed CX programs, the most successful focused on governance, combining executive actions with proof that CX improves organizational outcomes.

CHAPTER 11

What Do I Need to Do to Get the Support of Senior Leaders?

CHANGE BEGINS WITH GIVING EXECUTIVES AND EMPLOYEES a reason for the change, represented by Awareness and Desire in ADKAR and "create a sense of urgency" in Kotter's model. Posters claiming that "the customer is our top priority" don't accomplish this. Even the organizations with the least effective customer experience have signs on the wall trumpeting "Customers First!" Customer-focused statements are important but hardly sufficient. Employees see when your actions don't back up your words, and they know when to pay attention and when to ignore you. Even Wells Fargo had a customer promise at the same time they were creating fake accounts. It's important to make a big promise, but it's more important to back that up with action. But let's start with that big promise. **Your case for change must show why and how to change.** This is the heart of our discussion in the chapter.

Steps to Getting the Buy-In of Senior Leaders

Engage with leadership first, then move on to frontline staff. In this chapter, I'll walk through the steps to get leadership buy-in, based on what has worked for our Change Makers. In the next chapter, we'll move on to the frontline staff.

CREATE A COMPELLING CASE FOR CHANGE

As reported in Adam Grant's book *Originals*, when analyzing organizational environmental initiatives, management professors Lynne Andersson and Thomas Bateman found that the most critical difference in outcomes was the sense of urgency created. Employees and leaders are continually being asked to change, adopt new processes, and efficiently deal with requests for action. It's only when there's a proven need to act do they get and stay active. Kotter found similar results, showing where over 50 percent of change efforts fall short is in developing an urgent case for change.

What constitutes a sense of emergency or an urgent need to change old habits and practices? There are several common scenarios. Executives have called me because their customers have complained that the company is too difficult to do business with. They tell me that these calls have taken them by surprise, but it's hardly shocking. These executives do not have an early warning signal to alert them to customer unhappiness outside of standard NPS reports (and most of their executive clients don't fill out surveys). Without Emotional North Stars and the ability to track the behavioral data that suggest customers have issues, they're at risk for just this sort of wake-up call.

Typically, the customer has built up a ton of frustration over time, and the easiest way for the customer to explain what is wrong is to say, "Your company is too difficult to work with." This anecdote can spur action, creating that sense of urgency. While this can be frustrating for the CX leader who's been working on this very issue for years, it does present the opportunity to drive change.

The second reason takes us back to Action 1, when a retention or share of wallet issue rears its ugly head and the cause is determined to be a poor customer experience. In this situation, the CX leader has the opportunity to demonstrate how the experience impacts the important KPIs and to drive action.

Absent of these outside influences, it is up to you to create that sense of urgency. Use a combination of emotions and data to make your case. Show how a specific percent of your customers are frustrated, and how those customers churn more often, as we have discussed throughout this book.

A common outcome of this case for change is a customer experience vision that communicates the future customer experience. CX thought leader (and friend) Megan Burns recommends three criteria for a CX vision[1]—make it clear, easy to remember, and useful. The usefulness of the vision cannot be understated. Employees should feel confident that, when they follow the vision, the decisions they make are the right ones.

The CX vision needs to flow from your brand. United Airlines requires a very different CX vision than Southwest. That doesn't mean that United has to settle for a lame CX vision—just that trying to build its CX vision around creating a fun experience won't be believable, while it will be for Southwest. There should be a clear line from your brand through your strategy to your CX vision.

This vision needs to be specific, showing *how* the experience will be different, such as Dow's "We aim to be easy, enjoyable, and effective to do business with through all our digital and personal interactions." What impressed me is that, as I interviewed Dow's employees, they all shared this vision unprompted, displaying obvious alignment. This vision also gives clarity, especially how the teams emphasize *enjoyable* as an outcome.

Inherent to this is the need to make this vision specific to your customers. Megan cites the example of Warby Parker, whose customer vision statement is "We believe that buying glasses should be easy and fun. It should leave you happy and good-looking, with money in your pocket." This fits the Warby Parker brand and gives solid direction as to what the experience should be. Experience designers should think twice about adding expensive options. (It goes without saying that this vision also guides them to avoid designing ugly frames.) Another benefit of this approach is that it is unique to Warby Parker; it certainly won't work for Dow or UKG!

USING JOURNEY MAPPING TO CREATE A VISION

Journey maps are a Change Maker's best friend, as their graphic nature helps create the Desire to change the experience, as well as to communicate the Knowledge of the current journey. Take a look at the current-state journey map from a global B2B services client (figure 11-1). It shows the current journey's Moments of Truth and friction points in a compelling way, highlighting how Phil's journey can be very positive or negative, depending on the organization's performance, while CIO Alex essentially disappears during much of the journey. This is a clear call to action to improve outcomes.

The client organization's customer success leader, Percy Rose, and his team then worked across the company to create a future-state version of the journey map that included a vision of the future, as shown in figure 11-2. You can see how the company used the current-state map to identify not only friction points but also the missed opportunity to engage Alex in the experience. Percy and his team then built a cross-functional vision as to how the future journey could look, including the initiatives required to bring this vision to life.

Percy and his team now have two powerful artifacts to communicate the current challenges, as well as a vision of how the company can come together as an organization to create a better journey for its customers.

ACTIVATE EXECUTIVES

The leading cause of death for CX programs is passive executive support—leaders who say all the right things but don't actively support customer experience in their day-to-day activities. ADKAR incorporates the need to create Desire and for the change to be Reinforced, both of which require executive participation. Kotter's language is more visual, talking about the need to create a "guiding coalition." Both models agree that, without giving executives an active role, your program will die a slow death.

Gaining active involvement first requires exposing your executives to the current customer experience, and then giving leaders specific roles and helping them to hold each other accountable for the results.

Executives are busy, and it's natural to prioritize immediate concerns over the long-term impact of visiting customers. But if they don't regularly visit customers, how do they truly understand the customer experience? It helps to recruit one senior executive to set the example and motivate the rest. It's especially critical to understand the customer experience in B2B companies, where the experience is opaque. Retail executives can stop by a store and healthcare executives visit their doctors. But what do you do if you're a B2B company? You can't just show up and work a day in your customer's factory.

IBM provides an excellent example of a way to engage executives. When Lou Gerstner became its CEO in the early 1990s, the company was in trouble. IBM's hardware strategy wasn't working, and the company was hemorrhaging money. To tackle this problem, Gerstner instituted Operation Bear Hug, sending his top fifty executives out to meet with at least five customers each. They weren't allowed to sell, but only to listen and document their learnings in memos. Then those executives' two hundred direct reports had to do the same thing. The learnings pushed the company to a new strategic direction that led to today's very different IBM.

Xerox has the Xerox Corporate Focus Executive Program, where

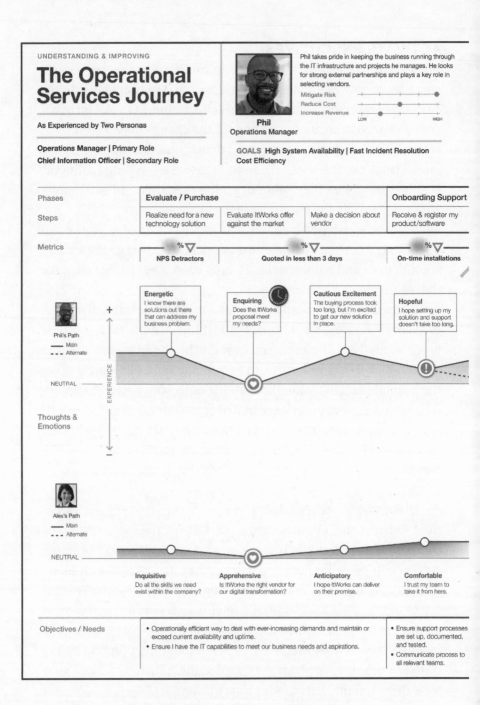

The Operational Services Journey

As Experienced by Two Personas

Operations Manager | Primary Role
Chief Information Officer | Secondary Role

Phil takes pride in keeping the business running through the IT infrastructure and projects he manages. He looks for strong external partnerships and plays a key role in selecting vendors.

Mitigate Risk
Reduce Cost
Increase Revenue
LOW — HIGH

Phil
Operations Manager

GOALS High System Availability | Fast Incident Resolution
Cost Efficiency

Phases	Evaluate / Purchase			Onboarding Support
Steps	Realize need for a new technology solution	Evaluate ItWorks offer against the market	Make a decision about vendor	Receive & register my product/software
Metrics	—% ▽— NPS Detractors	—% ▽— Quoted in less than 3 days		—% ▽— On-time installations

Phil's Path
— Main
- - - Alternate

Energetic
I know there are solutions out there that can address my business problem.

Enquiring
Does the ItWorks proposal meet my needs?

Cautious Excitement
The buying process took too long, but I'm excited to get our new solution in place.

Hopeful
I hope setting up my solution and support doesn't take too long.

EXPERIENCE

NEUTRAL

Thoughts & Emotions

Alex's Path
— Main
- - - Alternate

NEUTRAL

Inquisitive
Do all the skills we need exist within the company?

Apprehensive
Is ItWorks the right vendor for our digital transformation?

Anticipatory
I hope ItWorks can deliver on their promise.

Comfortable
I trust my team to take it from here.

Objectives / Needs
• Operationally efficient way to deal with ever-increasing demands and maintain or exceed current availability and uptime.
• Ensure I have the IT capabilities to meet our business needs and aspirations.

• Ensure support processes are set up, documented, and tested.
• Communicate process to all relevant teams.

Figure 11-1: Sample operational services journey of global B2B services company.

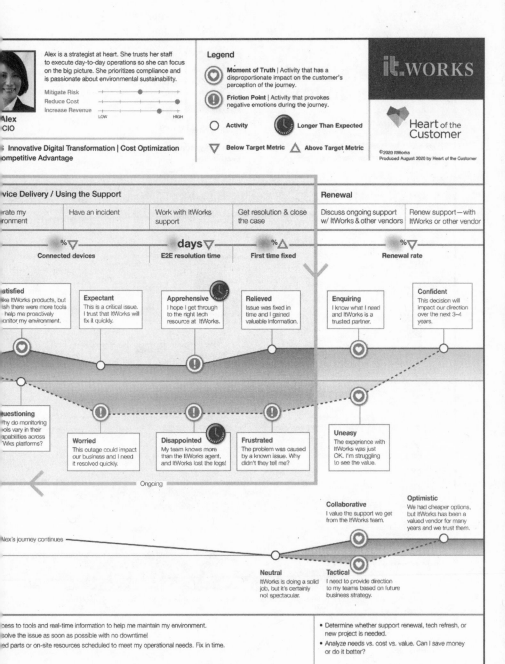

Alex is a strategist at heart. She trusts her staff to execute day-to-day operations so she can focus on the big picture. She prioritizes compliance and is passionate about environmental sustainability.

Mitigate Risk
Reduce Cost
Increase Revenue
LOW — HIGH

Alex
CIO

Innovative Digital Transformation | Cost Optimization
ompetitive Advantage

it.WORKS

Heart of the Customer

©2020 ItWorks
Produced August 2020 by Heart of the Customer

vice Delivery / Using the Support

rate my ronment	Have an incident	Work with ItWorks support	Get resolution & close the case

Renewal

Discuss ongoing support w/ ItWorks & other vendors	Renew support—with ItWorks or other vendor

%▽ **Connected devices**   **days**▽ **E2E resolution time**   %△ **First time fixed**   %▽ **Renewal rate**

atisfied
ike ItWorks products, but ish there were more tools help me proactively onitor my environment.

Expectant
This is a critical issue. I trust that ItWorks will fix it quickly.

Apprehensive
I hope I get through to the right tech resource at ItWorks.

Relieved
Issue was fixed in time and I gained valuable information.

Enquiring
I know what I need and ItWorks is a trusted partner.

Confident
This decision will impact our direction over the next 3–4 years.

uestioning
hy do monitoring ols vary in their apabilities across Wks platforms?

Worried
This outage could impact our business and I need it resolved quickly.

Disappointed
My team knows more than the ItWorks agent, and ItWorks lost the logs!

Frustrated
The problem was caused by a known issue. Why didn't they tell me?

Uneasy
The experience with ItWorks was just OK. I'm struggling to see the value.

Ongoing

Collaborative
I value the support we get from the ItWorks team.

Optimistic
We had cheaper options, but ItWorks has been a valued vendor for many years and we trust them.

Alex's journey continues

Neutral
ItWorks is doing a solid job, but it's certainly not spectacular.

Tactical
I need to provide direction to my teams based on future business strategy.

cess to tools and real-time information to help me maintain my environment.
solve the issue as soon as possible with no downtime!
ed parts or on-site resources scheduled to meet my operational needs. Fix in time.

- Determine whether support renewal, tech refresh, or new project is needed.
- Analyze needs vs. cost vs. value. Can I save money or do it better?

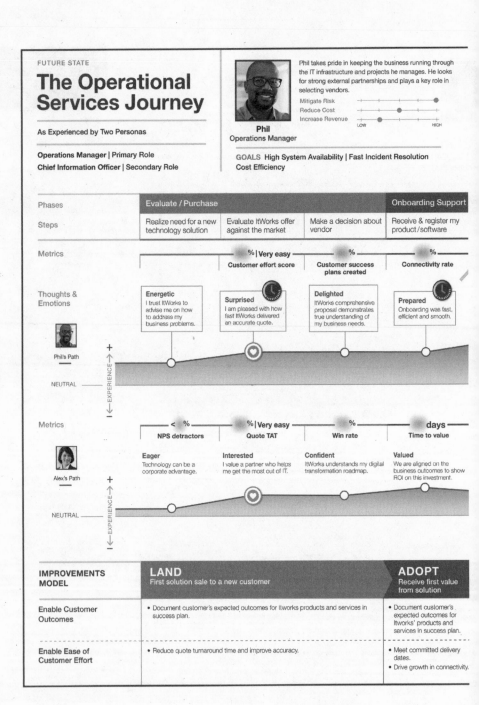

Figure 11-2: Sample future-state operational services journey.

Alex is a strategist at heart. She trusts her staff to execute day-to-day operations so she can focus on the big picture. She prioritizes compliance and is passionate about environmental sustainability.

Mitigate Risk
Reduce Cost
Increase Revenue

LOW — HIGH

Alex
CIO

...LS Innovative Digital Transformation | Cost Optimization
Competitive Advantage

Legend

Moment of Truth | Activity that has a disproportionate impact on the customer's perception of the journey.

Time Critical Activity

Activity

it.WORKS

Heart of the **Customer**

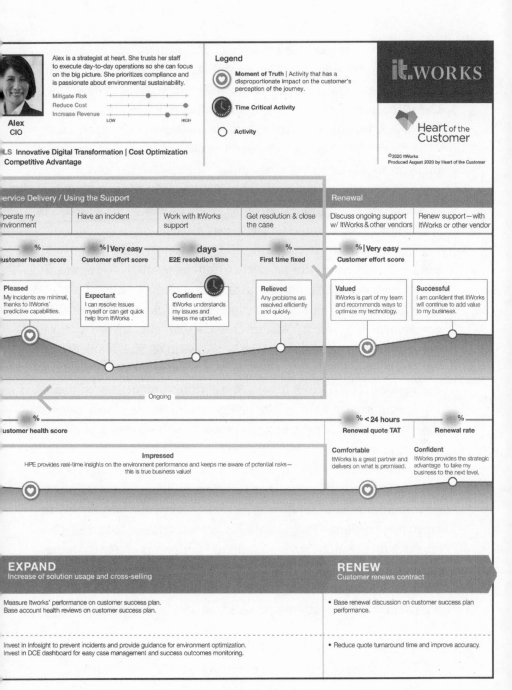

...ervice Delivery / Using the Support

...perate my nvironment	Have an incident	Work with ItWorks support	Get resolution & close the case	Discuss ongoing support w/ ItWorks & other vendors	Renew support — with ItWorks or other vendor

Renewal

___%	___%	Very easy	___days	___%	___%	Very easy
...ustomer health score	Customer effort score	E2E resolution time	First time fixed	Customer effort score		

Pleased
My incidents are minimal, thanks to ItWorks' predictive capabilities.

Expectant
I can resolve issues myself or can get quick help from ItWorks.

Confident
ItWorks understands my issues and keeps me updated.

Relieved
Any problems are resolved efficiently and quickly.

Valued
ItWorks is part of my team and recommends ways to optimize my technology.

Successful
I am confident that ItWorks will continue to add value to my business.

Ongoing

___%		___% < 24 hours	___%
...ustomer health score		Renewal quote TAT	Renewal rate

Impressed
HPE provides real-time insights on the environment performance and keeps me aware of potential risks — this is true business value!

Comfortable
ItWorks is a great partner and delivers on what is promised.

Confident
ItWorks provides the strategic advantage to take my business to the next level.

EXPAND
Increase of solution usage and cross-selling

Measure Itworks' performance on customer success plan.
Base account health reviews on customer success plan.

Invest in Infosight to prevent incidents and provide guidance for environment optimization.
Invest in DCE dashboard for easy case management and success outcomes monitoring.

RENEW
Customer renews contract

• Base renewal discussion on customer success plan performance.

• Reduce quote turnaround time and improve accuracy.

top executives are assigned to an account team for one of their clients, similar to what Darin Byrne at Wolters Kluwer shared.[2] Additionally, Xerox assigned corporate officers to serve as its Customer Care Officers of the Day. This put these officers directly in touch with customers, helping them to internalize their customer experiences.

According to Xerox's website, "The Officer of the Day has three main priorities: listen to the customer, address the customer's problem and take the necessary action to fix the underlying cause. It is a time-honored commitment to our customer focus." This helps keep the customer top of mind for these executives.

Use the lessons from Darin, IBM, and Xerox, and find ways to send your executives out to meet customers regularly. Once executives begin to understand the current state of the customer experience, give them active roles in designing it, which is a practice called governance. Since most CX issues cross departments, involving those departmental leaders is one of the best ways to resolve conflicts.

Roxie Strohmenger at UKG provides more detail on how she engages with UKG's executives. She conducts recurring CX Steering Committee meetings, involving senior leaders and C-level executives, in which she reviews key topics she wants to socialize or get guidance on to help overcome roadblocks to customer success. Historically, these meetings focused on reviewing reports. Now, Roxie uses the meetings to inform, manage obstacles and opportunities, and invite executives to actively participate in creating solutions. This also helps the executives have full perspective on organization-wide impacts across the entire customer journey, as there can be the potential to not always have full line of sight to the ripple effects—how a decision in one sphere impacts another from the customer perspective. As she explains:

> We have a recurring Steering Committee meeting with senior leaders and C-level executives, and this is where we share the work that's being done. But more importantly, we ask, "What are the roadblocks, what are the barriers?"

This gets them bought into participating in CX actively because they're part of the solutioning conversation. This is way more effective than just offering a high-level read-out—"This is what was done; this is what we're going to do next." Instead, we discuss, "Here's what we need to focus on because we have this hiccup or this element. Let's brainstorm it as an entire company and understand the ramifications of the effects from one decision to another from the customer perspective." So, engaging the senior executives has helped tremendously.

Roxie also conducts recurring meetings with each executive, discussing key strategic initiatives and how her CX strategy team can connect the executive and customer experience. Her team also attends and presents at each business unit's monthly or quarterly review meeting to showcase the work her team has done and the impact the team is having.

Nancy at Hagerty also talks about the criticality of an ongoing effort to engage executives:

I would say that, especially when you have a mature program, executive engagement ebbs and flows. You have to constantly reinvent how you engage with them. We used to do a quarterly report, but as you get out of that find-and-fix mode, how do you keep them engaged? I sit on the executive council, so we kick off that meeting with a client or member story every meeting, and that's been great. We used to do these lengthy stat reports, and I could see engagement waning, so now we use a lot of video feedback to highlight a pain point or a positive loyalty driver.

But I think one of the biggest challenges for our roles is just constantly re-engaging the executives. Luckily, we are blessed to have a culture and a CEO and owner who constantly reinforce that the customer needs to be in the center

of everything we're doing. Of course, we fall short sometimes, so that's where this executive engagement is critical.
If we have a billing issue, we're investing in that and we're
fixing it. If we have a customer-facing issue, we're all over it.

And this engagement helps us to justify the need to
invest in foundational CX capabilities, such as new listening tools, survey tools, analytics for digital listening, things
like that.

Creating a sustainable customer-focused approach requires first
exposing executives to the customer experience, then giving them
specific roles, holding each other accountable to efforts to improve
the customer experience.

Hydro-Québec: Creating a Customer Experience Movement at a Monopoly

The case for change goes beyond simply creating the vision,
requiring you to surround it with communications showing
why continuing to work on the customer experience is critical for the organization's—and the individual's—success. It's
not B2B, but one of my favorite examples of showing the
importance of the customer experience is Canada's largest
utility, Hydro-Québec. The company is a monopoly, so it may
seem an unlikely place for a customer experience focus. Yet,
Hydro-Québec's leadership saw the threat of deregulation and
knew it was important to focus on customers to ensure better
outcomes today, as well as tomorrow.

Hydro-Québec won the overall prize at the 2020 North
American Customer Centricity Awards. In its submission, it
explains how the utility built its case for change:

> Our sector has changed very little in recent decades.
> Electricity providers have been generating and deliv-
> ering electricity in a way where consumers have been

considered passive. However, with adoption and development of new technologies, customers are likely to have more options and could play an active role in the electric grid of the future. In fact, they are already starting to produce, sell and even exchange electricity. This trend will eventually completely change the relationship between clients and service providers. Moreover, customer expectations are also changing. Today's customers compare their experience to their interactions with technology giants such as Amazon, Apple and Google.

In this context, we had to reimagine our relationship with customers, our business model, and the optimization of the electric grid. Therefore, in 2015 Hydro-Québec set out to become a leader in terms of customer service and customer experience. This led to the development of a road map—called Customer-Centered Culture 2017–2021—designed to engage every employee in fostering a customer-centric culture and adopting the related mindset.

Even though Hydro-Québec is a monopoly, it used the risk of competition to create its case for change.

Hydro-Québec began its customer experience efforts by exposing executives to the current state of the customer experience, represented by support calls. Most companies locate contact centers in secondary markets miles away from headquarters, where rent and staff are cheaper. The unintended consequence is that it is "out of sight, out of mind," and executives have no exposure to what happens in this critical customer-facing channel.[3] Hydro-Québec addressed this situation by asking executives to visit and participate on calls at the contact center. Executives didn't lead the calls;[4] they were introduced at the beginning and asked follow-up questions at the end. The program really took off when their former CFO attended. Eric Filion, the president of distribution, tells the story with relish:

> When she [the CFO] came to visit us, there was tremendous excitement because at that time, executives

rarely visited. On one call, a customer contacted us because he was behind on payments, and she and the contact center rep had an engaging conversation on how to handle this and how much to ask the customer to pay.

The photos we shared of her visiting went viral, and suddenly every executive wanted to visit. I received many calls asking, "When can I come? I want to show my support, too!" But executives were also nervous, as they didn't want to make a mistake in front of the team, so we provided them training on the contact center and how to participate in calls. This executive shadowing provided a much stronger visibility of our customer experience to our executive team and created buy-in for our customer experience approach.

This led to a far more expansive customer experience effort. As Director of Client Experience, Martine Chartrand explains:

The employees involved in collecting and analyzing the customer's voice are also helping our culture to evolve. The goal is to use customers' insights in real time at every stage of their experience to improve, personalize, and simplify our offers and services. By getting to know our customers better, we're able to make insightful decisions and thus, improve their experience. Each month, we hold a customer voice forum—a community that includes members of senior management—where we listen to customer calls, share thoughts on the customer experience, and identify areas for improvement. In this forum, the customer literally has a place at the decision table.

Hydro-Québec's efforts focused on creating desire in its executive team for a more active approach to customer experience, which flowed down to the staff. In its submission, the utility showed multiple examples of employees—both unionized and not—committing to improve the customer experience.

Hydro-Québec even created cards for ambassadors to give to friends and neighbors who encountered troubles with the utility, providing a special phone number for them to call to resolve their issues. Martine further explains:

> The frontline employees who interact directly with customers [line workers, customer service representatives, vegetation control team, and technicians] are considered our sensors in the field to whom we listen and provide support. They receive customer orientation training through classroom sessions, video capsules, and coaching. The ambassador line has also been made available to all employees to give them the means to take care of their customers, whatever their needs are.

> In 2019, over 1,375 calls were handled by the ambassador line to support customers with specific questions or concerns. This further reinforced the importance of focusing on the customers—even for a monopoly.

Engage Middle Management

The life of a middle manager is hard. Managers are promoted based on their abilities to follow a process and do a job as outlined. Radical innovation is typically discouraged in favor of small changes. Social scientists even have a name for this—"the middle-status conformity effect"—which shows that simply being *called* a middle manager lowers creativity. It can be tough to convince middle managers that they need to change how they operate in order to improve the customer experience. While leaders and frontline employees generally see how customer-focused change benefits the organization, middle managers are secure in meeting KPIs that provide job security and a bonus. Success requires showing how they can benefit from a customer experience focus.

KPIs measure how a business unit is performing, such as working capital, customer complaints, or process time. Each is connected in some way to the customer experience, but that linkage isn't always clear. Since middle managers are judged according to the performance of their respective KPIs, successful CX leaders co-opt these metrics and demonstrate to the manager the link between performance metrics and the customer experience. As Jen likes to tell Dow's managers, "An improved customer experience will make it easier for you to accomplish your goals." Use the examples provided in this book to prove your case to the middle management group. There are two critical approaches toward KPIs: replace those that lead to bad behavior and co-opt the rest.

KPIs were created for good reasons but may have the unintended consequences of harming the customer experience. For example, customer complaints are clearly bad for both your organization and customers. But when customer service is responsible for both measuring and managing the complaints KPI, staff can circumvent the system by closing complaints before the issue is fully resolved. This artificially improves the KPI but frustrates customers and doesn't solve the problem. More than a few companies have discovered that, in order to look better on KPI scorecards, cases are prematurely closed or never logged in the first place. Holding customer service employees accountable to the number or length of complaints invites them to game the system. When held accountable to the number of complaints or length of time to resolution, even those with the purest intent can convince themselves that this issue doesn't require logging. It's better to separate the accountability for the issue from those who service it.

That's what Jen and her team did at Dow, addressing the KPI on the length of time it takes to resolve an issue. They first mapped the complaints experience to understand the scope of the problem, including how it impacted customers and enjoyability and thus, their future orders. (The flywheel in action.) Jen's team discovered that teams were transferring tickets to other departments because they didn't want to show too many complaints with their names attached. This had the unintended consequence of delaying resolution.

The CX team then met with a customer experience governance team made up of executives from across departments and geographies. Their goal was to shorten the time it took to resolve complaints, and their constraint was to do it without increasing headcount. They accomplished this goal by creating a new organization to own and manage complaints through to resolution, staffed with existing customer service employees. The company piloted this effort in Latin America and discovered that the team was able to get to the root causes of complaints and respond to the customer more quickly than had been the case previously. As a result, the KPI improved, as did both customer and Dow outcomes, without additional investment. After a successful trial, this process was scaled globally.

Another common example of unfortunate contact center KPIs is measuring average handle time (AHT). The reason to make this a KPI is logical; long calls are expensive, which encourage contact center employees to manage their time. Unfortunately, this creates unintended consequences in which employees end calls as quickly as they can, often before confirming the issue is resolved. I am amazed that, with research that clearly shows how this KPI hurts the customer experience, I still find it in many organizations. I remember one time I called a customer service provider with multiple questions. When the first question was answered, the rep asked me to call back with my second question so I wouldn't ruin his call handle time! AHT is a rational concern, but using it as a KPI leads to repeat calls, as agents often don't take the time to explore the other needs of the callers or to ensure advice or a solution to the first problem worked.

In the *Harvard Business Review* article "Call Length Is the Worst Way to Measure Customer Service,"[5] authors Pete Slease, Rick DeLisi, and Matthew Dixon report that companies that move away from AHT as a metric saw almost no increase in costs, as the longer calls were offset by fewer repeat calls.

Most KPIs are not so actively destructive to the customer experience. Many of them are easily addressed through customer experience, assuming you implemented the ideas from Action 1: Point the Flywheel. Remember that Roxie showed that, when customers are confident, they are far more likely to use self-service when issues arise, helping the KPI of reducing calls. It's easier to reduce product defects if you create such a strong experience that customers are willing to partner with you to track down the source of a software bug or a manufacturing defect. Co-opting KPIs is the best way to gain the trust of middle managers.

■ ■ ■

Change management requires effective sponsorship, typically from the C-suite. Change rolls downhill, which is why Kotter places "Build a guiding coalition" as the second step, right after a powerful case for change (which is required to create that coalition).

It begins by exposing the current state of the customer experience to those executives, which requires personal exposure. As we'll discuss in the next chapter, Roxie sent executives to interview customers as part of her journey mapping initiative, helping those executives understand the good and bad of the current experience, and the reasons behind that dichotomy of experience. We will also discuss strategies to ensure change management is sustainable by involving your frontline employees. It will likely not come as a surprise to discover that customer experience and change management are a natural combination.

Cari's Story

Dale and Cari were getting ready for the upcoming CX council meeting. Dale asked Cari for an update on the system integrator standardization project, which was tasked with ensuring that all partners could create outcomes like Creative Consulting's. "I'm sorry," Cari responded. "I've been working on the customer experience training initiative, and the meetings often overlap. And Stephen's been so focused on the reporting that he also can't attend."

"Well, working on project teams really isn't Stephen's strength," Dale concurred. "We've had some terrific momentum across the organization. Teams are really starting to get how customer experience impacts customers. But they still don't always understand how their specific roles tie in to CX. This training will help, but it's not really where I need you to spend your time—I need you pushing these teams to improve the experience. Shirley asked whether you had the resources needed to keep up the momentum. I think it's time for us to bring in additional help."

"The CEO's asking about me? I don't know if that's good or bad," thought Cari. But out loud, she said, "Well, I could certainly use help. I've never designed training before, so it's not really a strength of mine. I'm also not so great at creating communications. I just want to say, 'Do what's right for the customer. It's not that hard!' But I don't think that's probably the most effective message."

"Yeah, that email to the service team saying, 'Get this *#&$ fixed' probably wasn't your finest moment, either. You're creating impact, but if we want to keep moving the needle, we're going to need to bring in some help. What do you need?"

Cari was ready for this. "If I'm going to continue to bring along leadership, I need people who can work across the organization. The first person I need is a CX architect—someone who can work with Stephen to take his great research and integrate it into our projects to ensure our work is targeted against customer needs. This architect may do some customer interviews but is less of a voice-of-the-customer person and more of a designer.

"The second person I need is a communicator, a change manager type. Someone to work with the internal communications team to build training and messaging across the organization.

This person can also help Stephen amp up his dashboards, so they look less like something that Excel puked up."

"Yeah," Dale agreed. "Stephen does great work, but he isn't a designer. Shirley's seeing the results you're driving and gave me approval to bring in two people. I don't really get this architect role, but it seems like you have a solid plan, so let's go for it. The way I see it, you and I own the executive relationships, and these two new people are working across the larger organization under your guidance. I may need to be careful, or I may be working for you some day!"

"Well," Cari thought, "McDonald's did put their chief customer officer in charge of marketing. Who knows?" But out loud, she just replied, "Thanks! I'll get those requisitions out right away."

My Thoughts

Change management is critical for customer experience, but it's tough to manage that while you're leading the overall program. It requires communication skills and the time to develop specific messages for different parts of the organization. While some organizations have an internal change management or employee communications group that CX can leverage, most organizations either don't have this capability or those that do exist are overwhelmed with existing needs. So, it often requires bringing in a resource who is already trained in change management.

The CX architect is another way to spread impact in project-based organizations. This role is a combination of designer and researcher, bringing design thinking and customer research to project teams. They are typically assigned to the organization's most important projects, bringing in the voice of the customer. Their function is to help the company make financially sound decisions in the short term while also developing an improved customer experience to build long-term growth.

I most often see the CX architect in B2C or B2B2C organizations, which likely speaks to the lower maturity of B2B programs. I first heard about the role when I interviewed Marlanges Simar for my blog.[6] She shared how she partners with her company's voice-of-the-customer team to help bring together the latest customer data with a broader understanding of how the business's actions affect its customers' experiences. Essentially, this role adds actionability to the voice of the customer, connecting customer needs with their project teams. It's a great role to consider as your teams grow.

CHAPTER 12

How Do I Engage My Frontline Staff?

NOW THAT YOU HAVE EXECUTIVES ALIGNED AGAINST THE power of customer experience, it's time to engage your employees. It is critical to start with executives. I've witnessed multiple examples where the CX leader started by engaging the frontline. They created a program where employees sign up to be "CX Advocates," giving feedback and sharing the program in their teams. This works great for a few months! But then, employees' day-to-day work starts to intrude. They show up at fewer meetings. The employees stop spreading the word because they're not able to keep up with what the CX team is doing. And, eventually, the program dies. This won't happen when leadership is engaged, as they will *encourage* the CX Advocates, especially if those same leaders nominated the advocates.

Engaging the employee base is even more critical in B2B organizations, where typically 90 percent of employees have never met a customer in person. Giving them a vision of what the customer experience could be, and its impact to the organization, is a great first step. But don't tell people you're "changing" them. Use the capabilities of change management, but I prefer to use words like *activating employees* instead. Nobody wants to be changed, but they may be fine with being activated.

Engage Employees, But Don't Call It "Change Management"

As Adam Grant shared in his book *Originals*, "The most inspiring way to convey a vision is to outsource it to the people who are actually affected by it. . . . People are inspired to achieve the highest performance when leaders describe a vision and then invite a customer to bring it to life with a personal story." This also applies to employees. Share the vision, then invite them to discover ways to improve the customer experience. That will build the Desire to follow through with the new experience design.

Just don't call it "change management." Nobody wants to *be* changed. Instead, Change Makers use terms like *activation* to show how they are involving employees in the effort.

Since they can't bring all their employees to the contact center or out to visit customers, Change Makers adopt different methods to bring the customer experience to life for employees. One of the most overlooked change management approaches is to specifically link employees' jobs to the customer experience. It's tough to be customer centric if you don't know how your role impacts customers. This is straightforward for some—every contact center employee knows how they impact customers. But other times it isn't that simple. Sam Wegman is the Vice President of Customer Experience at Univar Solutions. She recalls how, early in her career, she was in accounts payable and didn't see any connection to the customer. As she explains it, "It wasn't until I was promoted to customer service that I realized how my work in accounts payable impacted customers. If I was late with a payment, our vendor didn't ship us new products. Which meant our customers couldn't order it from us, creating severe issues for them. But at the time, I never understood how critical my role was."

Now that she leads customer experience, ensuring that everyone from finance to IT understands how their roles impact customers is a central part of her program.

Connect Employee Activities to Customer Outcomes

We can demonstrate the connection between employees and customers by doing a linkage exercise, which works particularly well as a team meeting activity. Start with the work the team does—let's say it's inventory control in a manufacturing plant, which doesn't *seem* related to customers. Identify the team's tasks and work forward to the impact on the customer. In this case, the team is responsible for making sure that the plant has the raw materials it needs to hit the production targets. While the inventory control team likely feels disconnected from customers because it is focused on suppliers, as you do the exercise, it becomes clear to the team that customers can't be successful if the team fails to do its work efficiently and well. Begin with the tasks the team carries out (e.g., maintain records of inventory and audit those) and who is impacted by those tasks (e.g., the manufacturing line).

1. If the inventory control team doesn't do its job well, who does that impact and how? (e.g., the manufacturing line can't hit its daily targets).

2. Next, what does that impact? (The production line can't hit its quota for that product, which means it needs to switch to another product to keep the line busy.)

3. Continue the process until you get to the customer. There may be branching lines, which, in this case, will result in the following:

4. The manufacturing line will lose four hours of productivity as it is forced to switch to another product.

5. Customers who needed the original product will either have to wait until we can get the supplies or our safety stock will be reduced, creating risk.

6. Those customers who couldn't get their products won't be able to hit their quotas for their own customers because they're waiting on us.

7. Another branching line: Since we're a lean operation, that four hours of missed productivity will mean either that we're not able to keep up with demand for other products or that we'll need to work overtime to make it up.

8. Working overtime will increase costs, which will eventually be passed on to customers, costing them more.

9. And a third branching line: If we solve the need by sending them our safety stock, then if another customer suddenly orders more products, we can't fulfill that order.

10. That other customer will buy from our competitors, which hurts our business—and that customer may lose business, too, if they can't find sufficient stock to fulfill their orders.

The exercise helps teams understand how they impact customers. It's a good idea to walk through this with the department's leaders first, so if the team gets stuck, you can give suggestions to help them see that, no matter how far removed they are from the customer, they have a role.

This effort reminds me of the story of President John F. Kennedy when he visited NASA. The story goes that he spoke with a janitor and asked what he does at NASA. "Well, Mr. President," the janitor responded, "I'm helping put a man on the moon."

Your organization's vision likely isn't as singular as NASA's was, so you can't assume that all employees are as connected to the mission as this janitor reportedly was. It's up to you to create that linkage.

Connect Teams to the Experience

Another way we've helped connect the customer experience with teams is to ask, "If the customer experience were to improve, how would that improve *your* outcomes?" This is a counterintuitive question, because when the team talks with me, it naturally assumes I'm asking how it improves the *customer's* outcomes. Once I redirect the team, doing so starts an intriguing conversation.

For example, when I did this with a claims team, team members first talked about how, by improving claims, they make it better for customers. When I repeated the goal, it stumped them for a minute. But then they realized that, when the experience gets better and customers get emotionally engaged, claimants are more likely to accept their initial offer for a settlement, as they see it as being fair. As a result, they are far less likely to engage in costly escalations. (In other words, the CX Loyalty Flywheel at work.) This led them to rethink how they do their work, to focus less on the rational ("Let's get customers a response to their claims.") and more on how they could act in a way that creates a better customer experience. This then led them to consider the experience before a claim was submitted. If they could work with other teams to create more transparency and education *before* an accident occurred, they could improve outcomes for both the claims team and customers.

Stacy Sherman, formerly the Head of Customer Experience at a large B2B firm, shared how she used the annual Customer Experience Day (CX Day)—the first Tuesday of October each year—to reach out across the organization:

> I have a team—we're eight people. But I actually sort of preach that everybody in the company—finance, HR, the field—I go to everyone and say, "You have a CX job." It's not just my team. And I help them understand what that means and how it affects them.
>
> When we first celebrated CX Day, people expressed how much they loved it. But then teams started saying to me,

"While I love it, I really don't do anything with CX." And I said, "Oh, yes, you do. Because everything you do supports the frontline to be able to do their jobs better, easier, with a lower level of effort." So, I was on a mission to speak to people about the customer journey. For example, I went to finance and explained, "If customers don't understand their invoices and can't get help, then not making it easy to pay their bills is on us." There's a domino effect, and so the beginning, middle, and end of the customer journey matter. If any part is difficult, a customer will likely not stay. Even worse, they'll tell others about their bad experience, which has more negative impacts.

CX Day was initiated by the CXPA and is also recognized by Congress. It's held the first Tuesday of October each year, and companies throughout the world use this as a time to celebrate customers—and the employees who make those customers' experiences great.[1] CX Day is the perfect opportunity to share your program with employees. Something about having a national day gives permission to put on larger events than may be available at other times. Activating employees around the customer experience is one of the more time-intensive requirements to creating and accelerating the CX Loyalty Flywheel, but unless you invest the time, your results will be unintentionally sabotaged by teams who don't start with the customer in mind.

Another popular way to help employees understand the customer experience is through videos. Technology improvements have made it simpler and less expensive to collect video feedback, while the COVID-19 pandemic has helped customers become comfortable with video recording. Foot Locker and Airbnb both include options for video recordings in customer surveys. As organizations conduct journey mapping or other qualitative research, this creates opportunities to reuse the content to educate employees.

You may remember Marlanges Simar from the last chapter. She

shares how in a previous role she used customer videos of real-life members' stories to create empathy and customer understanding within her company's culture:

> We try to be creative and insert the voice of the customer in a number of different ways. For example, we produced a year-long video series that ran on our company intranet. Each week, a one- to two-minute video featured a different member telling a bit about themselves and an experience they'd had when using their pharmacy benefit. It gave employees a chance to empathize with our members and to gain a better understanding of the experience from their perspective. People loved it. The videos illustrate that every member has a story, which seems to reduce decision-making based on assumptions and generates more interest in collaborating with CX instead of assuming what customers need, want, and expect.

Customer Rooms: More Work, More Impact

Another way to expose employees to the current experience is a customer room, which is a place to bring all the elements of your customer's story into one location. A typical room shares a customer persona, showcases their pain points and needs, and builds everything into a cohesive story. While you can spend over a hundred thousand dollars on this initiative, you can also do it much more modestly, with more elbow grease than flash.

Jason Kapel, the Director of CX, Insights and Reporting, at a global B2B2C financial services firm, is an example of the latter. He needed his room to be transportable, as his organization has locations throughout the country; he also needed it to be ready in six weeks. He booked conference rooms in each location and customized the experience to fit whatever room he was in. He kicked off each location with an executive breakfast to engage the local leadership. Then he used a combination of emails and literature on employees' desks to create buzz.

Jason created a portable display with five main sections, including why CX is important (and difficult), understanding customers, journey mapping, measuring advocacy and future-state vision, and how employees can get involved. As Jason explains:

> We wanted to use different methods of presenting information in order to engage people in different ways, so we used large posters on the wall, infographics, lift-the-flap signs, stand-up banners, a rotating PowerPoint presentation of customer quotes on a projector screen, interactive iPad games, phone calls, opportunities to contribute to the room by putting Post-it Notes with ideas on the wall, a sectioned-off area where employees could videotape themselves providing an idea or story, and the presence of CX leadership stationed around the room ready to explain and engage. Our goal wasn't for every visitor to memorize our journey map or to be able to recite statistics on customer satisfaction—the goal was to capture the excitement around CX and help them share and internalize that excitement.

Interactivity is a definite best practice, improving engagement and retention. Other common practices are recorded customer calls and challenges to "figure out this communication" that was sent to customers, helping employees understand that their jargon isn't always understandable to customers.

To Compensate or Not to Compensate

At this point, you may be wondering about bonusing on improved CX scores. The research on this is quite mixed, but my opinion is that basing bonuses on CX scores will certainly get your executives' and teams' attention and will drive results. However, these may not be the results you hoped for.

One big issue with bonusing on CX scores is that teams can game the system. Teams find ways to manipulate customers to artificially create higher survey scores. While many public gaming examples are in B2C companies, it also happens in B2B, just differently and less publicly. Account managers neglect to send survey reminders to unhappy customers, or even try to keep the unhappy customer's name off of the survey invitation. Policies may be altered right before the survey goes out. Bad news may be delayed until after the survey is complete, while discounts appear just beforehand. Some of our Change Makers do give bonuses for CX scores. The difference is, while that may happen, it isn't the focus of the programs.

One Change Maker explained why he actively advocates against a bonus based on survey scores. He recalled:

> At my previous bank, we rewarded loan officers for customer satisfaction scores. And in the beginning, when we were getting the platform off the ground, and we wanted people to really think about the customer, it was a great way to motivate teams to deliver an improved experience. But over ten years, it created the worst kind of behavior; it almost turned into the auto-dealer kind of approach: "If I don't get a ten, I don't get a bonus." So, I will never do that again, anywhere I go.

In June 2021, I posted online to ask why many programs base bonuses on survey scores even though most thought leaders (including myself) recommend against it. Why is there this difference?[2] Most respondents didn't speak specifically to why the discrepancy exists but did share their philosophy.

Greg Bowell, a senior marketing executive, posted:

My thoughts are this: Companies have many competing priorities. What gets measured, gets done. So executive compensation and STIs [short-term incentives] are usually driven by the three to four Lag measures—high level, retrospective goals; e.g., Revenue, Profit, NPS, Engagement, etc. What should happen . . . is the organization should then be driven and compensated by the Lead Measures that drive those outcomes—i.e., the Drivers of NPS, not the same Lag Measures. Then everyone knows the part they are playing and can be recognized vs. a lofty goal they feel disconnected from or do not understand.

Michelle Morris, Managing Client Partner, Customer Experience and Contact Center, at Verizon, shared:

It's about what you're trying to accomplish. Is the org trying to motivate/drive change to increase CX, or is the org trying to reward or penalize behavior? Delivering great CX shouldn't be motivated by a carrot or a stick. Delivering great CX should be motivated by doing one's job well. Just like any other thing that an employee does well, rewarding exceptional behavior reemphasizes to the organization where the right thing was done.

Yes, compensation drives behavior. But so do clear role expectations and accountability. If the expectations of the role are defined and communicated and assessed properly, then orgs can use money for rewards of going above and beyond. If a job isn't done well, performance management plans should be the method for the correction plan just like any other negative behaviors.

Lee Kemp, Director of Customer Experience at the distributor Univar, shared:

I also struggle with the notion of compensating financially for NPS scores as it drives too much focus to the score rather than to the actions that will drive an improved experience for your customers. CXi and NPS are indicators, and not a definitive, absolute measure of customer sentiment. So don't chase the score. Chase your customers' priorities instead! That said, I'd rather see compensation/incentives that reward the positive behaviors that will in turn naturally improve your NPS/VoC results. Anything you can do to draw attention to and prioritize your customers' needs! Make CX cool! People will want to be a part of that and that will ultimately drive an improved experience for your customers *and* your employees!

My take: While compensation is an effective way to get employees to care about the customer, it's a blunt tool that creates unintended consequences. Think carefully before advocating for such a program, as you may find yourself spending time cleaning up messes created from gaming. When you compensate based on survey scores, you essentially make three assumptions:

1. **The score you are bonusing on matters.** And that it's worth paying more to accomplish this survey outcome. We discussed this in Action 1: most programs can't show that improving their survey scores actually impacts the company's success.
2. **Employees know how to improve that score.** This is also often untrue. Our research shows that few employees know the top drivers of the survey scores, let alone know how to impact that outcome.
3. **Employees won't do this unless you pay them extra.** I do understand a goal of matching the bonuses you offer for financial outcomes with a customer metric, but only do it if the first two are true.

This lack of knowledge on how to create improved survey scores is what leads to gaming. If you can't determine which changed behaviors will result in an improved score, then you're forced to ask customers to rate you more highly. As you'll soon see, Roxie ties the bonus to specific behaviors, which are far harder to game. It also provides more ownership. I remember when I worked at Best Buy, my annual bonus was tied to customer satisfaction. As only one of 130,000 employees, I felt that, while my work was good, my impact on that score was infinitesimal. However, if instead my bonus was based on the products I profiled—a behavior tied to my work—I would have been far more engaged. But, since most of my work was focused on experimental stores, I saw little relationship between my work and what my bonus was based on.

Dow Has a Deliberate Change-Management Approach

Change management is central to how Jen Zamora and her team at Dow approach CX, with Jen assigning three employees to change management: one on employee experience, one on customer experience, and a director who oversees their approach.

As Amy Sanborn, Director of Change Management, explains, "Success is going from talking about wanting to be different, talking about different terms that we should be using or different vocabulary and language, but then getting to the point where you actually see people doing that. They are actually changing their voice, their vocabulary that they're using."

Dow is a complex organization, with over thirty-five thousand employees in five businesses operating around the world, so changing such a complex organization isn't easy. Evidence of the program's impact is that, in addition to Jen's team, Dow's business units and functions have hired over twenty others *of their own headcount* to partner with her team and to work on CX within their respective businesses.

A global chemical manufacturer isn't the first place you'd look for a customer experience revolution, but that's exactly what has happened. Dow's customer experience vision is shared publicly on the company's website and in its investor reports, and Chairman and CEO Jim Fitterling regularly talks about the importance of being the most customer-centric materials science company in the world. And it's working. Customers report higher enjoyability in working with Dow, and that has translated to increasing growth.

A CEO talking about being customer centric isn't unique. Customer centricity is an easy talking point. But a CEO who specifically connects the dots between the deliberate decisions Dow makes to improve the customer experience and financial outcomes *is* rare. When my team and I met with Jim, we were impressed with his deep knowledge of the Dow customer experience, including details on how customers work across Dow's business units to order and receive products.

Dow has used a deliberate change-management approach to rally the entire organization to improve the customer experience, providing an effective template for other companies. Jen even wrote about the company's customer experience transformation in five articles on LinkedIn, providing a level of transparency unique for a B2B firm.

One of the tools Dow uses is called the Change Champions Network. As Dow conducted its first journey-mapping initiative, it found that employees kept raising their hands, wanting to help. From every geography and department, employees saw the importance of an improved customer experience and wanted to take part in the initiative. So, Jen's team created the network to foster communication. The program continues to grow, with over six hundred employees engaged with the Change Champions Network, sharing updates with their teams on what is being done with the customer experience and what it means to them.

The most common way to connect individual employees with the customer experience is through training. Jen describes how 60 percent of Dow's employees are in manufacturing, and it can be difficult to make a direct connection with the customer experience. Of course, they're creating products that customers buy. But how do they connect with the experience? Jen lets us in on her methods:

> We developed a program for educating the manufacturing employees and helping them understand how their roles are integral to the customer experience. For example, if we have to shut down, do our maintenance, and come back up, are we coming back up and producing prime product immediately? I spent an hour with manufacturing folks the other day who came to me with the customer experience impact on our internal customers, whom they consider clients. But when we got done with the conversation, they were like, "Wow, I never realized that I impacted the actual customer in that way."
>
> I thought we had made massive progress against our CX goals—and we have. And yet, I realized that we still were not always connecting the dots for our manufacturing folks. And so, that was a tiny taste of people who were finally getting there, and I was amazed at what they proposed as far as how they were going to impact the customer, and it felt so good.

Truly improving the long-term customer experience requires the entire company to be on board. By showing the current state of the customer experience and then linking the individuals' roles to that experience, you can ensure that the change to an improved customer experience continues.

Hagerty Engages Staff through Videos

Hagerty has over two thousand employees, which the company needs to motivate to create a superior experience. Hagerty's vision provides an excellent example: "Deliver exceptional experiences with every single interaction, creating clients that not only stay with Hagerty, but tell their friends about Hagerty."

To engage and inspire employees, Nancy Flowers has introduced videos into her toolbox. As she explains:

> One of the new innovations for us this year has been video feedback. And I have to tell you, it's been a tremendous tool because you can only report out on comments so often before people's eyes start to gloss over. Clients love our people; they are knowledgeable and friendly. But saying or reading that over and over can fall flat. When you play a video of a client raving about one of our fabulous service representatives, it rings true and brings the value of great service to life. In our relationship survey that we do twice a year, we have the option for people to leave a message to senior management. Bringing that feedback in has been really effective. And because I sit on the executive committee, two weeks ago, I played almost three and a half minutes of member feedback, some good and some bad. And that's a great catalyst for change.

It's so effective that Nancy now begins many executive meetings with a three- to five-minute video montage showing "the good, the bad, and the ugly" of the customer experience. She also shared an issue in which a fee was bringing in revenue but frustrating customers. She explains:

> Rationally, there was nothing wrong with it—this fee actually offset other costs and allowed us to make it easier for customers. But we are making money off it. I can't really do a cost analysis on why eliminating the fee is good for Hagerty's bottom line, right? But what I can do is show videos of people saying, "What the *bleep* is this fee for? I thought you are a trustworthy company." So, it's been great for those softer issues where not *everything* you solve for in client experience has a bottom-line ROI. We get into trouble when we think that way. If our mission in customer experience

is *always* efficiency and cost savings, we're doing it wrong. So, we use this as a change management approach to do the right thing for customers. And I know that eventually that will come back in benefits for the company.

Nancy also shares how she works to bring the customer experience to life for her employees:

We have a *member promise*, and every single employee goes through the Member Promise Workshop, whether customer facing or not. And that workshop is fundamental in making that connection. It was cocreated by Kate Hogan, who is in our human resources department, and Tracy Konzer, who's in the member experience group, and they won an award for it through CX of M, which is the professional organization that Michigan State runs. They do these exercises, where they show, for example, someone in accounting, seeing their response time to a question or a vendor contract does matter. We start with their response time and follow that through a chain of events to see the impact on the customer. So that even if you aren't customer facing, you absolutely impact the customer experience. And so that workshop is cross-functional. You have people in IT and accounting with field people, and they do these exercises to understand how they impact the client experience. It's foundational to connect employees' work to the member experience.

Video is just one of many tools, but it's one that Nancy has found effective at her organization.

Engaging Teams at XYZ Software

XYZ relies on multiple tools to align its teams to improve the customer experience. Executives participate in customer advisory boards and attend customer listening tours. Also, similar to Darin Byrne's program, XYZ has executive sponsors for key strategic accounts. In aligning the frontlines, Natasha shares:

A few years ago, we created an internal program called the XYZ Pledge, which is an initiative to reinforce the importance of putting our customer in the center of everything we do. The program brings teams together and breaks down silos to solve for customer issues across their journey with XYZ; for example, how can we make our customer's experience more seamless and easy? It's about harnessing the full power of XYZ to live our value of customer success.

We also use our training product and created a path called the Power of Customer Experience. To date, over thirty-four thousand employees have completed the trail, one of the top three paths completed by our employees. We also created a CX ambassador program, where we put employees through training on fundamentals of CX as a practice, and [teach them] how they can apply these concepts to their day-to-day job. With everything virtual in this pandemic environment, we created videos highlighting "customer stories" to showcase how employees are impacting customer experience. This serves as an inspiration for our employees and a great way to provide recognition.

We recently created a dedicated program for our CX ambassadors that includes training and certification. We create this cohort who goes through a twelve-week program. We have guided conversations every week, and every other week we host a learning session where we watch videos, go through the material, and do the exercises together as a team. And we talk about how the learning applies to our company, and so we have very pointed discussions led by a member of our team.

There are three series: a beginner, an intermediate, and then an advanced version, where we've created our own course on what CX means. This is a two-day in-classroom training course, but it is now available online, too. We take classrooms of twenty to thirty participants, and we talk through key areas that are very specific to XYZ and how we do customer experience. For example, we've focused on measurement because everyone is very interested in terms of how we measure customer experience. This is a great way for us to educate how, while it might not be easy to measure customer experience, it is possible. And we have teams to look at NPS, CSAT, sentiment, analysis, and usage data because we always convey that it's not only what customers say, but what they do.

This leads the CX team to do journey mapping. And then, from an advanced standpoint, we are beginning to teach them about service mapping because at the end of the day, a lot of them are in operational roles and are looking to improve our internal processes to meet the customer needs and improve the experience. And service maps are a great way to teach them. They are a great intersection and consolidation of the touchpoints in a customer journey and from the customer's point of view, and then we can bring in the back office to assess how we set up our processes and programs to really deliver on those experiences.

We've had two to three hundred participants go through the program. But that's just a beginning. Now, we engage them on a monthly and quarterly basis. We encourage word of mouth about the program and share the resources that we have to bring more people into the fold. They evangelize the program, so as they do in their day-to-day job, so where there are opportunities for improvement in customer experience, they let the team know.

The second part of this program is that these evangelists have their ears to the ground, so we discover where we can be better from an experience standpoint. And then the third part is connection. It's such an amazing platform, where they get to see all of these different priorities and initiatives that are being worked in the company. And they're connecting the dots and breaking down silos.

The feedback we have been getting is that it's a great platform for our teams to have vision across the company, for removing any duplication in projects, and for breaking down silos. All of this just sort of evolved naturally.

Educating on customer experience strikes at the second A (or Ability) in ADKAR, needed to drive change and is something I haven't discovered nearly often enough.

UKG: A Strong Believer in ADKAR

UKG is a strong believer in ADKAR, with a specific change management team certified in the capability, offering guidance and certified training throughout the organization. Roxie Strohmenger walks through how she applies ADKAR into building customer experience into UKG's culture:

Once I started with UKG, I had a brief amount of time to do a listening tour and hear from the organization's leaders about their current efforts and how CX might fit in. After that, I focused on Awareness, building internal campaigns to share what customer experience was all about, and how it can help us be more successful, which was more about the Desire. And I went back and forth between the two, building Awareness and Desire. This was especially critical when we changed our measurement approach, as how we captured CX and interpreted the numbers weren't what our organization was used to seeing. We traditionally looked at overall satisfaction and NPS, but then we switched over to expectations, ease, and emotion—and specifically, confidence. So, I spent a lot of time building Awareness and Desire so they'd have the trust in the numbers. And while I started with the executives, I worked my way down to the frontlines, cascading the purpose and the numbers.

Once that was complete, we started working on Knowledge and Ability, sharing, "Okay, now let me show you tips that you could leverage." By that time, I had been invited to present at our internal conferences. That got everybody into the knowledge play: "Here's why we're doing CX, here's how to do it, here's tips, here's tricks."

That's when we started to work with the change management team and with training, rolling out playbooks on how they could improve the experience, which focused on the Ability for them to execute. So then, after a couple rounds that lasted over a year, Reinforcement started to happen because then they started to see the quarter-over-quarter change. At the end of 2020, it was monumental because that's when they saw all the uptick. And then the teams were saying, "We're going to double down on this even further," because they could see it working in both our CX numbers and our overall performance.

A good example of this was with our account managers. Our journey mapping showed how, through our rapid growth, our account managers were getting stretched. So, the organization doubled down and when our research showed the importance of them being trusted advisors, we built specific playbooks on how they could serve this role more effectively. And that's when we saw the double-digit growth in our CX scores, which we know tie in to retention and growth of accounts.

UKG's focus on change management continues to strengthen, and Roxie and her team are earning ADKAR certification to add this important tool to their skill sets.

When it comes to tying CX to bonuses, Roxie isn't a fan of basing the bonus off high-level scores, whether NPS, satisfaction, or anything else. Instead, she focuses on more actionable items that the individual can impact.

For example, UKG's research shows that a Knowledgeable U Krewer[3] is one of the top drivers of satisfaction with a support call. To drive good quality of CX, UKG focuses on incenting employees on more actionable items that employees could impact. As a result, when it's looked for people chasing scores—common when bonuses are based on higher-level metrics—it hasn't been able to find any.

The critical component is to base the bonus on something actionable. As Roxie shares, "The bonus should be based on performance drivers that are behaviorally driven. If we need to do a bonus based on CX scores, then let's do it based on behaviors the employee can control and on things that we can coach the employee on. It's pretty tough to build coaching on how to improve overall satisfaction. That's what makes it work, as opposed to the used-car approach you see at organizations that base their bonuses on higher-level metrics."

That's the best practice. Bonuses in and of themselves aren't bad. But lazy bonuses—applying the bonus to the same high-level, indirect survey score to everyone in the company—is a bad practice. While I'm a fan of the concept of bonusing, it only makes sense if you can draw a straight line from the item being bonused to improved outcomes.

■ ■ ■

At the top of the chapter, I wrote "engaging the employee base is even more critical in B2B organizations, where typically 90 percent of employees have never met a customer in person. Giving them a vision of what the customer experience could be, and its impact to the organization, is a great first step." A great example of someone who connects the dots that is worth repeating is Jim Fitterling at Dow.

Even though he's at the very highest level of the organization, Jim has a laser focus on the customer experience. As I mentioned earlier, a CEO talking about being customer centric isn't unique. Nearly every CEO mentions customers because it's an easy talking point. But Jim is an example of that rare CEO who specifically connects the dots on the deliberate decisions Dow makes to improve the customer experience, and then links these to financial outcomes. And that *is* rare.

I hope that you have enjoyed your journey reading this book and can begin to see ways of connecting the dots between customer experience and results in your organization. I invite you to contact me directly at jim@heartofthecustomer.com or on LinkedIn (linkedin.com/in/jimtincher) if you have any questions or just wish to talk. Thank you.

Cari's Story

Cari's search for a communicator resulted in an addition to her team—Addie—who had been with Sycamore for almost three years in a marketing support role. Addie's enthusiasm and smarts were soon paying dividends.

Dale and Cari were in their weekly one-on-one, and Dale shared a request he'd received. "The executive team is jazzed about the journey mapping and surveys, but they feel they're always trying to push the message," said Dale. "It helps that Addie is providing them with their talking points, so they are up to speed in their team meetings, but the meetings aren't as productive as they could be. The execs feel they have to keep explaining CX and how it connects to the business. So, how do we activate our software designers and engineers? Oddly enough, even Sue, who runs the customer success teams, feels like her team doesn't feel engaged with this work. How can we extend our impact?"

Cari thought about it. "I'm glad to hear there's a sense of ownership from the execs," she said. "It's actually an ideal problem to have—they want us to move faster. I'll check with Addie, but two ideas come right to mind.

"First, let's give the execs some help by engaging lower-level managers. We've been talking about putting together a CX-in-a-Box initiative, tools to help our midlevel managers engage their teams. We can do it virtually, but I'd love to make it a physical box if there's budget for it. We'll include a kickoff PowerPoint that walks through our CX vision and what it means to our various teams, with a targeted slide for our major functions, showing how CX impacts product, quality assurance, finance, and others. It will also include some of the improvements we've made. Maybe we can show a few of the videos from the journey mapping, and then communicate how we've responded to those needs to increase confidence.

"If we can do the physical boxes, I'd like to include hoodies or some other fun swag. Maybe even have one bigger prize that they can hand out to the winner of a quiz about our customer experience."

"That would be good," Dale replied. "I know when I was a marketing manager, I never knew what to say to my teams. Having something I could use to engage my team—and that I didn't have to write—would be terrific. I think you'll get a ton of uptake."

"We're also far enough along that I'd like to put together what I'm calling the CX Champions Network," Cari continued. "We can put the invitation into the box. We'll ask each manager to nominate one member of their team for this role. It won't take much of their time—an hour or two a week for a meeting with us to share what's happening with their teams. That will give the managers support, and it also gives us advocates throughout the company. Maybe we can put a special badge on their photo on the intranet."

"Now that we're all remote, it probably makes more sense to do this virtually," Dale suggested. "But I love the idea of doing a contest. Maybe we make it bigger—put together a company-wide quiz on the state of the customer experience, and those with the top scores win some serious swag. If we announce it in the box, that will also drive adoption. Let me see if we can't find the budget for some sweet items. Like maybe some Google glasses! I always thought those were cool."

"Why don't you find the budget, and I'll work on the prizes," Cari suggested. She thought, "Google glasses? Wow. There's no way I'm letting my program be associated with those." As she left the meeting, Cari had a sense of pride. Having executives request her help in sharing the good news about customer experience? It's the goal she always hoped for, and now that it's happening, she was pumped.

My Thoughts

Getting the frontline teams engaged is where your program's impact accelerates. But there are reasons this comes last in the book. First, the surest way to make customer experience a "flavor of the day" is to rush into sharing the program with the entire company before you build a sustainable infrastructure. Unless executives can see the big picture and how CX helps them accomplish their goals, they won't give the resources needed to be successful. The ultimate example is from Dow, where the business units hired over twenty people to work on CX outside of the central CX department. But other organizations also have big successes by contributing people to be a part of a CX advocates group.

The only way to create this buy-in is to tackle the hard work from the first three sections of the book. Establish how your program impacts the financials, engage customers emotionally so those financials improve, and connect your work to the data so you can prove it. These three sections were all about building the muscle so that, when it comes time to spread the word, you're ready.

Takeaways

Identifying Sources of Value in the CX Loyalty Flywheel

Please use the workbook that you can download from DoB2BBetter .com/workbook to complete the exercises and activities. Completing this work will result in a playbook that will help you plan your CX program and provide insight into questions and challenges that your fellow CX colleagues everywhere are facing. We will continue on from Action 3 and use the story of Cari as an example of how she would respond to questions from her colleagues. Here are the questions I'd ask her, if I were consulting with her on her CX strategy.

Who are the most important leaders to engage in your customer experience governance? Is there an existing committee where they already meet, or do you need to create a new governance team?

CARI: We did form a CX council that includes most of our C-suite plus some other product and operational leaders.

How can you give them an active role to play in supporting the customer experience?

CARI: For the first few months, I can share high-level results from our journey mapping and the relationship survey. We can break down the biggest needs and involve them in ideating on what a new experience can be. Ideally, I can then ask each leader for resources to improve the outcomes, then come back to them next month with progress, and ask for their feedback going forward.

Who are the most important advocates for your program? How can you engage them to work on the customer experience?

CARI: Operations and product are the two leaders I need to engage. We need to get a handle on how we manage incident resolution and give customers visibility to those outcomes. We won't make significant improvements unless I can get them both to participate. I'll have to start with meeting with each one separately, and see if I can get buy-in on the concept, before I bring them together.

What are the critical overall needs you need to communicate globally?

CARI: Transparency is a big deal. When customers do an implementation or open a support ticket, it feels to them like it goes into a big black hole. If we can provide improved transparency, that will go a long way into mediating the frustration coming through in our surveys.

Empathy is the other one. Many of our customers report that we're talking at them, rather than with them. Taking the time to actively listen would go a long way.

Are you able to tie customer experience needs to individual departments to engage them with the customer experience?

CARI: We have a large number of issues that we need to address. It's easier to engage some areas—such as product and customer success—than others, such as finance. I initially thought the project management office could be an issue, but we're actually finding a number of items where we can work together.

How can you support managers in sharing the CX program?

CARI: The CX-in-a-Box concept seems to be working well. We plan to redo this every October for CX Day, to keep it top of mind. We can also create larger activities—maybe even get people back to the offices for a day to celebrate.

AFTERWORD

LEADING A CUSTOMER EXPERIENCE TRANSFORMATION IS THE most thrilling way to improve company outcomes that I know. Done right, customer experience isn't fluff but instead, is an art and a science focused on creating an experience that leads a customer to go out of their way to find more ways to work with your company, spending more and building a mutually beneficial relationship.

Doing so requires you to create a disciplined approach to measure and accelerate the CX Loyalty Flywheel, identifying the financial results from the flywheel, the Emotional North Star that accelerates its pace, and the Customer Ecosystem Data that allow you to track it, as well as greasing it through a deliberate approach to change management to help bring everyone in your company along.

Spending time with our Change Makers has inspired me and changed the way I think about customer experience. I hope they've had the same effect on you. As I mentioned in the introduction, all four of our Change Maker heroines were promoted while I wrote the book. Two—Nancy and Roxie—have expanded their scopes, and the other two—Jen and Natasha—have moved on to new capabilities to help their companies succeed.

At Heart of the Customer, one so-called soft outcome I celebrate is the promotion of our clients, including the four I have mentioned, as well as other Change Makers profiled in the book—among them Darin, Laurie, and Christine.[1]

If you haven't already done this, I encourage you to download the companion workbook, which you can find at DoB2BBetter.com /workbook.

There are also multiple ways to keep the conversation going. You can always find me on LinkedIn at linkedin.com/in/jimtincher. Also, with the launch of this book, we're creating a new membership program called the CX Fellowship, where a small group of proven Change Makers get together on a regular basis to share best practices.

But before I let you go, let's finish up Cari's story.

A Bright Future for Change Maker Cari

The year-end meeting with Yolanda went well, with the CX program accomplishing Dale's two big goals, creating the environment where Sycamore had more customers willing to be references and accelerating upsells. Cari was pumped when her budget request for next year was approved. She had recently onboarded Jose to her team, filling the critical CX architect's position. She had support for adding another analyst, along with a new text analytics system, which would enable them to get even deeper into understanding challenges with the customer experience.

Jose was already guiding multiple projects, so budget approval for a second architect was also gratifying. Sycamore's focus on agile meant that Jose had to be in daily stand-ups on projects; expanding this team would ensure that all major projects incorporate the voice of the customer into its design.

Even so, she was a bit nervous when CEO Shirley's admin messaged her yesterday, asking if she could attend an early morning meeting—in person, no less. Cari got ready to step into the room. On the few occasions when Shirley had invited her into her office, it didn't always go well. For example, when she initially integrated emotions into the customer survey, it had been an uncomfortable meeting explaining to Shirley why she gave clients the option to report they were "embarrassed" when talking about Sycamore. She couldn't think of any specific problems that were happening, so she hoped it would be good news.

But when she walked into the office, Dale was there—he hadn't said a thing to her about this! She relaxed when she saw the big smile on Shirley's face.

"Cari, I admit I was a bit uncertain at putting somebody in operations in charge of our customer experience. It seemed such a different skill set that I had my doubts," said Shirley. "But these last two years have been amazing. As I've met with customers, I've noticed the tone has changed. Tom, First American's CIO, even told me that he's considering a major expansion of our products—something that's always been off the table. He actually used the words 'my confidence in Sycamore has really increased,' just as you've been designing for."

"Thanks!" Cari responded, not sure where this was headed.

"That's why I invited you and Dale this morning. You've made a great start, but it's time to take it to another level. That's why I'm asking you to become Sycamore's first Chief Customer Officer. Your insights to our customers are invaluable, and I want you to be a part of our senior leadership team, ensuring that we continue to grow by creating great outcomes from our customers, who want to grow with us."

"I don't know what to say!" Cari stammered.

"Why don't you just say yes?" Dale suggested. "I'll miss having you as a part of my team. But I will enjoy even more having you as a peer on leadership."

"Then, yes. Yes, I'm excited!" Cari responded.

"That settles it, then," Shirley concluded. "Welcome aboard. I'm excited to see what we'll do next."

As she walked to her car, Cari's thoughts were swirling. She already had big ideas of what to do next—Sycamore's user conference could use an overhaul to be more customer focused, and she knew that a bigger investment in Sycamore's online community could pay dividends.

Maybe Dale didn't report to her yet. But with another few years of progress, who knows?

My Thoughts

CX pays! By building an approach where you focus on both the customer and business benefits and include the change management to ensure the organization follows through on improvements, you can gain the executive visibility and support needed to become a real Change Maker. Cari is obviously a fictional character. But she is an accurate portrayal of amazing Change Makers who are having huge impacts in their organizations.

It's my hope that you, too, dear reader, will be able to use these tools to drive change and increase your influence.

So, let's get started!

ACKNOWLEDGMENTS

THE LEARNINGS IN THIS BOOK AREN'T MINE ALONE BUT come from our team at Heart of the Customer and our incredible clients.

From Diane, who by now has probably interviewed more customer experience leaders than anybody in the world, and from Nicole, Jenita, Shawn, Jean, and Ben, who have helped me craft my thoughts; and Tamika, Marcie, Ann, Ty, Eduardo, Sue, Brian, Cameron, and Kristen, who help our clients to become Change Makers.

A big thanks to Kris LaFavor of Design Ahead, who makes everything we do look amazing, including many of the graphics in this book, and Sage Troolin, who thoroughly researched many of the topics where I needed help.

I also want to acknowledge all the Change Makers—not all of whom could be included in this book—who inspire me and keep me learning. Without your time and involvement, this book could never have happened. Roxie, Jen, and Darin let me shadow them for days, listening into their conversations and asking questions. Nancy, Laurie, Renae, and Marlanges let us interview a bunch of their team members to learn about their excellent programs, and all the others who agreed to be interviewed.

I owe an incredible debt of gratitude to two amazing Change Makers. Roxie Strohmenger, CCXP of UKG, and Andrea Krohnberg, CCXP of Kelly Services, read through multiple revisions of the manuscript, helping to guide it from a bunch of raw thoughts to what you have before you now. Anything that doesn't ring true is something I probably added after their reviews!

And not to be forgotten, the CXPA, which serves as a beacon for the customer experience community and has been an amazing resource for me in my career and learning.

NOTES

Introduction

1 I first ran across this in the CustomerThink report, *Customer Experience at a Crossroads*, by CEO Bob Thompson. His report analyzed which programs could show business or competitive value, which he called "Winning" programs, and reported that 25 percent of all programs in his study were "Winning," while 58 percent were "Developing," and 17 percent were "Starting." Our research was similar, showing that 22 percent were Change Makers—those who reported that they could prove business impact from their work.

2 I am indebted to the work of Jim Collins, who published the concept of a flywheel in his seminar book, *Good to Great*. You can learn more about his writing on the flywheel at jimcollins.com/concepts/the-flywheel.html.

3 Troy, "B2B vs B2C Market Size?," *ICTSD* (blog), accessed April 6, 2022, ictsd.org/b2b-vs-b2c-market-size.

4 Aimee Lucas, "B2B CX Management Efforts Have Room to Improve," *Experience Matters Blog*, Qualtrics XM Institute, August 24, 2020, xminstitute.com/blog /b2b-cx-room-improve.

5 LaserMaster made high-resolution laser printers. The company is defunct.

6 We've now been married for twenty-eight years!

7 Half of Hagerty's revenue comes from direct relationships, and the other half comes from its B2B distribution partners. Here, we're of course focusing on the B2B half of its business.

8 See CXPA.org.

9 Readers of my first book, *How Hard Is It to Be Your Customer? Using Journey Mapping to Drive Customer-Focused Change*, may remember that there was a reference to ABC Software. This is a separate organization from that one.

10 This opinion was not a notion shared by most of our Change Makers!

Chapter 1

1 Pointillist, *2021 State of Customer Journey Management and CX Measurement*, July 2021, myjourney.pointillist.com/content-customer-journey-cx-measure-report.html. Pointillist has since been purchased by Genesys.

2 NPS asks a loyalty question, "How likely are you to recommend _____ to a friend or colleague," on a 0 to 10 scale. The Net Promoter Score is calculated by taking the percentage of customers who give a 9 or 10 and subtracting the percentage who give between 0 to 6, then turning that into a whole number. For example, if 30 percent of customers rate their likelihood to recommend your company as a 9 or 10, and 10 percent rate it between 0 to 6, the Net Promoter Score is 30 minus 10, or 20.

3 Watermark Consulting, *The Customer Experience ROI Study*, October 2021, www.watermarkconsult.net/cx-roi.

4 Qualtrics XM Institute, *ROI of Customer Experience, 2020*, August 2020, xminstitute.com/research/2020-roi-cx.

5 American Marketing Association, *Customer Satisfaction and Its Impact on the Future Costs of Selling*, June 2020, ama.org/2020/06/11/customer-satisfaction-and -its-impact-on-the-future-costs-of-selling.

6 Watermark Consulting, *The Customer Experience ROI Study*, October 2021, www.watermarkconsult.net/cx-roi.

7 Forrester Research, Inc., *Top Tactics for Making a More Successful CX Business Case*, August 2018, forrester.com/report/The-Top-14-Hacks-For-Your-CX-Business -Case/RES144052.

8 CustomerThink Corp., *Customer Experience at a Crossroads: What Drives CX Success?*, January 2019, customerthink.com/customer-experience-at-a-crossroads -what-drives-cx-success.

9 Dave has since started his own consulting company. I'm proud to say we've worked with him on a few projects. He truly *is* a Change Maker!

Chapter 2

1 With TCF Bank merging with Huntington Bank, Noah is now Huntington Bank's Commercial Banking CFO.

2 Distributors are the link between manufacturers and their customers. The end customer can order from multiple manufacturers but only have to work with one company and receive a single shipment.

3 For clarity's sake, this is not a reference to Hagerty.

4 There are exceptions where the numerator isn't available. For example, companies that sell through distributors may not be able to learn how much each end customer spent with them, since that revenue number is held by the distribution partner. If you can't get your distribution partner to share it with you, it will be very difficult to calculate share of wallet for the end customer, although it is still useful to show the *distributor's* share of wallet with you.

5 Heart of the Customer study.

6 SaaS Capital staff, "Growth and Revenue Retention in SaaS Businesses," *SaaS Capital Blog*, SaaS Capital, April 5, 2017, saas-capital.com/blog-posts/growth-and -revenue-retention-in-saas-businesses.

7 SaaS Capital, LLC (www.saas-capital.com).

8 After being asked this third question, one participant in particular had no response. After a few seconds of silence, he responded, "Jim, you're assuming I know somebody from finance." Okay, he got me. Yes, that *was* an assumption of mine—one that was obviously incorrect!

Chapter 3

1 Our survey, which primarily involved CXPA members, showed that about one-third of respondents had none or one person leading customer experience in their organization; another one-third had two to five, and the final third had six or more people involved in their customer experience efforts.

2 We'll go more into this in Action 3.

Chapter 4

1 Scott Magids, Alan Zorfas, and Daniel Leemon, "The New Science of Customer Emotions," *Harvard Business Review*, November 2015, hbr.org/2015/11/the-new -science-of-customer-emotions.

2 "Executive Order on Transforming Federal Customer Experience and Service Delivery to Rebuild Trust in Government," The White House, December 13, 2021, whitehouse.gov/briefing-room/presidential-actions/2021/12/13/executive-order -on-transforming-federal-customer-experience-and-service-delivery-to-rebuild -trust-in-government.

3 Measuring effectiveness, ease, and emotion are metrics embedded in Forrester's CX Index score. For further information, see forrester.com/research/cx-index.

4 It's interesting that I created the concept of the Emotional North Star before interviewing Barbara. It appears that we both came up with the same concept (and name) independently.

5 "I CARE Core Values, Characteristics, and Customer Experience Principles," US Department of Veterans Affairs, last modified November 16, 2021, va.gov/icare /core-values.asp.

6 The VA measurement is defined as giving a 4 or 5 to the survey question.

7 VA staff, "Serving America's Veterans," *VAntage Point* (blog), US Department of Veterans Affairs, December 31, 2021, blogs.va.gov/VAntage/wp-content/uploads /2022/03/Serving-Americas-Veterans_VA-FY2022-Q1-Trust-Report-External.pdf.

8 A sample is at va.gov/welcome-kit.

9 Jim Tincher, "When CX Is a Matter of Life or Death," *Heart of the Customer* (blog), Heart of the Customer, January 9, 2020, heartofthecustomer.com/when -cx-is-a-matter-of-life-or-death.

10 For more details on these cognitive biases, see Daniel Kahneman, Olivier Sibony, and Cass R. Sunstein, *Noise: A Flaw in Human Judgment* (New York: Little, Brown and Company, 2021).

11 Alex Edmans et al., "Music Sentiment and Stock Returns Around the World," *Journal of Financial Economics* 145, no. 2 (2022): 234–254, doi.org/10.1016 /j.jfineco.2021.08.014.

12 Readers of my first book, *How Hard Is It to Be Your Customer? Driving Customer-Focused Change Through Journey Mapping*, may wonder whether this is the same Darin of "ABC Software" that we featured in that book. It is!

13 If you've recently purchased a home, look at the bottom of the disclosure documents. Odds are, you'll see Wolters Kluwer's name there.

14 Gartner, Inc. acquired CEB, a best practice insight and technology company, in 2017.

15 With the purchase of CEB by Gartner, the original study has been removed, but it was also quoted in the *Harvard Business Review* article "Making the Consensus Sale," which you can find at hbr.org/2015/03/making-the-consensus-sale.

16 Social proof is a concept discovered by Robert Cialdini, introduced in his book *Influence*. People often rely on others to help make decisions, whether they are experts, celebrities, peers, or fellow customers.

17 "Left Brain vs. Right Brain: What Does This Mean for Me?," *Healthline*, last modified May 31, 2022, healthline.com/health/left-brain-vs-right-brain.

18 Qualtrics XM Institute, *ROI of Customer Experience, 2020*, August 2020, xminstitute.com/research/2020-roi-cx.

19 This focus on the low end of the survey scale makes sense. Angry customers capture the imagination. Most CX consultancies use this same approach: contact detractors to discover their problems and fix them. While we don't recommend you ignore customers experiencing problems, this narrow "find and fix" mentality doesn't go far enough to create loyal customers who will buy more from you and refer you to others.

20 To be clear, this story was not from the VA.

21 Jackson Noel, "How TurboTax Turns a Dreadful User Experience into a Delightful One," *Appcues* (blog), Appcues, February 7, 2019, appcues.com/blog/ how-turbotax-makes-a-dreadful-user-experience-a-delightful-one.

Chapter 5

1 Being from the north, I have never understood the delight that their customers have with their subs. But, having tried a few, I have to agree that they're amazing!

2 Amazon staff, "Statement by Jeff Bezos to the U.S. House Committee on the Judiciary," Amazon, July 29, 2020, aboutamazon.com/news/policy-news-views/ statement-by-jeff-bezos-to-the-u-s-house-committee-on-the-judiciary.

3 Jeffrey P. Bezos, "2008 Letter to Shareholders," US Securities and Exchange Commission, April 2009, sec.gov/Archives/edgar/data/1018724/000119312509081096/dex991.htm.

4 Randall Lane, "Bezos Unbound: Exclusive Interview with the Amazon Founder on What He Plans to Conquer Next," *Forbes*, September 4, 2018, forbes.com/sites/randalllane/2018/08/30/bezos-unbound-exclusive-interview-with-the-amazon-founder-on-what-he-plans-to-conquer-next.

5 Since the time of this interview, the marketplace has launched and is seeing strong success.

Chapter 6

1 Wolters Kluwer's Darin Byrne created my favorite name for a project: the Human Readable Invoice Initiative.

2 See *In the Hands of a Change Maker* at heartofthecustomer.com/resource/in-the-hands-of-a-change-maker.

3 It was important to do it blind (meaning that participants could not see what company sponsored the research) so that she could ask about the emotions from competitors' customers, to see if other companies were creating different emotions.

4 If you want to go deep on the research on emotions and how they impact decision-making, Roxie recommends Paul Ekman's work, as well as the summary available at doi.org/10.1016/j.jcps.2015.04.003.

5 A break-fix issue is something tactical that needs to be repaired to restore the experience.

Chapter 7

1 There is also a ton of literature on how this applies to B2B companies as well. The most successful B2B organizations understand their customers' customers, so they can help create mutually beneficial outcomes.

2 Leaders, 28 percent of all organizations represented, are those that claim a very good understanding of customer satisfaction across all three of the main phases of the customer journey: prepurchase/consumption, purchase/consumption, and postpurchase/consumption.

3 New York AMA Communication Services, Inc., *Jiffy Lube: Identifying Key Revenue Drivers in Customer Comment Data*, January 2018, greenbook.org/mr/insights-that-work/shell-oil-identifying-key-revenue-drivers-in-customer-comment-data. I love this case study and have talked about it for years. When I spoke to the Portland CXAIPDX chapter, I brought up this case study. It turned out that one of the original analysts, Tim Lynch, was attending that night. We totally geeked out! It was great to hear more details on the study.

4 Most manufacturers require orders be submitted at least a certain number of days before delivery, called lead time.

5 Ryan W. Buell, "Operational Transparency," *Harvard Business Review*, March 15, 2019, hbr.org/2019/03/operational-transparency.

Chapter 8

1 I realize that some companies do ask customers whether they had to call multiple times. But this is a terrible idea. First, you're asking customers to tell you something you should already know. Second, it isn't reliable.

2 It's okay if you don't have friends in IT yet, but now's probably the time to do that. I spent years in IT, and we were always hungry to connect with the rest of the organization!

3 XM refers to eXperience Management. You can find the report at qualtrics.com /xm-institute/global-state-xm.

4 Pointillist is now owned by Genesys.

5 Pointillist, *2021 State of Customer Journey Management and CX Measurement*, July 2021, myjourney.pointillist.com/content-customer-journey-cx-measure-report .html.

6 The inverse is not true; there are multiple journey analytics platforms without orchestration.

7 As you have probably guessed by now, during the writing of this book, Christine was promoted—to Global Digital Customer Experience Manager at Schneider Electric.

8 Schneider Electric doesn't measure emotions but focuses on behaviors that link to emotions.

9 Customer Experience Index is Forrester's measurement of effectiveness, ease, and emotion.

10 Captive agents are those who do not have a choice of providers; all relevant business goes to Hagerty. Independent agents may send all, some, or no business to the company. For example, Hagerty has a partnership with Allstate, which uses captive agents, whereas most of Hagerty's business comes from those who are independent.

11 Customer lifetime value and annual recurring revenue.

Chapter 9

1 In a continuing theme, he's since left the organization and is now a Senior Vice President at VoC software provider Medallia.

2 One of our clients at a different financial services institution shared the results from a qualitative journey-mapping program that included interviews with distri- bution partners. One of the underwriters asked, "You conducted thirty interviews. What's the confidence interval on that data?" At financial services, quant data rules!

3 Technical debt reflects the implied cost of additional rework caused by choosing an easy (limited) solution now instead of using a better approach that would take longer. Over time, that debt accumulates, as it becomes harder to implement changes. By making more-informed decisions, the agile teams prevent expensive rework and can even reduce this technical debt.

4 Bill's company works with other financial institutions to manage their debt products, so a success is when that financial institution sends more products its way.

5 For example, with one software client we survey the decision-makers, the IT team implementing the software, and the users. Decision-makers consistently rate our client higher than do the other groups. At a manufacturer, however, we find that the installers love our client, but leadership feels far less love. It varies by company.

6 At one point, Bill told me, "Data is the love language."

7 To help people adopt, they must become aware of the need to change, desire to change, know what to change, be able to change, and have it reinforced.

8 This analysis is current as of early 2022 as I write this book. I do expect journey analytics to make its way to CRM and other platforms, which will change this calculation.

9 Genesys, *Beyond Net Promoter Score: Customer Experience Reimagined*, March 2022, genesys.com/resources/beyond-nps-cx-measurement-reimagined.

Chapter 10

1 Darin has now been promoted to lead professional services globally for another business unit within Wolters Kluwer.

2 As with most of our Change Makers, Lisa Hagen has moved to a new role.

3 I first saw this in the Temkin Group's (the forerunner of Qualtrics XM Institute) June 2010 report, *The Current State of Customer Experience*, where 71 percent of respondents said that this was a significant obstacle. While the percentage isn't as high, it's still one of the top issues cited in the November 2019 report, *The Global State of XM*.

4 McKinsey & Company, *Unlocking Success in Digital Transformations*, October 2018, mckinsey.com/business-functions/people-and-organizational-performance /our-insights/unlocking-success-in-digital-transformations.

5 Jeffrey Pfeffer, "Are There Stars in Banking—or Anywhere Else?," CBS News, last modified August 5, 2009, cbsnews.com/news/are-there-stars-in-banking-or -anywhere-else.

6 "The Prosci ADKAR Model," Prosci, Inc., last modified April 7, 2021, www.prosci.com/methodology/adkar.

7 "The 8-Step Process for Leading Change," Kotter, Inc., December 17, 2017, kotterinc.com/8-step-process-for-leading-change.

8 Diane Schnitker, aka the "rock star."

9 A rack builder was a website tool that allowed customers to select a few products, and it would then provide all the materials needed to mount the equipment into a standard IT rack—a common activity in audiovisual systems.

10 Pointillist, *2021 State of Customer Journey Management and CX Measurement*, July 2021, myjourney.pointillist.com/content-customer-journey-cx-measure -report.html.

11 See linkedin.com/posts/jimtincher_cx-activity-6807995311194296320-4W4o.

Chapter 11

1 Megan has a helpful YouTube video entitled "How to Write a Clear, Useful Customer Experience Vision Statement" at youtube.com/watch?v=82pq5qEXSLw.

2 Xerox Corporation, *2018 Corporate Social Responsibility Report*, October 2018, xerox.com/corporate-social-responsibility/2018/society/customer-first-focus.html.

3 When I was in my CX role at the health insurance organization, our nearest call center was three hours away. I did get the executives to travel up there. Once. In two and a half years.

4 Although there is the story about the CEO trying to explain a bill to a customer . . .

5 Pete Slease, Rick DeLisi, and Matthew Dixon, "Call Length Is the Worst Way to Measure Customer Service," *Harvard Business Review*, February 22, 2017, hbr.org/2017/02/call-length-is-the-worst-way-to-measure-customer-service.

6 Jim Tincher, "Interview with Marlanges Simar – Director of CX at Prime Therapeutics," *Heart of the Customer* (blog), Heart of the Customer, February 12, 2019, heartofthecustomer.com/interview-marlanges-simar.

Chapter 12

1 You can learn more about CX Day at cxday.org.

2 See linkedin.com/posts/jimtincher_customerexperience-cxtransformation -activity-6815256595778404352-pNH0.

3 UKG's name for its employees.

Afterword

1 And not just clients! Heart of the Customer employees Nicole and Diane mentioned in this book were also promoted during this time.

INDEX